Suicide and Social Justice

Suicide and Social Justice unites diverse scholarly and social justice perspectives on the international problem of suicide and suicidal behavior.

With a focus on social justice, the book seeks to understand the complex interactions between individual and group experiences with suicidality and various social pathologies, including inequality, intergenerational poverty, racism, sexism, and homophobia. Chapters investigate the underlying and often overlooked connections that link rising rates and disproportionate concentrations of suicide within specific populations to wider social, political, and economic conditions.

This edited volume brings diverse scholarly and social justice perspectives to bear on the problem of suicide and suicidal behavior, equipping researchers and practitioners with the knowledge they need to fundamentally rethink suicide and suicide prevention.

Mark E. Button, PhD, Dean, College of Arts and Sciences and Professor of Political Science, University of Nebraska-Lincoln (USA).

Ian Marsh, PhD, is Reader in the School of Allied Health Professions at Canterbury Christ Church University (UK).

"Finally—a book that examines the growing suicide crisis from a social justice perspective that powerfully disrupts traditional assumptions and frameworks. This timely book provides an exceptional body of critical knowledge by highlighting the importance of understanding the effects of social, political, and economic forces on human pain and suffering that can make life unliveable. The unique multidisciplinary scholarship throughout the volume is brilliant, rigorous, thoughtful, and encourages the reader to reflect on the social systemic factors involved in the modern suicide epidemic. The essays within this collection are lifesaving. *Suicide and Social Justice* is essential reading for anyone, and everyone, concerned with the public health crisis of the century."

—**Heidi Rimke**, PhD, Associate Professor of Sociology, University of Winnipeg

"This volume is an important, compelling and original contribution to the emerging field of critical suicide studies. By providing a diverse range of perspectives on the connection between suicide and social justice, the authors set out new and vital ways to approach and understand suicide. The book challenges many conventional views and approaches to the issue of suicide by cogently and carefully showing how suicide must be framed through the lens of inequality and social justice. Only by such an approach, in my view, will it be possible to critically and meaningfully engage with suicide prevention in a realistic, experiential, and holistic manner. Nothing could be more urgent."

—**Baden Offord**, Director and Dr Haruhisa Handa Chair of Human Rights, Centre for Human Rights Education, Curtin University

"Mark E. Button and Ian Marsh have woven together an impressive assemblage of practitioners, persons directly impacted by suicide, and academics, connected in solidarity with a collective ethics for justice doing. These tenacious authors/activists challenge the very descriptions used to express suffering and offer emergent, just practices, rich critiques, alternative critical analysis of how the harms of suicide are caused and framed, and ways to better respond with dignity, justice, liberation, and hope."

—**Vikki Reynolds**, PhD, Activist, Therapeutic Supervisor, and Adjunct Professor

Suicide and Social Justice

New Perspectives on the Politics of Suicide and Suicide Prevention

Edited by Mark E. Button and Ian Marsh

Routledge
Taylor & Francis Group
NEW YORK AND LONDON

First published 2020
by Routledge
52 Vanderbilt Avenue, New York, NY 10017

and by Routledge
2 Park Square, Milton Park, Abingdon, Oxon OX14 4RN

Routledge is an imprint of the Taylor & Francis Group, an informa business

Library of Congress Cataloguing in Publication Data
Names: Button, Mark E., editor. | Marsh, Ian, 1967- editor.
Title: Suicide and social justice : new perspectives on the politics of suicide and suicide prevention / edited by Mark E. Button and Ian Marsh.
Identifiers: LCCN 2019046188 | ISBN 9781138601833 (hardback) | ISBN 9781138601840 (paperback) | ISBN 9780429460494 (ebook)
Subjects: LCSH: Suicide. | Suicide—Prevention. | Suicidal behavior—Social aspects.
Classification: LCC HV6545 .S8257 2020 | DDC 362.28—dc23
LC record available at https://lccn.loc.gov/2019046188

ISBN: 978-1-138-60183-3 (hbk)
ISBN: 978-1-138-60184-0 (pbk)
ISBN: 978-0-429-46049-4 (ebk)

Typeset in Sabon
by Swales & Willis Ltd, Exeter, Devon, UK

Contents

Acknowledgments

The inspiration for this book began at the Critical Suicidology Conference in Canterbury, UK, June 29–July 1, 2017. Many of the contributors to this volume were assembled in Canterbury in the summer of 2017 and this book would have likely never been imagined (let alone completed) without the supportive international network of academics and activists that the Critical Suicide Studies group brings together each year. Our deepest thanks go to the diverse scholars who have contributed to this volume. We thank all of our contributors for their passion, dedication, and hard work in helping us to rethink what suicide and suicide prevention might begin to look like when social justice is placed at the center of our attention.

We also wish to thank Anna Moore of Routledge for her support of this book idea and for her thoughtful editorial guidance and assistance in bringing this volume to press.

Mark Button: I want to express my deepest gratitude for my co-editor Ian Marsh. Without Ian's wide scholarly influence, his passionate commitment to rethinking dominant approaches to suicide and suicide prevention, and his warm generosity and kindness, I likely would have never been drawn into the critical suicide studies community. It has been a genuine pleasure working with Ian on this book project and I thank him for the inspiring example he sets of a scholar and global citizen committed to making the world a better place for all people.

I also want to thank several people who have been particularly influential to me in approaching the complexities of suicide and suicide prevention: Dr. Margaret Battin, Dr. Craig J. Bryan, documentary film maker Lisa Klein, Dr. Ella Myers, Dr. Jennifer White, and Utah State Representative Steven Eliason.

Ian Marsh: I wish to express my sincere thanks to those scholars whose intellectual, ethical, and practical commitment to more critical and just approaches to the study of suicide and suicide prevention continues to inspire me: Jennifer White, Rob Cover, Katrina Jaworski, Heidi Hjelmeland, Michael Kral, Jonathan Morris, Ludek Broz, Scott Fitzpatrick, David Mosse, Erminia Colucci, Marnie Sather, Heidi Rimke, China Mills, and

Amy Chandler. Two papers have been particularly influential in opening my mind to the possibilities of a social justice approach to suicide—Vikki Reynolds' "Hate Kills: A Social Justice Response to 'Suicide'", and Mark Button's "Suicide and Social Justice: Toward a Political Account of Suicide"—and I would like to express my deep gratitude to both authors. Vikki and Mark's work directly influenced the genesis and development of this book, and their passionate advocacy for more compassionate and just approaches to suicide has, I know, inspired many scholars and activists around the world. It was also a great pleasure to collaborate with Mark as co-editor of this volume.

Regrettably, Dr. Michael Chandler passed away during the course of the production of this volume and so was unable to see his contribution to this book in print. In honor of his life-long scholarly work and activism in the field of suicide prevention, we dedicate this volume in memory of Michael Chandler.

Contributors

AnnaBelle O. Bryan, MS, Director of Operations, National Center for Veterans Studies, University of Utah

Craig J. Bryan, PsyD, ABPP, Associate Professor, Department of Psychology, Executive Director, National Center for Veterans Studies, University of Utah

Mark E. Button, PhD, Dean, College of Arts and Sciences and Professor of Political Science, University of Nebraska-Lincoln

Silvia Sara Canetto, PhD, Professor, Department of Psychology, Colorado State University

Amy Chandler, PhD, Chancellor's Fellow, School of Health in Social Science, University of Edinburgh

Michael J. Chandler, Professor Emeritus, Department of Psychology, University of British Columbia

Lory Barsdate Easton, JD, Institute for the Psychological Sciences

Michael J. Kral, PhD, Associate Professor, School of Social Work, Wayne State University

Christopher E. Lalonde, PhD, Professor, Psychology, University of Victoria

Feea R. Leifker, PhD, MPH, Director of Clinical Services, National Center for Veterans Studies, University of Utah

Ian Marsh, PhD, Reader, School of Allied and Public Health Professions, Canterbury Christ Church University

Alexis M. May, PhD, Post-Doctoral Fellow, National Center for Veterans Studies, University of Utah

Janet McCord, PhD, Professor of Thanatology, Marian University

Maura McFadden, MS, Institute for the Psychological Sciences

China Mills, PhD, Senior Lecturer in Public Health, City University of London

Rebecca S. Morse, PhD, Associate Professor of Psychology, Institute for the Psychological Sciences

Joseph Osafo, PhD, Associate Professor, School of Social Sciences, Department of Psychology, University of Ghana

Mohsen Rezaeian, PhD, Professor, Epidemiology and Biostatistics Department, Rafsanjan Medical School, Occupational Environmental Research Center, Rafsanjan University of Medical Sciences, Iran

David C. Rozek, PhD, Director of Training, National Center for Veterans Studies, University of Utah

Bee Scherer, PhD, Professor of Religious Studies and Gender Studies, Canterbury Christ Church University

Daniel G. Scott, Artistic Director, Planet Earth Poetry; Associate Professor Emeritus, School of Child and Youth Care, University of Victoria

Jennifer White, EdD, Professor, School of Child and Youth Care, University of Victoria

Introduction

Mark E. Button and Ian Marsh

Suicide is a vital issue of social justice for our times. That is the core philosophical and practical-political claim of this book. The purpose of this edited volume is to bring diverse scholarly and social justice perspectives to bear on the problem of suicide and suicidal behavior for a variety of populations within many different regions of the world today.

What do we mean by a social justice approach to suicide? Analyses of the relationship between particular social concerns such as unemployment, rising levels of inequality, poverty, social integration or exclusion, and deaths by suicide have been a fairly consistent feature of modern bio-political engagements with the issue. With 79% of global suicides occurring in low- and middle-income countries (WHO 2018) and with more than half of all people dying by suicide in the United States without any known mental health condition (CDC 2018), the complex relationships between key demographic factors (gender, age, ethnicity, sexuality, socio-economic status, rurality, veteran status, etc.) and suicide remains a vital and ongoing concern. Indeed, over the last decade or more, there has been a growing willingness to see suicide as a *public* health issue and not one that is reducible to any singular or mono-casual explanation (WHO 2018).

Yet, there is still a limit in how far scholars, public officials, clinicians, and concerned citizens are willing to go in thinking about the constitutive interactions between individuals and the entrenched and long-term social-structural conditions and processes in relation to which individuals live. A social justice approach to suicide and suicide prevention—inspired by scholars such as Iris Marion Young (2006; 2011)—emphasizes that we need to develop a greater understanding for the ways in which structural social processes create enduring background conditions—with their own cultural, economic, and policy histories—that generate and consolidate more suicide risk factors (and undermine protective factors) for some people more than others. To adopt a social justice approach to patterns and specific concentrations of suicide ideation, attempts, and deaths within different countries and communities neither presumes nor requires that we identify a particular set of actors or institutions that are liable for this differential positioning in relation to suicide. But a social justice approach to suicide does require that we examine the relationship among multiple and simultaneous risk factors like poverty, ethnicity, sexuality, rurality, veteran status, and limited access to health care as more than the operation of fate or mere bad luck. Generalized and differential individual positioning in relation to suicide arises out of the interaction of multiple subjective, interpersonal, and external factors operating over time that are rarely reducible to individual choices or the easily specifiable actions of liable persons or institutions. The analytic and normative framework of social justice is appropriate and necessary in the case of suicide because it highlights the role that social-structural processes can play in the formation of vulnerability to suicide without presuming that this framework could ever serve as the full or complete account of all deaths by suicide.

Such an approach moves beyond traditional sociological or social determinants of health perspectives. For while a relationship between suicide and various forms of social disadvantage and marginalization has been long recognized by researchers, a social justice approach posits that behind these issues and inequalities are also socio-political drivers or forces—including colonialism, racism, heteronormativity, patriarchy, and downward economic mobility—that also influence patterns and rates of suicide around the world. These "social facts" of suicide tell a political story—a story (or a series of stories) that is frequently punctuated by marginalization, persistent public policy neglect, cultivated indifference, and bad faith.

Given that the "social facts" of suicide have been long established, we can legitimately ask why it is that a more explicitly political and socio-structural narrative around suicide has not previously emerged, or, put another way, why it is that knowledge of the relationship between various dimensions of inequality and suicide has not led to a more organized or systematic political response within global suicide prevention efforts. One answer is that for nearly two centuries the dominant way of framing the issue has been as an individual mental health problem, and this has strongly shaped the ways in which suicide is conceptualized and responded to in practice. Since the early nineteenth century, suicide and suicidality has been for the most part seen as arising from, and located within, the interiority of a separate, singular, individual subject. Constituted in relation to a "compulsory ontology of pathology" (Marsh, 2010), such deaths are read as private, individual events largely divorced from long term social-structural processes and questions about the distribution of equal opportunities for human flourishing and a life of dignity, that is, social justice. While this formulation of suicide in relation to pathology has undoubtedly been productive in terms of opening up possibilities for thought and action, it has also come to limit what can authoritatively be said and done in relation to the issue. Despite recent engagement with suicide from a broader public health perspective (Department of Health 2017; Public Health England 2015a, 2015b, 2016), and the efforts of critical suicide studies scholars and activists to widen the disciplinary and theoretical base of suicidology (e.g. Button 2016; Cover 2012; Jaworski 2014; Kral and Idlout 2016; Marsh 2016; Mills 2017; Reynolds 2016; Wexler and Gone 2012; White 2016, 2017; White and Kral 2014; White et al. 2016), suicide continues to be conceptualized as primarily a question of individual mental health.

For Heidi Rimke (2000; 2010a; 2010b; 2016), the ways in which human problems come to be framed as innate pathologies of the individual mind and/or body can be conceptualized as "psychocentrism," and the social production of psychocentric knowledge in relation to suicide has meant that not only are the complex social and political contexts of such deaths obscured, but also responses to the issue have tended towards the individual level with collective and political responses marginalized or absent. Suicide has thus remained outside of politics, although we would also argue that to frame suicide primarily as an issue of individual mental health is itself a political act. Thus, part of a social justice response to suicide requires that we understand, as Chloe Taylor argues, "the political nature of our current ontology of suicide as pathology" (2015, 20).

The exact nature of the relationship between currently existing dominant "psy" approaches and emerging social justice formulations—the extent to which they could be said to be complementary or necessarily in opposition—is a yet-to-be settled question, and the authors in this volume take up various positions in this ongoing debate. For most, the aim of a social justice approach to suicide is not to refute dominant biomedical and psychological approaches to suicide that focus on the role of individual psychopathology in suicidal behavior. Rather, a social justice approach—conceived and anchored in normative commitments to equal moral freedom and human dignity— seeks to contextualize and supplement this dominant understanding with more explicitly political, structural, and socio-cultural accounts of the factors involved in rising rates of suicide, especially as these rates are concentrated within vulnerable populations and the intersections among them (native peoples, the elderly, veterans and military personnel, individuals in poverty, rural residents, LGBTQ youth, and others). Whereas the dominant framework in the analysis and prevention of suicide sees *individual* psychopathology at work, a social justice approach *also* sees historically and structurally embedded *social* pathologies that call for both deeper contextual analysis and more organized social and political responses. A social justice approach also seeks to understand the complex interactions between various social pathologies (inequality, intergenerational poverty, racism, sexism, heteronormativity, marginalization, stigma, and social isolation) and individual or group experiences with suicidality. As such, a social justice approach to suicide requires that scholars, policy makers, and practitioners investigate the underlying and often overlooked connections that link the rising rates and disproportionate concentrations of suicide within specific populations to the wider social, political, and economic conditions bearing on individuals' lives.

With persistent rising rates of suicide in numerous countries throughout the world, public health officials are increasingly calling for the development of a wider range of prevention efforts than we have seen before (see CDC 2018). We think that this is the precise entry point for a social justice approach to suicide because it asks us to examine the ways in which congealed cultural and social practices and entrenched policy regimes have helped to distribute and consolidate vulnerability to suicide in unequal ways. We understand this work as a necessary precursor to more thorough-going suicide prevention efforts aimed at primary social and political institutions at multiple levels of organization—from neighborhoods and villages, to churches and schools, states, and international organizations. As Iris Marion Young has argued:

> To judge that a suffering or disadvantage is unjust . . . implies that we acknowledge the circumstance as grounded at least partly in institutions and the social processes they generate. When we acknowledge such social causes of suffering or disadvantage, we thereby at least implicitly recognize an obligation to try to improve those social processes.
>
> (2011, 33)

As Jennifer White argues in this volume, such recognition and call to action also needs to be accompanied by a shared understanding of our interdependence and relational accountability, and the taking of a stance that "does not shy away from acknowledging and addressing our potential *complicity with harm.*" Once we accept that suicide emerges from contexts of social injustice of which we are all a part, suicide prevention can be re-imagined from a social justice perspective as a collective responsibility and social movement to mediate the harmful effects of "the cruelties, forms of dispossession, and injustices of the present, while at the same time never 'forgetting' the historical harms that have contributed to the experience of suffering and suicidal despair." Suicide prevention from a social justice perspective thus becomes more of a collective, relational, and political endeavor than is currently the case, redrawing the boundaries of the field in ways many within existing mainstream suicidology might find challenging.

To sum up, a social justice approach to suicide combines socio-political and/or cultural-historical analyses of the determinants and experiences of suicide with the elaboration and defense of new political, social, and cultural efforts at suicide prevention. Promoting justice in the context of suicide prevention means preventing the social processes and structural conditions that interact with personal-psychological factors that increase suicidal ideation, attempts, and deaths. This unique volume brings together an intellectually diverse groups of scholars and practitioners from a range of different academic and professional fields to fundamentally re-think suicide and suicide prevention today.

Volume Overview

Part I of this volume is dedicated to a critical assessment of some of the philosophical and ethical sources from which an engagement with suicide as a question of social justice can be developed and practiced today. As we have already noted, suicide is usually described and framed as primarily a question of individual mental health, with wider economic, social, historical, and political contexts relatively under-examined. However, new forms of scholarship and public health advocacy that link suicide to structural issues of injustice, inequality, exclusion, and oppression have started to emerge—constituting what could be called a political or social justice approach to suicide and suicide prevention. In his chapter for this volume, "Suicide and Social Justice: Discourse, Politics and Experience," Ian Marsh discusses some of the different ways in which the relationship between social injustice and suicide is formulated, analyzes the assumptions underlying such accounts, and considers the possibilities for thought and action that are opened up through the discursive construction of suicide as a question of social justice. Marsh argues that social justice approaches to suicide can provide valuable new ways of understanding and responding to suicide, but only if certain assumptions embedded in mainstream suicidology—particularly those pertaining to notions of personhood and agency—are called into question. Drawing on poststructuralist theory, Marsh shows how theoretical accounts that explore the relationship between language, power, oppression, and experience can cast light on how suicidal subjects are formed over time within particular social and political environments. Historically, suicidology has only rarely engaged with the question of how experiences of inequality and injustice contribute to suicide, but emerging social justice approaches offer some hope that this oversight is now being redressed.

In Chapter 2, "Shame as Affective Injustice: Qualitative, Sociological Explorations of Self-Harm, Suicide and Socioeconomic Inequalities," Amy Chandler considers the complex relationship between socioeconomic disadvantage, emotions, and self-harm and suicide. The unequal distribution of rates of self-harm and suicide across different social groups is a key indicator that these practices should be considered in terms of social justice. In the UK, for example, rates of hospital treated self-harm and completed suicide are concentrated among people who have experienced socioeconomic disadvantage. This concentration can be understood as an inequity—unfair and unjust treatment, with far-reaching effects on families and communities. Epidemiological approaches have been pivotal in identifying inequalities in the distribution of self-harm and suicide. However, such approaches are less helpful when it comes to *explaining* the deeper reasons for such distributions. In this chapter, Chandler asks: What is it about the experience of socioeconomic disadvantage that leads to higher numbers of people taking their own lives, or harming themselves? Chandler shows that a careful consideration of the role of emotions—and especially the role of shame—helps to explain how structural conditions of oppression and inequality can shape individual actions, including self-harm and suicide.

Part II of this volume explores the intersections of specific populations affected by high rates of suicide and the role of public policies therein. The chapters in Part II draw from a diverse range of global, political perspectives on suicide and suicide prevention. In Chapter 3, "Cultural Continuity and Indigenous Youth Suicide," Michael J. Chandler and Christopher E. Lalonde draw upon a three decade-long program of research aimed at better understanding two deeply puzzling issues. The first of these concerns how it could possibly be that so many young persons can and do so regularly choose to end their own lives. Relatedly, the second puzzle focuses special attention on Indigenous youth, and the "epidemics" of youth suicide alleged to characterize such special populations. Euro-American thoughts about health and well-being continue to be dominated by what Cushman (1990) has labeled the West's historical commitment to "self-contained individualism." Few still seriously doubt that poverty, discrimination, and disenfranchisement, along with a whole raft of related social troubles, naturally count among the possible "up-stream" causes of many of our subsequent miseries. Nonetheless, as Chandler and Lalonde argue, the particular location where the consequences of such socio-cultural problems are standardly imagined to come home to roost, and the preferred targets of most planned intervention efforts, too often continue to be understood as located somewhere in the troubled hearts and minds of single individuals. As a result, whenever we are moved to minister to such troubles, the familiar impulse—the usual treatment strategy—is to attempt to save one soul at a time. Chandler and Lalonde show that this approach is not a particularly well-thought out public health strategy. The alternative they promote attempts instead to identify problem-related socio-cultural markers characteristic of whole communities—factors intended to monitor the collective efforts of whole communities to right earlier social injustices. Their chapter focuses on the problem of youth suicide as it manifests itself in the Indigenous First Nations communities in Western Canada.

In Chapter 4, "Strengthening Borders and Toughening Up on Welfare: Deaths by Suicide in the UK's Hostile Environment," China Mills traces some of the ways in which post-recession austerity policies in Britain—shaped by deterrence technologies, bordering practices, and hierarchy—create conditions that make life, for some, unlivable, and that incite, elicit, and invite suicidality. Focusing on border practices, Mills emphasizes that hostile government policies are not new, are tied up with histories of colonialism, and are pervasive across a range of what she calls "classificatory politics." Mills' chapter details the relevance of bordering practices for thinking about suicide, and explores the ways some organizations move away from psychocentric, individualizing, and depoliticizing agendas by making visible the ways detention and welfare reform exacerbate and cause distress and suicide. Mills argues that hostile environments facilitated by specific public policies are neither new nor singular, nor can they be "fixed" by tweaking public policies, given that the pervasive underlying logic of these policies intersects with other systems to create conditions that elicit suicidality.

Chapter 5 by Mark E. Button presents a statistical index and analysis of "suicidal regimes" by correlating the rates and distribution of suicide with reference to key public policy actions and inactions at the state level in the United States. Button's chapter aims to show that many suicidal persons do not simply "fall" into at risk categories owing to exclusively individual (endogenous) mental health challenges; rather, individuals and populations at risk for suicide are also *formed* by political and structural conditions that undermine a life of equal freedom, flourishing, and human dignity. Suicide prevention is therefore a matter of both mental health and social justice because the rates and distribution of suicidality are, in part, the product of public policy choices and a corresponding bad faith (or willful blindness) about the effect of these choices on the formation of distinctive suicidal subjectivities. Button argues that important "symptoms" relevant to suicide prevention efforts include the political and ideological constitution of suicidal regimes: those states with high rates of concentrated poverty, racial and ethnic marginalization, unsupportive environments for LGBTQ youth, lax firearm regulations, and inadequate and unequal access to comprehensive health care. The tragedy of suicide is not restricted to individuals in crisis; the tragedy of suicide also refers to the deeper structural crises that are constituted by the persistence of suicidal regimes: those governing political bodies that consistently score poorly on the suicidal regime policy index. Concerned citizens and public health advocates should therefore be trained to identify not only those individuals who are in crisis, but to identify the underlying institutional and political factors that help to constitute these crises and take appropriate *political* action to prevent them and pursue alternative public policy directions.

Moving beyond the United States and Europe, Chapter 6 by Silvia Sara Canetto and Mohsen Rezaeian provides an analysis of protest suicides among women in Muslim-majority countries. In most countries around the world, women have lower suicide rates than men. However, five of the six countries where women's suicide rates are higher than men's are Muslim-majority countries. A recurring female suicide-script in these countries is of suicide as a way of protesting against, and to escape from the institutionalized oppression and abuse they endure in their family and community. Uneducated, poor, adult women living in rural areas are especially likely to engage in protest suicide. Canetto and Rezaeian show that Muslim women's protest suicides challenge the dominant theory that women are protected from suicide, especially during their reproductive years, and when they have significant family and community ties. Muslim women's protest suicides require moving beyond dominant suicide-prevention paradigms such as the belief that social ties are protective against suicide and the widely accepted view that suicide is nearly always a symptom of a mental disorder. Muslim women's protest suicides also require the adoption of a human rights perspective on suicide prevention. As Canetto and Rezaeian argue, this means that suicide prevention strategies must be understood as a commitment to social justice and that Muslim-majority communities and countries commit to achieving full educational, economic, and social rights for women.

Chapter 7 by Joseph Osafo, "From Psychocentric Explanations to Social Troubles: Challenging Dominant Discourse on Suicide in Ghana," is dedicated to an analysis of the legal and discursive forces that shape the realities of suicide in Ghana. As Osafo shows, pathological and moral perspectives that locate the risks for suicide within the individual are dominant in Ghana. Nonetheless, wider social issues such as domestic violence, economic hardships, bullying in public schools, and a host of other external difficulties continue to be overlooked factors in suicidal behavior in Ghana and other countries. The situation for suicide attempt survivors in Ghana is particularly precarious given the existence of a state law that vigorously prosecutes them. Osafo's chapter examines the complex dimensions of suicide risks in Ghana from a social-existential perspective. From this angle, the criminalization of attempted suicide in Ghana is viewed as primarily a human rights issue and thus decriminalization is a central priority for social justice. Osafo argues that suicide prevention in Ghana should not rest solely with psychocentric academics and practitioners, and that civil society groups such as human rights campaigners, religious-based pressure groups, and NGOs are also essential to this effort.

Part III of this volume begins with a turn to the embodied experience of those living with and confronting suicide and suicidal ideation. Chapter 8 by Bee Scherer provides powerful testimony of living with traumatic experiences and understanding oneself as a "suicide waiting to happen." Scherer's chapter is a passionate call for the end of the judgmental language and "patronizing pathologization" of people living with suicidal thoughts. For Scherer, the term "suicide" itself wrongly over-emphasizes self-agency and individual burdens over more systemic "phonoïc" wounds and forms of victimization. Scherer's chapter concludes with a poem—inspired by Bee Scherer's life, persistence, and political resistance—by Daniel G. Scott, "self murder."

The remaining chapters in Part III of this volume seek to reorient contemporary clinical and community-based practices of suicide prevention. In Chapter 9, Rebecca S. Morse, Michael J. Kral, Maura McFadden, Janet McCord and Lory Barsdate Easton focus on the emergence of the paraprofessional mental health movement; the work of "ordinary" or lay people to help individuals with mental health issues through the use of hotlines, survivor support groups, and social media crisis supports (such as crisis text lines). They frame this work as a counterbalance to the dominant biomedical approach to mental health care and argue that engaging trained nonprofessional volunteers in such socially responsible action can reduce impediments to access to care and ultimately decrease social disparity in the provision of mental health support.

Similarly, Chapter 10 by Craig J. Bryan, AnnaBelle O. Bryan, David C. Rozek, Feea R. Leifker and Alexis M. May also engages with issues of equity and justice regarding the availability and quality of mental healthcare services, but this time in relation to U.S. veterans at risk for suicide. U.S. military veterans are a vulnerable group owing to their high rates of physical and psychological injury and disability, and these vulnerabilities increase their risk for suicide. Bryan et al. argue that veterans often receive low quality healthcare due in large part to deficient training practices in the U.S. mental healthcare professional training programs. The authors detail institutional and systems-based changes in accreditation requirements, regulatory processes, and institutional policies which would act as corrections to these flaws, and argue that addressing these issues could significantly improve the quality of mental healthcare services for veterans and, by extension, reduce suicide rates in this high-risk community.

Chapter 11 by Jennifer White, "Hello Cruel World! Embracing a Collective Ethics for Suicide Prevention," concludes this volume with her eloquent call for a reconsideration of the project of suicide prevention itself. Highlighting the growing dissatisfaction with biomedical framings of suicide and individualistic approaches to prevention, White argues for richer and more nuanced vocabularies to reflect more politically informed, historically situated, and relational conceptualizations of living, dying, suffering, and suicide. For White, there is a need to develop an ethical vision for suicide prevention that takes account of the social, historical, and political contexts of people's lives, one that can capture our deep interdependency, complicity, and potential for collective action. Inspired by Alexis Shotwell's (2016) work on collective forms of ethics that eschews purity, White maps out what a re-vitalized ethical and political vision for suicide prevention might look like, one that recognizes that we are always living and working in the midst of interlocking systems, structures, and discourses that both reproduce harm and also shape understandings of what counts as a worthwhile life.

Possibilities for Social Justice or Political Approaches to Suicide

As the editors of this volume, our aim has been to assemble in one volume scholarship that would explore how various social justice and political perspectives and approaches might confront the issue of suicide in different parts of the world. It is our belief that these kinds of critical engagements have the potential to open up new possibilities for thought and action in relation to suicide and suicide prevention beyond traditional philosophical, sociological, medical, or psychiatric approaches. The work collected in this volume amply demonstrates how social justice perspectives and political analysis can help us understand more fully how suicide arises within specific social, economic, political, and historical contexts. Each contribution to the volume seeks to make connections between inequalities and injustices perpetuated through the creation and maintenance of particular social structures and hierarchies, and deaths by suicide. Many of the chapters describe the very real psychic/emotional impact on those caught up in such assemblages, some from first-person perspectives and many from first-hand experience of others' suffering. All suggest possibilities for informed action. The framing of suicide as a question of politics and social justice perhaps represents a challenge to current dominant constructions of the act, but in our view, it is one that is full of possibilities and is long overdue.

References

Button, Mark. 2016. Suicide and social justice: Toward a political approach to suicide. *Political Research Quarterly*, 69(2), 270–280.

Center for Disease Control and Prevention (CDC). 2018. Suicide Mortality in the United States, 1999–2017. National Center for Health Statistics (accessed 17 December 2018).

Cover, Rob. 2012. *Queer Youth Suicide, Culture and Identity: Unliveable Lives?* Farnham: Ashgate.

Cushman, Pauline. 1990. Why the self is empty: Towards a historically situated psychology. *American Psychologist*, 45, 599–611.

Department of Health. 2017. Preventing Suicide in England: Third Progress Report of the Cross-Government Outcomes Strategy to Save Lives. Available online: www.gov.uk/government/uploads/system/uploads/attachment_data/file/582117/Suicide_report_2016_A.pdf (accessed 17 July 2018).

Jaworski, Katrina. 2014. *The Gender of Suicide: Knowledge Production, Theory and Suicidology*. Farnham: Ashgate.

Kral, Michael J., and Idlout, Lori. 2016. Indigenous best practices: Community-based suicide prevention in Nunavut, Canada. In Jennifer White, Ian Marsh, Michael J. Kral, and Jonathan Morris (Eds.), *Critical Suicidology: Transforming Suicide Research and Prevention for the 21st Century* (pp. 229–243). Vancouver: University of British Columbia Press.

Marsh, Ian. 2010. *Suicide: Foucault, History and Truth*. New York: Cambridge University Press.

Marsh, Ian. 2016. Critiquing contemporary suicidology. In Jennifer White, Ian Marsh, Michael J. Kral, and Jonathan Morris (Eds.), *Critical Suicidology: Transforming Suicide Research and Prevention for the 21st Century* (pp. 15–30). Vancouver: University of British Columbia Press.

Mills, China. 2017. 'Dead people don't claim': A psychopolitical autopsy of UK austerity suicides. *Critical Social Policy*, 38(2), 302–322.

Public Health England. 2015a. Suicide Prevention: Identifying and Responding to Suicide Clusters. Published September 2015. Available online: https://assets.publishing.service.gov.uk/government/uploads/system/uploads/attachment_data/file/459303/Identifying_and_responding_to_suicide_clusters_and_contagion.pdf (accessed 17 July 2018).

Public Health England. 2015b. Preventing Suicides in Public Places: A Practice Resource. Available online: https://assets.publishing.service.gov.uk/government/uploads/system/uploads/attachment_data/file/481224/Preventing_suicides_in_public_places.pdf (accessed 17 July 2018).

Public Health England. 2016. Local Suicide Prevention Planning: A Practice Resource. Available online: www.nspa.org.uk/wp-content/uploads/2016/10/PHE_LA_guidance-NB241016.pdf (accessed 17 July 2018).

Reynolds, Vikki. 2016. Hate kills: A social justice response to suicide. In Jennifer White, Ian Marsh, Michael J. Kral, and Jonathan Morris (Eds.), *Critical Suicidology: Transforming Suicide Research and Prevention for the 21st Century* (pp. 169–187). Vancouver: University of British Columbia Press.

Rimke, Heidi. 2000. Governing citizens through self-help literature. *Cultural Studies*, 14(1), 61–78.

Rimke, Heidi. 2010a. Consuming fears: Neoliberal in/securities, cannibalization, and psychopolitics. In Jeff Shantz (Ed.), *Racism and Borders: Representation, Repression, Resistance* (pp. 95–113). New York: Algora Publishing.

Rimke, Heidi. 2010b. Beheading aboard a Greyhound bus: Security politics, bloodlust justice, and the mass consumption of criminalized cannibalism. *The Annual Review of Interdisciplinary Justice Research*, 1, 172–192.

Rimke, Heidi. 2016. Introduction – Mental and emotional distress as a social justice issue: Beyond psychocentrism. *Studies in Social Justice*, 10(1), 4–17.

Shotwell, A. 2016. *Against Purity: Living Ethically in Compromised Times.* Minneapolis: University of Minnesota Press.

Taylor, Chloe. 2015. Birth of the suicidal subject: Nelly Arcan, Michel Foucault and voluntary death. *Culture Theory and Critique*. doi:101080/147357842014937820

Wexler, Lisa M., and Gone, Joseph P. 2012. Culturally responsive suicide prevention in Indigenous communities: Unexamined assumptions and new possibilities. *American Journal of Public Health*, 102(5), 800–806.

White, Jennifer. 2016. Reimagining youth suicide prevention education. In Jennifer White, Ian Marsh, Michael J. Kral, and Jonathan Morris (Eds.), *Critical Suicidology: Transforming Suicide Research and Prevention for the 21st Century* (pp. 244–263). Vancouver: University of British Columbia Press.

White, Jennifer. 2017. What can critical suicidology do? *Death Studies*, 41(8), 472–480. doi:10.1080/07481187.2017.1332901. Epub 2017 May 19.

White, Jennifer, and Kral, Michael. 2014. Re-thinking youth suicide: Language, culture and power. *Journal of Social Action for Counselling and Psychology*, 6(1), 122–142.

White, Jennifer, Marsh, Ian, Kral, Michael J., and Morris, Jonathan (Eds.). 2016. *Critical Suicidology: Transforming Suicide Research and Prevention for the 21st Century*. Vancouver: University of British Columbia Press.

World Health Organization (WHO). 2018. Suicide Data. Available online: www.who.int/mental_health/prevention/suicide/suicideprevent/en/ (accessed 10 December 2018).

Young, I. M. 2006. 'Responsibility and global justice: A social connection model'. *Social Philosophy and Policy Foundation*, 23(1), 102–130.

Young, I. M. 2011. *Responsibility for Justice*. New York: Oxford University Press.

Part I

1 Suicide and Social Justice

Discourse, Politics and Experience

Ian Marsh

Introduction

Over time, suicide has variously been considered from theological, philosophical, moral, ethical, sociological, psychological, literary, autobiographical, psychiatric, epidemiological and medical perspectives (to name just some of the most obvious). One way to approach the subject of suicide is to examine how the issue is framed in such accounts, and the relationship of representation to practices and experience. Obviously, it would be a huge task to attempt to map all perspectives and related practices. However, a tighter focus on the dominant ways in which suicide is constructed at particular times in specific places allows us to cast light on not only the meanings that get attached to suicide, but maybe, more complexly, on the relationship between the ways in which suicide is represented or framed, what gets done in relation to the issue, and the effects in terms of people's experiences of suicidality and suicide.

In previous work (Marsh, 2010, 2016) I have suggested that contemporary mainstream ways of framing suicide are grounded on particular assumptions that decisively shape thought and practice: namely, that suicide is pathological ("People who kill themselves are mentally ill"); suicidology is science ("We will come to the best understanding of suicide through studying it objectively, using the tools of Western medical science"); and suicide is individual ("Suicidality arises from, and is located within, the 'interiority' of a separate, singular, individual subject"). I would argue that despite the advances of a broader public health approach in the field of prevention, suicide is still, for the most part, understood as primarily a question of individual mental health, and that as a consequence, wider economic, social, historical and political contexts of suicide have remained relatively under-examined. More recently, however, work explicitly linking suicide to issues of injustice, inequality, exclusion and oppression has emerged – constituting what could be called a political or social justice approach to suicide. In this chapter, I am interested in what links these approaches, in how the relationship between social injustice and suicide is variously formulated, in the assumptions underlying such accounts, and also in what possibilities for thought and action are opened up through the discursive construction of suicide as a question of social justice.

Approach

The aim here is not to survey all papers, chapters and books that have dealt with suicide in relation to issues such as poverty, social exclusion, oppression of minority groups, and so on – a historical mapping of texts that link suicide to social problems is not the purpose of the chapter. Rather, it has more modest and focused goals. The approach taken here is, broadly speaking, a discourse analytic one (Bacchi, 2009; Marsh, 2010, 2016). I am interested in how, within particular texts, questions of social justice are brought into relationship with suicide; that is, in how that relationship is conceptualised, and on the styles of thought (Rose, 2000), vocabularies, stories, ideas and images which are drawn on in accounts that link social injustice to suicide. Of particular interest are the ways in which traditional bio-medical, psychiatric and psychological approaches to suicide are conceptualised within social justice discourse – as I believe a yet-to-be settled question is the extent to which the relationship between existing dominant "psy" approaches and emerging political or social justice formulations of the issue could be said to be complementary or necessarily in opposition.

There are also questions relating to the assumptions which could be said to underlie different accounts of suicide – how the relationship between language and experience is formulated, what sort of claims to truth are made and on what basis, and how notions such as personhood, agency, intention and causation are conceptualised, and to what effect.

I am also interested in what possibilities for thought and action are opened up through the discursive construction of suicide as explicitly a question of social justice. By this I mean, what might the different ways of framing suicide as a political or social justice issue mean for practice, for research, and for how people might come to understand and experience suicide and suicidality differently. Or to put it another way, what alternative ways of understanding and responding to suicide are made possible through a social justice approach to the issue. The question of how suicidal subjects are formed in relation to social-political conditions is central here.

The analysis thus focusses on addressing the following interrelated questions:

1 How is the relationship between social injustice and suicide formulated (that is, what style of thought, vocabularies, stories, images and conceptual schema are drawn upon in making the link between suicide and social justice issues)?

2 How are traditional bio-medical, psychiatric and psychological approaches to suicide conceptualised within social justice discourse?
3 What assumptions underlie such accounts (particularly in relation to ideas of personhood, agency and causation)?
4 What possibilities for thought and action are opened up through the discursive construction of suicide as a question of social justice?

In terms of selection of papers, I have sought out ones that explicitly take a social justice stance towards the issue of suicide, and these are analysed in terms of the divergences and convergences in their formulations, conceptualisations, and theoretical assumptions in relation to the above questions.

The Formulation of the Relationship between Social Injustice and Suicide

Most obviously, social justice approaches to suicide emphasise the contexts – political, economic, social, cultural and historical – within which suicide occurs (Mills, 2017; Reynolds, 2016; Wexler & Gone, 2012; White, 2016, 2017; White & Kral, 2014). Often, this consideration of wider contexts is explicitly contrasted with dominant "psy" (psychiatric, psychological, psychotherapeutic) approaches, where the main focus tends to be on the individual, somewhat separated or seen in isolation from these factors. White and Kral (2014), for instance, argue that traditional psychological theories provide, an "excessively individualistic and technical account of suicide, which serves to both de-contextualize the act and strip away its inherently relational, ethical, historical, and political nature" (p123). Rather than seeing distress and suicidality as somehow being free of these contexts, such experiences are instead taken as socially and culturally constituted, and the relationship between them theorised. Drawing on social justice approaches in mental health (e.g. Morrow & Weisser, 2012), White and Kral (2014) argue that social and historical contexts "produce environments of discrimination and social inequality, which place a disproportionate burden of suffering on some groups of people and not others" (p130). Reviewing the extensive research on risk factors for suicide, White and Kral (2014) point to adverse living conditions, socioeconomic disadvantage, unemployment and economic hardship, poverty and social fragmentation as factors that increase the likelihood of suicide. Research on racism, prejudice and discrimination in relation to suicide is also cited, as is that relating to postcolonial trauma of indigenous peoples, and the specific experiences of sexual minority youth. They conclude, "suicide is thus tied to social inequalities and injustice" (p130), yet individualised, "psycho-centric" (Rimke & Brock, 2012) understandings of the act have tended to dominate the field of prevention. By such means, as White (2017) argues elsewhere "colonial violence, racism, heteronormativity, patriarchy, social exclusion, capitalist greed, and injustice" come to be obscured (p474).

It is arguably this step, from evidence of the relationship between inequality and suicide, to the framing of the issue in terms of injustice and politics, which marks the application of a social justice (as opposed to say, a "social determinants") approach. For whilst a relationship between social status or level of integration, economic hardship, unemployment and so on, and deaths by suicide may have been recognised by researchers for a long time, arguing that behind those issues and inequalities there are socio-political drivers or forces – such as colonialism, racism, heteronormativity, patriarchy and capitalism (Cover, 2012, 2016; Kral & Idlout, 2016; Mills, 2017; Reynolds, 2016; Wexler & Gone, 2012; White, 2017; White & Kral, 2014) – that have a direct and systematic effect on rates of suicide, is fairly new.

Once that move has been made, a number of further questions open up. How to formulate and represent the relationship between social injustice and suicide? What forms of research to undertake and draw upon in making claims to truth, based on what epistemological and ontological commitments? For whilst "traditional" psychological, psychiatric and epidemiological (and even sociological) research on suicide has tended to look for variables which could be isolated and measured, a social justice approach has, arguably, a need to make use of means and methods of knowledge production more suited to understanding complex relationships and contexts.

For the most part, this has led to the use of qualitative research methods over quantitative (but not exclusively, see for example Mark E. Button's chapter in this collection), marking a further shift away from mainstream suicidology, where the quantitative is usually (strongly) favoured over the qualitative (see Joiner, 2011). In a way, there is no categorical imperative to use one form of research method over another, as the nature of the evidence is such that the link between socioeconomic disadvantage, say, and suicidal behaviours is sufficiently well-established that fairly well-grounded claims to truth can be made (see Platt, Stace, & Morrissey, 2017). Rather, it is in the bringing together and foregrounding of that evidence, and the nature of its interpretation, that social justice approaches distinguish themselves from more traditional sociological and epidemiological ones.

So, in terms of the representation and interpretation of knowledge on the relationship between inequalities and suicide, social justice approaches can be distinguished from more traditional ways of framing the issue by the primary, and overt, focus being on the ethical and political context of such a relationship. This can perhaps be illustrated by comparing two studies into deaths by suicide in the UK in recent years: a report by The Samaritans, "Dying from inequality" (Platt, Stace, & Morrissey, 2017), which draws on academic research to analyse the relationship between "socioeconomic disadvantage and suicidal behaviour" (p3), and China Mills' (2017) paper, "'Dead people don't claim': A psychopolitical autopsy of UK austerity suicides".

"Dying from inequality" presents evidence of a "significant association between socioeconomic disadvantage and suicidal behaviour" (Platt, Stace, & Morrissey, 2017, p4), and poses questions as to why this might be: what it is about socioeconomic disadvantage that increases the risk of suicidal behaviour, and what can be done about it (ibid). The report considers research evidence at three levels: societal, community and individual, and "sets out the actions needed to reduce the number of disadvantaged people taking their own lives" (p6). Whilst making clear connections between socioeconomic disadvantage – including homelessness, poor housing, unemployment, job loss and financial crises – and poor mental health and suicidal behaviours, "Dying from inequality" stops short of taking a social justice stance on these issues. By this, I mean the connections and associations highlighted, the analysis in terms of increased risk, and the recommendations for policy and practice changes, are framed rather narrowly as economic and public health inequalities and only implicitly as political issues. Suicide, the report concludes, "is everybody's business and recommendations arising from this report are aimed at a range of agencies, both local and national, to address issues at societal, community and individual levels" (p179). So at a society level, improved mental health services, a focus on high risk groups, the provision of "adequate social welfare payments" and "universal high quality public service provision in health, education, housing and social security" (ibid), the destigmatisation of poverty and debt; at community and individual levels, greater awareness of the impact of economic hardship, specialist training for staff dealing with those experiencing economic hardship on "recognising, understanding and responding compassionately" (p181) to those in distress or suicidal. These are all, undoubtedly, important recommendations, but there is a sense that the report remains conservative in its analysis and proposals for change.

By contrast, China Mills' (2017) "Dead people don't claim" utilises a "psychopolitical autopsy" approach to analyse the relationship between specific policies, socially produced and maintained structures and hierarchies, moral economies of human worth, the psychic/emotional life of people caught up in such a regime (specifically experiences of shame and anxiety), and deaths by suicide. On the surface, China Mills' paper bears many similarities to "Dying from inequality" – analysis at different levels (national policy, community and individual/psychological), drawing on empirical epidemiological and public health data to support arguments, and a desire to understand the ways in which socioeconomic hardship relate to deaths by suicide. I would argue, though, that the approaches diverge in terms of the extent to which the analysis of such deaths takes into account, in Vikki Reynolds' (2016) terms, the context of social injustice in which they occurred. The Samaritans, as a UK charity, are perhaps limited in the extent to which they can produce reports that frame suicide as a social justice issue, or to make calls for political accountability or change. But suicide can be understood as political in the broad sense (rather than a narrow, party political, sense) of the term, and a social justice discourse on suicide is constituted, in part, by a consideration of how these wider political aspects can relate to suicide.

Mark Button's (2016) political approach to suicide as a matter of social justice explores these issues in detail. Button attends to the ways in which suicide could be constituted as a political and social justice issue, and explores the ethical and moral grounds upon which such a claim can be made, arguing that there is "a compelling collective obligation, grounded in the moral equality and dignity of persons, to ameliorate the social, economic, and material conditions that are correlated with higher rates of suicide" (2016, p271). Like China Mills (2017) and others (Cover, 2012, 2016; Kral & Idlout, 2016; Reynolds, 2016; Wexler & Gone, 2012; White, 2017; White & Kral, 2014), there is an explicit step taken beyond the acknowledgement of evidence that economic conditions or inequality are related to rates of suicide, to the framing of the issue in terms of injustice and politics. As Button states, a political analysis moves beyond

> structural sociology by arguing that the "social facts" of suicide (the patterns and trends of suicide rates in certain populations) also tell a political story – a story (or a series of stories) that is frequently punctuated by marginalization, persistent neglect, cultivated indifference, and bad faith.
>
> (2016, p274)

For Button,

> [a]n organized political approach to suicide would not allow a society and its major institutions (legislative bodies, the health care industry, schools and universities, the mass media, etc.) to characterize suicide as a strictly personal or family problem because such an approach would start with the acknowledgment that suicide is also a collective burden of social justice tied to the distribution of primary goods within a political system.
>
> (ibid)

Button's analysis draws attention to the "persistent structural injustices that both mirror and further aggravate wider injustices in relation to socioeconomic class, race, ethnicity, age, sexuality, and disability". Such a situation necessitates a response, "not only in relation to the background conditions of possibility for patterns of suicide but also in relation to the formation of an integrated and politically responsible engagement with these patterns" (2016, p276). Suicide, in such an account, is political in the broadest sense, and encompasses an ethical and moral imperative to recognise the harm not only of unequal conditions but the harm of allowing these to continue.

A social justice approach to suicide, in these accounts, is taken to be a political, ethical and moral endeavour. There is a shared understanding that a desire to die expresses something more than a disordered or pathological mind or brain, that it is formed over time within social, economic and political contexts, and these conditions are foregrounded and interpreted as a question of justice and politics. Further, the framing of suicide as solely an issue of individual mental health is argued to have social, political and ethical consequences (Button, 2016; Mills, 2017; Reynolds, 2016; Wexler & Gone, 2012; White, 2016, 2017; White & Kral, 2014).

Conceptualisation of Traditional Bio-Medical, Psychiatric and Psychological Approaches to Suicide within Social Justice Discourse

A theme throughout social justice texts is of psy-discourse obscuring the socio-economic and political contexts of suicide, and the argument that the framing of suicide as a question primarily of individual mental health is itself not a politically neutral act (Button, 2016; Mills, 2017; Reynolds, 2016; Wexler & Gone, 2012; White, 2016, 2017; White & Kral, 2014). There are often, too, acknowledgements that a political or social justice approach can complement existing mental health theory and practice (Button, 2016; Reynolds, 2016; White, 2017), with the aim being "to supplement (not fully dislodge) the dominant psychological and psychiatric approaches to the study of suicide with greater overall attention to the sociocultural dynamics that are part of the enduring conditions of possibility for suicide today" (Button, 2016, p270).

The engagement with psychological theory from a social justice perspective can be productive. Mark Button (2016), for example, provides an interesting analysis of one of the most well-known psychological theories of suicidal behaviour – Thomas Joiner's (2005) Interpersonal Theory of Suicide. For Joiner (following Edwin Shneidman), suicide arises due to mental pain, and mental pain is experienced due to unmet human needs – specifically thwarted belongingness and perceived burdensomeness – and it is these factors, alongside an acquired capacity for suicide, that are taken to be the main drivers behind acts of suicide. Button interrogates these concepts, asking about their sociocultural sources and how it is that "these specific forms of self-consciousness take root within an individual psyche and within members of larger social groups" (2016, p274). Within this account, belongingness and burdensomeness are not located solely within, or read as arising from, separate individual minds, but are seen as emerging from socio-political contexts and conditions, and analysis of the social and political sources of "burdensomeness"opens up the concept beyond its narrow, individual-level deployment in psychological theories of suicide, but in a way which could be said to complement and extend an existing "psy" approach.

In other accounts, though, the utility of psychiatric and psychological theory, concepts and practices are contested more strongly. China Mills (2017), for example, also takes up the social construction and political deployment of "burdensomeness" in relation to media reporting of benefit claimants, but in a way that more pointedly challenges the usefulness of mainstream "psy" theorising. Within China Mills' "psychopolitical autopsy" approach, social structures and hierarchies are taken to interact with the moral economies of human value and worth, and ideological policy making, to produce the psychic life of those subjected to such a regime. Suicide thus comes to be read not as an outcome of a disembodied, pathological mind or brain – not as a form of "derangement" (Joiner et al., 2016) – but as "embedded within an affective economy of the anxiety caused by punitive welfare retrenchment, the stigmatisation of being a recipient of benefits, and the internalisation of market logic that assigns value through 'productivity' and conceptualises welfare entitlement as economic 'burden'" (Mills, 2017, p1). Within such an environment, it is argued, suicides arise that are linked to people's fears of being a "burden" and reflect "the internalisation of market and eugenic logic, where stigmatisation is made flesh, and through which people come to think of, and act on, themselves as though their lives have no value" (p12). Whilst drawing on a vocabulary of "psychic life", emotional distress and "internalization", Mills is careful to distinguish those aspects of human life from the medicalised language of psychiatry. Indeed, Mills resists any attempt to reconfigure the effects of economic crisis as "mental illness", framing psychopolitical analysis as a way of understanding the psychological impact of social injustice whilst "remaining alert to the ways psy-expertise, particularly in relation to mental health, can operate to depoliticise and individualise austerity suicides" (p15). Mills' work here echoes other writers working from social justice perspectives in terms of critiquing psycho-centrism (Rimke and Brock, 2012) – the ways in which social problems get read as flaws in individual bodies/minds (e.g. Cover, 2016; Reynolds, 2016; White, 2017; White & Kral, 2014).

For Vikki Reynolds (2016), writing from a social justice activism stance, it is necessary to critically engage with the language around suicide, arguing that psychiatric and psychological discourse can mask

> the heart-rending suffering, daily indignities, and desolation many people struggle with. The language of suicide quiets our collective discomfort and provides a 'cause' for the stolen lives, normalizing the social contexts of exclusion, stigma, and hate in which these horrid deaths occur.
>
> (pp169–170)

Locating issues of social injustice inside the minds of clients, Reynolds argues, risks replicating oppression. Drawing on the work of Linda Coates and Allan Wade (2004, 2007), Reynolds points to ways in which the individualising and pathologising language of suicide obscures the contexts of violence within which such acts can occur, hides the victim's resistance to violence, obscures the perpetrator's responsibility, and blames the victim (p171).

A number of social justice and political analyses address the ways in which suicidal subjects are formed within political, economic, social and discursive environments (e.g. Button, 2016; Mills, 2017; Reynolds, 2016; Taylor, 2015), and here the relationship between psy discourse, processes of subject-formation, and a social justice stance is complex. In Chloë Taylor's (2015) analysis of the death by suicide in 2009 of Québécois author Isabelle Fortier (whose pen name was Nelly Arcan), it is argued that not only is psy discourse deployed to turn attention from political complicity (as others have asserted) but, more strongly, that suicidal subjects themselves are formed in relation to psy-expertise and practice. Arcan, who had attempted suicide on previous occasions, reflected upon this form of death in many of her writings, and Taylor argues that Arcan's view of the suicidal subject – as an identity reflective of an essential part of herself – is a product of the bio-medicalisation of suicide. Taylor writes that Arcan's reading of suicide in general, and of her own experience of suicidality in particular (which Arcan wrote about in 'La Honte', 2007), is significant since it reflects the dominant view of suicide today in that "the essentialisation of suicidal subjectivity is the result of the biopoliticisation of death and of biopolitical expert discourses which produce the subjects about which they purport to provide knowledge" (p3).

Taylor's analysis of the contexts of Arcan's life and death resonates with Mills' (2017) psychopolitical approach, in that systemic and structural social injustices and related moral economies of worth are understood as implicated in experiences of emotional distress and subsequent deaths by suicide. Yet, such is the power of psy-discourse that, in Arcan's case at least, distress and a desire to die are primarily read as indicative of personal deficit and pathology. So, for Arcan, an inability to live is innate, and this is a belief that is repeated again and again in her writings. As Taylor (2015) writes,

> [r]ather than considering the possible relation between her consistent critiques of gender, her experiences of sexual oppression, and her sense that she could not live in the world, Arcan accepted that she was not made to live and that her problem was medical and primordial. That is, she was convinced that something was wrong with her and not with the world, and that something could not be changed because it was innate.
>
> (p17)

Taylor (2015) warns against replacing "a compulsory ontology of pathology with a compulsory ontology of oppression", but is also clear that, from a Foucauldian perspective, "the suicidal subject, similar to the mentally ill subject, the delinquent, and the sexual subject, is not so much an object of scientific knowledge as a product of it" (p18). This is a radical claim, and as Taylor acknowledges, a troubling one, for "this means that the discourses and practices that we draw upon to understand and to prevent suicide may in fact contribute to creating subjects bound to kill themselves, or at least to contemplate suicide throughout their lives" (ibid). Such a stance, though, does open up possibilities for resistance, and ways of framing suicide and suicide prevention beyond the individual and pathological, and Taylor (2015) argues that instead of seeking "the biological or psychopathological sources of suicide within the subject, we should seek a political recognition of and response to the reasons that lead some people to take their lives" (p20). Taylor's analysis, as with other social justice writings on suicide, highlights the many contingencies of suicidal desire, as well as "the political nature of our current ontology of suicide as pathology" (ibid).

Underlying Assumptions

It is on this point, the nature of the suicidal subject if you like, that social justice approaches perhaps depart most radically from traditional "psy" understandings of suicide and suicidality. The "taken-for-granted, bounded, consciously aware, agentic self that has become so natural that it is almost impossible to think it otherwise" (White, 2017, p473) is questioned and different assumptions brought to bear on notions of personhood, subjectivity, and agency in relation to suicide. Mark Button (2016) draws attention to the "dark underside" of the modern, Western conception of "responsible autonomous agency" that brings with it impossible demands and standards to live up to in a world of "contingency, rupture, and precariousness", with failure to do so leading to "self-loathing and potential self-destruction" (p275). Culturally and historically formed notions of selfhood thus can come to be implicated in suicide itself.

Alternative formulations of subjectivity, personhood and agency more generally are a feature of social justice thinking in relation to suicide (Button, 2017; Mills, 2017; Taylor, 2015; White, 2017; White & Kral, 2014), and Chloë Taylor's (2015) analysis of the death of Nelly Arcan demonstrates the productiveness of understanding suicidal subjects as formed over time within political, economic, social and historical contexts. As Judith Butler (2015) notes, conceptualising personhood as an outcome of processes of subject-formation allows us to ask, "[w]hat destroys a person when that person appears to be destroying himself or herself? Do we find the social within the psychic at such moments, and if so, how?" (2015, p10). Psychopolitical analysis (of the type discussed earlier) strongly affirms the social in the psychic, but Butler raises interesting questions not only as to how that which is "external" becomes "internal", but also the processes by which elements of the "external" come to be "the driving force of psychic life" (ibid). Butler invites us to think about the role of language, or discourse, in this process, and it is here, again, where ontological and epistemological assumptions of many social justice or psychopolitical ways of thinking differ from traditional suicidological approaches. The suicidal person is taken to be formed in relation to contingent (even if "astonishingly stable, continuous, and slow to change" (Foucault, 2017, p36)) social norms and structures rather than existing as a pathologised, essentialised, unchanging "type". As with Mills' psychopolitical analysis, Butler (2015) points to the importance of those interconnected norms that precede and exceed us, that circulate in the world before impressing themselves upon us. That impression, Butler argues,

> opens up an affective register. Norms form us, but only because there is already some proximate and involuntary relation to their impress; they require and intensify our impressionability. Norms act on us from all sides, that is, in multiple and sometimes contradictory ways; they act upon a sensibility at the same time that they form it; they lead us to feel in certain ways, and those feelings can enter into our thinking even, as we might well end up thinking about them. They condition and form us, and yet they are hardly finished with that work once we start to emerge as thinking and speaking beings. Rather, they continue to act according to an iterative logic that ends for any of us only when life ends, though the life of norms, of discourse more generally, continues on with a tenacity that is quite indifferent to our finitude.
>
> (p5)

What Butler is pointing to is a process more complex than "a single norm acting as a kind of 'cause' and the 'subject' as something formed in the wake of that norm's action" (ibid). Rather, the process of formation is continuous and repeated in relation to a network or matrix of "norms, conventions, institutional forms of power" (p6). It is these, identified as oppressive structures and hierarchies, alongside corrosive moral economies of worth and value, which a psychopolitical analysis takes as important elements in the formation of suicidal subjects, and it is those elements which can impress upon the psychic life of such subjects and be experienced as distress and suicidality. And, importantly, it is those factors and forces which can be rendered visible within social justice and political framings of suicide. As Butler (2015) argues, the process of subject-formation is ongoing – we are never fully formed, but always still being formed, and never fully forming, and such a stance contains within it possibilities for resistance not available to traditional "psy" ways of thinking, in that it points to a radical contingency of suicidal selfhood and experience (Marsh, 2018).

Possibilities for Thought and Action Opened Up through the Discursive Construction of Suicide as a Question of Social Justice

Reconceptualised as a political issue, what new possibilities for understanding and responding to suicide emerge in these texts? What alternative forms of collective practices and social action are made apparent? (White, 2017).

The construction of suicide as a question of politics and social justice contains, most obviously, a demand for more just social arrangements and the fair and equitable distribution of societal resources, to enable all members of society to flourish (Morrow & Weisser, 2012; White & Kral, 2014). Framing distress and suicide as social justice issues aims to move thought beyond narrow, reductionist psychological explanations (Mills, 2017). Individualistic ways of framing and responding to suicide are taken to be limited in their effectiveness due to their restricted focus; "solutions that are developed typically target individuals for change but leave the specific social, political, and cultural contexts of people's lives – including the corrosive effects of structural inequalities – unaccounted for" (White, p472). Instead, there is a call to have an approach to prevention "that is compassionate and responsive to individuals who are suffering" but also at the same time, one "capable of creating more just social arrangements by interrupting and subverting the structural, discursive, material, and social-historical relations that both produce and reproduce colonial violence, entrench social inequalities, and create vulnerabilities among certain groups but not others" (White, pp472–473). Central, here, is a resistance to characterising suicide as a narrowly personal or family problem, and the need to acknowledge "that suicide is also a collective burden of social justice tied to the distribution of primary goods within a political system" (Button, 2016, p274).

A widening of the conversation on suicide and suicide prevention is taken to be one way to move the field away from limited and limiting "psy" framings. Through the inclusion of social justice activists, political, postcolonial, feminist and queer theorists, community activists, service users, practitioners, policy makers, family members, and persons with lived experience, it is argued new voices could be drawn into the conversation on what it means to study suicide and to enact practices of suicide prevention. polanco, Mancías and LeFeber (2017) read this "as something other than advocating for scientific or intellectual diversity for the sake of inclusion of additional professional paradigms", but rather interpret it to be "a proposal of expanding human interest and recapturing the human edge (Wilkinson & Kleinman, 2016) in suicidology's social inquiry" (p1). Such an approach seeks "more diverse and creative, less psychocentric and less depoliticized" ways of thinking and acting (White, 2017, p472), which can lead to the development of new conceptual formations and analytic frameworks, more generative and creative knowledge production practices, the challenging of disciplinary norms, and a critical interrogation of the intellectual and ethical grounds of long-accepted practices (Button, 2016, p277).

An overarching aim of such processes would be to "secure the conditions of human dignity for all persons" through a "new right to life movement for the already born" (Button, 2016, p271). The affirmation of life in relation to suicide through political means, Button argues, requires addressing the ways in which suicidal subjectivities within a population are formed and distributed (ibid). An analysis of the formation of such subjectivities would entail "a wider, macroscopic analysis of sociopolitical conditions" (Button, 2016, p276). As a consequence, the list of risk factors for suicide would

> need to be expanded to incorporate things like social fragmentation (Trovato and Jarvis, 1986) and social isolation; community depopulation, blight, and crime; unemployment (Platt and Hawton, 2000), measures of union concentration, and real median incomes for working-class citizens; degree of community investment and community programming, especially for youth and LGBTQ and Native American youth in particular; access to mental health services, especially in rural areas (where suicide rates are higher); and regulations governing the possession and safe storage of firearms (Brent and Bridge 2003).
>
> (Button, 2016, pp276–277; see Button, this volume, for an example of this work)

In terms of knowledge production, polanco et al. (2017) discuss the "moral care" required of researchers working from a social justice perspective. Drawing on feminist and critical methodologies, they discuss how recognition of the relational and ethico-political dimensions of the research process requires not only the sharing of power in relation to the "co-interpretation or co-construction of knowledge" (pp527–528), but also the "putting forth" of "a political, social, and moral agenda committed to the undoing of social, historical, political, and cultural effects that result in suicide" (p528). Locating suicide within a context of social suffering, there follows an imperative to engage in research, which resists forces that seek to represent suicide in "decontextualized, individual, and pathological" ways (polanco et al., 2017, p521).

Such a situating of distress and suicidality within a context of social suffering also resonates with possibilities for therapeutic work. As White (2017) argues,

> [n]arrative therapists and community workers have long understood the importance of resituating problems like depression, hopelessness, and suicidality within a broader sociopolitical context as a way to make visible many of the sources of human suffering (including, e.g., social inequality, racism, patriarchy, ageism, ableism, competition, gender violence, colonialism, etc.).
>
> (p478)

Such therapeutic work can bring to the fore the social, historical and political barriers individuals and communities have faced and continue to face, the resources of resistance and survival they have drawn upon and possess, and to "restory" "lives in ways that are much richer, more nuanced, and in keeping with their hopes, aspirations, and preferred futures (Sather & Newman, 2016)" (p478).

Conclusions

The framing of suicide as a question of politics and social justice represents a challenge to the individualised, "internalised", pathologised and depoliticised understanding (and experience) of suicide which has come to be produced in relation to dominant psy constructions of the act. The challenge is primarily ethico-political, but also to the foundational epistemological and ontological premises the field of suicidology works under. If, it is argued, rather than starting from a belief in some unchanging, universal "essence"of suicidality, we worked on the assumption that each age and place creates its own suicide, social justice analysis can provide the tools to understand more fully the processes involved in the formation of suicidal subjects within specific social, economic, political and historical contexts. A psychopolitical approach, for example, makes connections between the inequalities and injustices perpetuated through the creation and maintenance of particular social structures and hierarchies, and the ways in which these interact with moral economies of human worth and ideological political policy making, in order to understand the psychic/emotional impact on those caught up in such assemblages.

Certain questions remain, however. If the focus of prevention shifts from the individual to wider social and political institutions, norms and practices, the number of possible sites of intervention broadens considerably, and would perhaps involve

> significant public investment in the kind of practices of care – health care, mental health services, workforce assistance, and family support services, to name a few – that could provide communities with the resources to respond humanely and with dignity to physical illness, unemployment, drug/alcohol dependency, and family conflict.
>
> (Button, 2016, p275)

The collective political response advocated by Button (2016) would require substantial thought, effort, will and material resources, but, as he also points out, the moral and political costs of not seeking to understand and address the relationship between inequality, injustice and suicide are also considerable.

Bantjes and Swartz (2017) raise questions regarding the claims of effectiveness made in relation to "culturally informed critical" approaches to preventing suicide, and also whether prevention is, or should be, always the primary aim. They argue that assertions of efficacy and utility are sometimes made despite the considerable difficulties involved in substantiating such claims (Bantjes & Swartz, 2017, p518). They also question whether much of the work is actually about preventing suicide, and that maybe the focus of efforts should be on "trying to understand a complex, contextually variable phenomenon, just as other researchers study consumer behavior, for example, without any intention or claim to be changing that behavior" (Bantjes & Swartz, 2017, p518). But, ethically, to identify the socio-political context of deaths by suicide is perhaps also to commit oneself to addressing such a situation, too.

The complex practical and ethical issues a social justice approach wrestles with are perhaps a reflection of genuine engagement with the complexities of suicide itself. Chloë Taylor (2015) rightly warns we should be wary of replacing "a compulsory ontology of pathology with a compulsory ontology of oppression" (p18), but her own nuanced and contextualised analysis, as with the various psychopolitical approaches described above, demonstrates the utility of trying to understand the ways in which suicidal subjects come to be formed in relation to modern regimes of truth and power.

References

Arcan, N. (2007). La honte. Available online at www.nellyarcan.com/pdf/Nelly-Arcan-La-honte.pdf (accessed 27 June 2018).

Bacchi, C. (2009). *Analysing Policy: What's the Problem Represented to Be?* Frenchs Forest: Pearson Australia.

Bantjes, J., & Swartz, L. (2017). The cultural turn in critical suicidology: What can we claim and what do we know? *Death Studies*, 41(8), 512–520. doi:10.1080/07481187.2017.1333355

Brent, D. A., & Bridge, J. (2003). Firearms availability and suicide: Evidence, interventions, and future directions." *American Behavioral Scientist*, 46(9), 1192–1210.

Butler, J. (2015). *Senses of the Subject*. New York: Fordham University Press.

Button, M. (2016). Suicide and social justice: Toward a political approach to suicide. *Political Research Quarterly*, 69(2), 270–280. doi:10.1177/1065912916636689

Coates, L., & Wade, A. (2004). Telling it like it isn't: Obscuring perpetrator responsibility for violence. *Discourse and Society*, 15(5), 499–526.

Coates, L., & Wade, A. (2007). Language and violence: Analysis of four discursive operations. *Journal of Family Violence*, 22(7), 511–522.

Cover, R. (2012). *Queer Youth Suicide, Culture and Identity: Unliveable Lives?* Farnham: Ashgate.

Cover, R. (2016). Queer youth suicide: Discourses of difference, framing suicidality, and the regimentation of identity. In J. White, I. Marsh, M. J. Kral, & J. Morris (Eds.), *Critical Suicidology: Transforming Suicide Research and Prevention for the 21st Century* (pp188–208). Vancouver: University of British Columbia Press.

Foucault, M. (2017). *Subjectivity and Truth: Lectures at the Collège de France, 1980–1981*, ed. Frédéric Gros, trans. Graham Burchell. New York: Palgrave MacMillan.

Joiner, T (2005). *Why People Die by Suicide*. Cambridge, MA: Harvard University Press.

Joiner, T. (2011). Editorial: Scientific rigor as the guiding heuristic for SLTB's editorial stance. *Suicide and Life-threatening Behavior*, 41(5), 471–473. doi:10.1111/j.1943-278X.2011.00056.x

Joiner, T. E., Hom, M. A., Hagan, C. R., & Silva, C. (2016). Suicide as a derangement of the self-sacrificial aspect of eusociality. *Psychological Review*, 123, 235–254.

Kral, M. J., & Idlout, L. (2016). Indigenous best practices: Community-based suicide prevention in Nunavut, Canada. In J. White, I. Marsh, M. J. Kral, & J. Morris (Eds.), *Critical Suicidology: Transforming Suicide Research and Prevention for the 21st Century* (pp229–243). Vancouver: University of British Columbia Press.

Marsh, I. (2010). *Suicide: Foucault, History and Truth*. Cambridge: Cambridge University Press.

Marsh, I. (2016). Critiquing contemporary suicidology. In J. White, I. Marsh, M. J. Kral, & J. Morris (Eds.), *Critical Suicidology: Transforming Suicide Research and Prevention for the 21st Century* (pp15–30). Vancouver: University of British Columbia Press.

Marsh, I. (2018). Historical phenomenology: Understanding experiences of suicide and suicidality across time. In M. Pompili (Ed.), *Phenomenology of Suicide: Unlocking the Suicidal Mind* (pp1–12). Cham: Springer International Publishing.

Mills, C. (2017). "Dead people don't claim" A psychopolitical autopsy of UK austerity suicides. *Critical Social Policy*, 38(2), 302–322.

Morrow, M., & Weisser, J. (2012). Towards a social justice framework of mental health recovery. *Studies in Social Justice*, 6(1), 27–43.

Platt, S., & Hawton, K. (2000). Suicidal behaviour and the labour market. In K. Hawton, & K. van Heeringen (Eds.), *The International Handbook of Suicide and Attempted Suicide* (pp309–384). Chichester: John Wiley.

Platt, S., Stace, S., & Morrissey, J. (Eds.) (2017). *Dying from Inequality: Socioeconomic Disadvantage and Suicidal Behaviour*. London: The Samaritans.

polanco, m., Mancías, S., & LeFeber, T. (2017). Reflections on moral care when conducting qualitative research about suicide in the United States military. *Death Studies*. Sep; 41(8), 521–531. doi:10.1080/07481187.2017.1333356. Epub 2017 May 22.

Reynolds, V. (2016). Hate kills: A social justice response to suicide. In J. White, I. Marsh, M. J. Kral, & J. Morris (Eds.), *Critical Suicidology: Transforming*

Suicide Research and Prevention for the 21st Century (pp169–187). Vancouver: University of British Columbia Press.

Rimke, H., & Brock, D. (2012). The culture of therapy: Psychocentrism in everyday life. In D. Brock, R. Raby, & M. Thomas (Eds.), *Power and Everyday Practices* (pp182–202). Toronto: Nelson Education.

Rose, N. (2000). *Biological Psychiatry as a Style of Thought.* Paper presented to a symposium on models and cases in scientific thought at Princeton University.

Sather, M., & Newman, D. (2016). "Being more than just your final act": Elevating the multiple storylines of suicide with narrative practice. In J. White, I. Marsh, M. J. Kral, & J. Morris (Eds.), *Critical Suicidology: Transforming Suicide Research and Prevention for the 21st Century* (pp115–132). Vancouver: University of British Columbia Press.

Taylor, C. (2015). Birth of the suicidal subject: Nelly Arcan, Michel Foucault and voluntary death. *Culture Theory and Critique.* doi:101080/147357842014937820

Trovato, F., & Jarvis, G. K. (1986). Immigrant suicide in Canada: 1971 and 1981. *Social Forces*, 65(2): 433–457.

Wexler, L., & Gone, J. (2012). Culturally responsive suicide prevention in Indigenous communities: Unexamined assumptions and new possibilities. *American Journal of Public Health*, 102(5), 800–806. doi:10.2105/ajph.2011.300432

White, J. (2012). Youth suicide as a "wild problem": Implications for prevention practice. *Suicidology Online*, 3, 42–50.

White, J. (2016). Reimagining youth suicide prevention education. In J. White, I. Marsh, M. J. Kral, & J. Morris (Eds.), *Critical Suicidology: Transforming Suicide Research and Prevention for the 21st Century* (pp244–263). Vancouver: University of British Columbia Press.

White, J. (2017). What can critical suicidology do? *Death Studies*, 41(8), 472–480. doi: 10.1080/07481187.2017.1332901. Epub 2017 May 19.

White, J., & Kral, M. (2014). Re-thinking youth suicide: Language, culture and power. *Journal of Social Action for Counseling and Psychology*, 6(1), 122–142.

White, J., Marsh, I., Kral, M. J., & Morris, J. (Eds.) (2016). *Critical Suicidology: Transforming Suicide Research and Prevention for the 21st Century.* Vancouver: University of British Columbia Press.

Wilkinson, I., & Kleinman, A. (2016). *A Passion for Society: How We Think about Human Suffering.* Oakland: University of California Press.

2 Shame as Affective Injustice

Qualitative, Sociological Explorations of Self-Harm, Suicide and Socioeconomic Inequalities

Amy Chandler

Introduction

The unequal distribution of rates of self-harm and suicide across different social groups is a key indicator that these practices should be considered in terms of social justice. In the UK, rates of hospital treated self-harm and completed suicide are concentrated among people who have experienced socioeconomic disadvantage (Haw et al., 2015; Mok et al., 2012). This concentration can be understood as an inequity – unfair, and unjust, with far-reaching effects on families and communities (Button, 2016; Platt, 2011). Epidemiological approaches have been pivotal in identifying inequalities in the distribution of self-harm and suicide. However, such approaches are less helpful when it comes to explaining such distributions. What is it about the experience of socioeconomic disadvantage that leads to higher numbers of people taking their own lives or harming themselves? There is a danger when considering such associations to engage in common-sense theorising: for instance, Marcus Redley's (2010) study of self-harm in an area of multiple deprivation in Scotland found that medics occasionally privately associated their patients' self-harm with "shite life disease" (p. 477). Such approaches rather fatalistically indicate that anyone facing so many problems (including poverty, and living in an area of multiple deprivation) might consider or enact self-harm. In this chapter, I sketch out an alternative approach to understanding the relationship between socioeconomic disadvantage, self-harm and suicide. I suggest that engaging with emotions helps to explain how structural conditions of oppression and inequality can shape individual actions, including self-harm and suicide.

Attending to emotions when considering self-harm and suicide is increasingly recognised as important (Abrutyn & Mueller, 2014). Clinically oriented research points to the salience of certain feeling states (e.g. entrapment), the absence of feeling states (e.g. hope) and the role of emotions (e.g. shame) in predicting suicide and self-harm (Lester, 1997; O'Connor, 2011; Williams, 1997). The way in which emotions are conceptualised in studies of suicide and self-harm varies widely:

from quantitative, clinical studies which quantify emotion, and seek to enrol particular emotional states in *predicting* suicide or self-harm; to qualitative, sociological research which has explored the way emotions shape *meanings* and accounts of suicide and self-harm (Fullagar, 2003; Scheff, 1990).

In contrast to the treatment of shame in much existing work on self-harm and suicide, this chapter moves away from the role of emotions in *predicting* suicide or self-harm, advancing a sociologically informed argument, which points to the role of emotion in illuminating the *meanings* of these practices. In doing so, I directly address the way that meanings and emotions are situated within a broader social context, including in relation to structural inequalities, histories of oppression and marginalisation (Abrutyn, 2017; Ahmed, 2014). I argue that centring emotions, examined via qualitative analysis of the accounts of those who have self-harmed or died by suicide, can form an important contribution to a social justice approach to understanding and responding to suicide.

Theorising Shame

While emotions are often associated with psychology, and the inner workings of the mind, sociological research and theory has established emotions as (also) thoroughly social. This does not mean that psychology or biology are neglected, rather the focus of sociological analysis is on the ways that social factors, from broad social structures, to intimate, interpersonal interactions shape, drive or even constitute emotion (Barbalet, 2001; Burkitt, 2014; Lupton, 1998; Turner & Stets, 2006). Contemporary sociological work on emotion engages with social and psychological aspects whilst seeking to attend to emotions as embodied: experienced and felt, often communicated through or by bodily responses or actions (Cobb, 2018). This is widely applicable to a range of emotions, not least shame, which is characterised by bodily features and practices: blushing, the act of turning away the face, of hiding the body from the gaze of others (Dolezal, 2015; Probyn, 2005).

The work of Thomas Scheff has been particularly influential in articulating a sociology of shame. For Scheff, shame, more than other emotions, is the "master emotion" of everyday life. This leads from Scheff's interactionist approach, which draws on classical sociology, particularly the work of Charles Cooley, to understand shame as intimately tied to our assessment of how others view us. Where we see, anticipate or imagine that others view us negatively, we feel shame (conversely, if we envision positive regard, we feel pride) (Scheff and Retzinger 2001, p. 8). Shame is characterised as an intensely negative emotion that individuals will seek to avoid experiencing *and* avoid acknowledging: Scheff argues shame is most often *hidden*. The deeply discomfiting nature of shame, according to Scheff, can be attributed to its role in maintaining – and signalling threat to – social bonds; and through this, its powerful connection with the self. Indeed, Scheff has argued that so strong is the taboo around shame that social theorists often avoid naming or facing it. For instance Goffman's studies of social micro-interaction use the terms embarrassment, and "saving face" rather than shame (Goffman, 1968; Goffman, 1973). The hidden, or "taboo" nature of shame is, for Scheff, characteristic of modern societies, and also deeply problematic. Across several publications he has connected *hidden* shame to a wide range of forms of violence, including suicide (Scheff, 2006; Scheff, 2014; Scheff & Retzinger, 2001).

Sociological research addressing shame is particularly relevant to a consideration of suicide and social justice since Scheff, and subsequent theorists, have argued that experiences of shame are unequally distributed across social groups, and can be tied to a range of social oppressions and inequalities. For instance, Sally Munt (2007) and Rob Cover (2012), have each drawn on sociologies of shame to explore the shaming of LGBT people, with Cover in particular tying this to an analysis of the "problem" of queer youth suicide, tying the shaming of "non-normative desires, behaviours and identities" to suicide deaths (Cover, 2012, p. 116). In a different arena, Larry Ray (2014) has enrolled shame to develop a sociological analysis of looting following the riots that took place in London 2011. According to Ray, Scheff's theories of shame implicate violence as an "automatic response" to shame. In contrast, Ray argues that connections between shame and (violent) action are shaped by "speech acts", which provide "normative [moral] justifications for violence with reference to perceived injustices" (p. 132). This underlines the importance of attending to accounts, as doing so offers insights into the ways in which social structures, cultural contexts and individual meaning-making may shape social action.

However, in contrast to Ray's focus on meaning-making and "lay" accounts, a feature of much social scientific writing on shame is that it tends to draw on material from literature, film, or other cultural materials representing narratives of or about shame (Ahmed, 2014; Munt, 2007). Indeed, Scheff has argued that in order to develop theories of shame, it is necessary to engage with such resources, due to the "hidden" nature of shame. He suggests that drawing on fictional accounts of shame facilitates access to minute by minute internal conversations that are not normally accessible to researchers. Of particular note, Scheff has drawn on a close reading of Goethe's *The Sorrows of Young Werther* (Scheff, 1990; Scheff & Retzinger, 2001). This is particularly relevant since in this analysis, Scheff points to some of the ways in which shame can arise out of structural inequalities, played out in more intimate interactions, and then reflected on internally by an individual, resulting – in this case – in the suicide of the eponymous Werther.

Scheff argues that Werther can be read partly as an autobiographical account of Goethe's own experiences of feeling shame related to being "out of place" in a social hierarchy. He suggests that the cumulative experiences Werther reports of experiencing rejection, ostracisation and discrimination on the basis of his social class, which are in turn repressed, hidden or obfuscated by Werther, can be causally linked to his eventual suicide. Further, Scheff suggests that experiences of shame by oppressed or marginalised social groups can be linked to their *continued* oppression and marginalisation, which he links to: "shame over its members' characteristics and *idealization* of the characteristics of the elite class" (1990, p. 131, emphasis in original).

This argument is taken up in the work of Andrew Sayer (2005), who emphasises the moral nature of emotions, and of class-based oppression. Sayer's work offers a useful expansion of Scheff's propositions regarding the role of shame in maintaining social bonds. His work emphasises the role of value, paralleling the focus on "interest", which emerges in queer readings of psychological literature on shame (Probyn, 2005; Sedgwick & Frank, 1995). These theories emphasise that in order to feel shame one must be *interested* or *ascribe value* to whatever is lacking, or to whomever is thought to view the self with contempt. Echoing Scheff, Sayer notes that

> [t]he worst kind of disrespect, the kind that is most likely to make one feel shame, is that which comes from those whose values and judgements one most respects. Class inequalities mean that the "social bases of respect" in terms of access to valued ways of living are unequally distributed, and therefore that shame is likely to be endemic to the experience of class.
>
> (p. 954–955)

These works also share a consideration of the role of resistance as a response to shame. A key limitation of Scheff's work on shame is that while he clearly articulates the existence of diverse responses to shame, his analyses tend to centre on those that are framed in negative terms, in particular conflict and violence (Ray, 2014). In contrast, Sayer, and others, have argued that responses to shame may involve a rejection of dominant social norms and the shame that accompanies a "failure" to live up to these (Cover, 2012; Munt, 2007; Ray, 2014; Sayer, 2005). These readings offer a potentially more transformative reading of shame, in contrast to the more fatalistic view articulated by Scheff.

The approach to shame which I draw on in this chapter is informed by the sociological treatments briefly summarised here. As such, my perspective differs markedly from clinical psychological treatments more usually found within suicide studies, which frame shame as an individual attribute. Some case studies go on to quantify (individual) feelings, and enrol these measurements in predicting and intervening in suicide and self-harm.

One study, for instance, operationalises shame as an "attitude" towards help-seeking, and argues that this can be more easily modified than more intractable, structural predictors of suicide, such as socioeconomic disadvantage (Reynders et al., 2016). In contrast, the sociological approach I draw on here sees shame (and stigma) as deeply embedded in social relations and social structures, such that approaching it as a modifiable "attitude" is both politically contentious and unlikely to meet much success (Tyler & Slater, 2018).

Centring Accounts in the Study of Emotions, Self-Harm and Suicide

Research which quantifies emotions can be seen as part of a broader tendency within suicide research, which has been subjected to long-standing critique for centring positivist, "objective" approaches, rather than more interpretive methods which address meaning or explanation (Chandler et al., 2011; Douglas, 1967; Fitzpatrick, 2011; Hjelmeland, 2016). Despite such critiques, suicide research remains dominated by quantitative approaches, and by particular disciplinary perspectives – clinical/health psychology and psychiatry (Wray et al., 2011). However, on the margins of suicidology a growing range of more critical, creative and qualitative methodologies are being brought to bear on understanding suicide and self-harm. This work clearly speaks to the importance of alternative methodological approaches, with well-rehearsed arguments supporting this (Chandler, in press; Fitzpatrick, 2011; Hjelmeland & Knizek, 2016; White et al., 2016).

In this chapter, I draw on a synthesis of published literature which used qualitative methods, and which addressed the socioeconomic contexts in which self-harm and suicide take place. The review was commissioned by UK-based suicide prevention charity, Samaritans, who sought to draw on diverse disciplinary perspectives and methods in order to better understand the association in the UK (and elsewhere) between socioeconomic disadvantage and higher rates of suicide and self-harm (Case & Deaton, 2015; Haw et al., 2015; Platt, 2011; Samaritans, 2017). Given the scarcity of qualitative research addressing suicide, and the equally limited engagement with socioeconomic context the review identified a limited number of appropriate and relevant papers (Chandler, 2017). Nine[1] studies were found, which explicitly engaged with socioeconomic context and which had used qualitative approaches (Abrams & Gordon, 2003; Barnes et al., 2016; Cleary, 2012; Elliott et al., 2014; Huey et al., 2014; Kidd, 2004; McDermott & Roen, 2016; Redley, 2003; Stack & Wasserman, 2007). The review only included studies which engaged with the accounts of those who had self-harmed or died by suicide. A further 24 studies where socioeconomic context was less central were also included (see Chandler, 2017 for a full list).

Box 2.1 Qualitative studies explicitly addressing socioeconomic disadvantage

Nine studies directly reported on SED, using qualitative methods: three from the US (Abrams & Gordon, 2003; Elliott et al., 2014; Stack & Wasserman, 2007), one from Canada (Kidd, 2004), and five from the UK (Barnes et al., 2016; Cleary, 2012; Huey et al., 2014; McDermott & Roen, 2016; Redley, 2003). Kidd and Huey et al. interviewed people experiencing homelessness or insecure housing, focusing on accounts of suicide and self-injury, respectively. Stack and Wasserman conducted a qualitative analysis of coroner reports, investigating the relevance of economic strain to understanding completed suicides. Cleary, Elliott et al. and Barnes et al. interviewed people admitted to hospital following self-harm, addressing the role of economic hardship in explaining acts of self-harm. Redley interviewed 50 people admitted to hospital following self-harm, all of whom lived in an area of socioeconomic deprivation. Abrams and Gordon contrasted the accounts of six young women who had self-harmed, three living in urban, socioeconomically deprived areas, and 3 living in more affluent, suburban areas. McDermott and Roen's monograph includes a chapter focusing on the impact of socioeconomic context in shaping LGBT young people's understandings and experiences of self-harm and suicide.

Papers included in the review were subject to multiple readings, attending both to the fragments of accounts presented in the papers, and to the interpretive statements made by researchers, drawing on an approach to qualitative synthesis set out by Rhodes and Treloar (2008). This approach to qualitative synthesis is explicit about the role of the reviewer's interpretation; and in this case, my focus on examining the potential "mechanisms"[2] driving the identified relationship between socioeconomic disadvantage and higher rates of suicide and self-harm was clearly foregrounded.

The role of theory and interpretation is vitally important in what follows. One of the findings from my review was that in many cases qualitative research addressing self-harm and suicide was characterised by two limitations. Firstly, a relatively limited engagement with the situated nature of accounts, and the well-established position in qualitative research that interviews provide data on how an individual, in a particular context, makes sense of a given phenomenon, but that interviews do not provide an unproblematic insight into "what happened" (Atkinson, 2009; Atkinson, 2010). Secondly, reviewed studies engaged very little with the importance of researcher positionality in shaping analysis. While "reflexivity" is an established practice in qualitative research, it is rare for researchers to incorporate evidence of the practice of reflexivity in published reports (Boden et al., 2016). In terms of social justice this is significant, as failure to engage with these aspects of qualitative work can mean that the "voices" of those analysed may be (however inadvertently) drawn on in a descriptive manner, potentially co-opted by researchers in ways which ultimately fail to understand accounts as productions of social interaction, shaped by structural, political and cultural contexts (Riessman, 2008; Scott & Lyman, 1968).

In this chapter, I suggest that such failures – along with the widespread failure to attend to accounts at all (Hjelmeland & Knizek, 2010) – can be understood as forms of epistemic injustice (Fricker, 2007). Fricker's concept of epistemic injustice, and particularly the variant of testimonial injustice, is highly relevant to suicide research. Testimonial injustice, according to Fricker, occurs when a person's account of themselves (their testimony) is disbelieved, ignored, or otherwise subject to question because of their social characteristics. Fricker uses the case of women's (particularly poor women of colour) accounts of sexual harassment as a case in point. Gender, race and class all combine to make the status of a claim about sexual harassment subject to query. The concept of epistemic injustice has recently been applied to thinking about the minimisation of patients' views in healthcare, and the particular marginalisation of "mad" voices in research addressing mental illness (Carel & Kidd, 2014; LeBlanc & Kinsella, 2016).

Accounts of those who have self-harmed or died by suicide are also – frequently – subject to question; both because the nature of the acts themselves are so often associated with "madness"; but perhaps even more so if the person engaging in these acts is a member of a devalued social group – poor, racialised, sexual minority, female or trans. Research with GPs, and medics in Accident and Emergency settings has identified enduring negative and stereotypical attitudes towards patients who self-harm (Chandler, 2016; Chandler et al., 2016; Cleaver et al., 2014; Saunders et al., 2012). There is a clear need for further work that engages more carefully in this area, to ascertain the extent to which the social features of patients might shape how they are responded to.

Fricker's concept of epistemic injustice also incorporates a second variant: hermeneutic injustice. This is also relevant to considering qualitative research on suicide. Hermeneutic injustice refers to disadvantages associated with a lack of "hermeneutical resources" among a marginalised group, such that they do not have the language or knowledge to name their experiences. Fricker draws on the example of sexual harassment here as well, suggesting that women were affected by "sexual harassment" long before they had a name to describe the experience. This is relevant to thinking about both shame and structural inequalities and disadvantage, since each of these may affect people's experiences, shape their actions, but each may also be "hidden" – difficult to identify, let alone name (Scheff, 2014).

In part related to the notion of hermeneutic injustice, I propose that "listening to" and "describing" accounts of self-harm and suicide is not sufficient. Recent critical scholarship has pointed to the way in which ethnographic and sociological research is historically rooted in colonial and imperialist projects (Denzin, 2016). As such, I suggest that the way in which qualitative research with accounts of self-harm and suicide are carried out can form an important part of reimagining suicide in terms of social justice. This relates also to Fricker's testimonial injustice which can, she writes, have the effect of demoting "the speaker from informant to source of information, from subject to object" (2007, p. 133). As such, and as this review will begin to show, researcher engagement with the accounts of those who enact self-harm or suicide must go beyond "listening" to marginalised voices. For qualitative approaches to suicide and self-harm to contribute meaningfully to social justice, it is vital that accounts are analysed and presented critically, theorised and tied to broader issues of justice, inequality and oppression. Further, the position of the researcher, and their relationship with their "informant" should be directly reflected on, carefully and with sensitivity to power (LeBlanc & Kinsella, 2016).

Excavating Shame in Accounts of Self-Harm and Suicide

Leading from the notion that shame is frequently a 'hidden' emotion, it was indeed uncommon for the papers I reviewed to explicitly name or discuss shame. However, papers frequently identified (if not always discussing in detail) a range of situations or circumstances which could be associated with a *devaluation* of the self-harming or suicided subject. Accounts in these cases often featured terms which have been suggested as substitutes for the explicit naming of shame in everyday accounts (Retzinger, 1995). For instance, Barnes et al.'s (2016) participants spoke of feeling "inadequate", "rejected", or of not being able to "face" particular situations or interactions (e.g. with banks, benefits processes, bailiffs). Such articulations were common across the reviewed studies.

> Because when I was working [prostitution] I was always just thinking "Well fuck I'm not worth it. I'm not worth anything . . . There's no reason to live".
>
> (Woman, 20, in Kidd, 2005 p. 40)

The direct identification of shame did occur in some analytic discussions. Huey et al. wrote of participants who had been bereaved feeling shame in relation to a lack of control over experiences of loss. Further, while less common, shame was present in some of the data presented in the reviewed papers. For instance, Everall et al. (2006) noted with some surprise that shame was a key theme and was "spontaneously discussed" (p. 379) by participants, tied in particular to a difficulty with seeking help, since shame was associated with "admitting" both distress and suicidal feelings.

> I didn't want people to know I was suicidal. I was just really ashamed and worried that people would find out and look down on me.
> (Stephanie, 19, in Everall et al., 2006 p. 379)

Shame was also present in relation to acts of self-harm framed as suicide attempts, perhaps relating to historical (often gendered) associations between "attempts" and "failure" (Jaworski, 2014). Elliott et al. (2014, p. 3) reported 11 of 12 participants "regretted what they had done and felt guilty and ashamed". While shame is framed as "hidden" in the theoretical literature, it is also clear that shame can more easily "stick" to some bodies and, perhaps, some practices more easily than others (Ahmed, 2014). While it is not the focus of this chapter, the importance of guilt and shame in relation to suicide and self-harm *after* they have been enacted, is one which is deserving of further critical, qualitative attention (Wiklander et al., 2003).

Although the potential presence of shame in the accounts was identified in the review, the analysis in most papers did not directly address shame, or engage with theoretically informed approaches to emotions. Leading from the arguments I set out earlier regarding the importance of more critical and nuanced analytic work within qualitative studies of suicide, I will now introduce two further ways in which qualitative, sociological engagement with shame can help to expand our understanding of the relationship between socioeconomic disadvantage, self-harm and suicide. The analysis I develop is designed to be suggestive of the need for further critical and theoretically informed work which engages with emotions as embodied, as communicative, which takes seriously the role of language and accounts, and which situates all of this within broader social and political contexts. Such approaches may go some way to ameliorating the epistemic injustice which is, I suggest, present in much suicide research, even where it enrols qualitative approaches.

Shame, Emotion and Language

Attending to the status of accounts provided in interview studies, or drawn from documents such as suicide notes, is central to critical qualitative analysis. The reviewed studies were somewhat variable in how far such critical engagement was evident. For instance, Stack and Wasserman's (2007) analysis of medical examiner's files of completed suicides in the US presented a rather sanitised thematic review, with no indication of how accounts (in notes, or reports) were constructed. The analysis focused instead on the excavation of "stressors" (e.g. job loss, car loss, relationship breakdown) with little sense of how these were interpreted by the individual who died, or those around them. This approach contrasts starkly with the more multifaceted analysis developed by Shiner and colleagues (Shiner et al., 2009), where they focus in detail on the situated nature of different pieces of evidence contained in coroner reports of suicide in the UK: showing how in one case, for instance, very different motives were implicated by suicide notes written by the same person for multiple audiences.

Shiner et al.'s approach also enables greater consideration of emotional and social contexts in which suicides take place – featuring revenge, anger – and shame. While challenging and undoubtedly complex, attending carefully to the way in which suicide, self-harm and emotion are narrated can offer important insights. Not least, such approaches offer contextual detail as to how relationships between self-harm, suicide and 'stressors' are understood and given meaning, often mediated through emotional language. When examined in light of relevant sociological theories of emotion and social structure, attending to the nature of accounts can provide an alternative perspective on how suicide and self-harm might come to be understood as an expected, reasonable response to socioeconomic disadvantage; one that moves beyond the quantification of "stressors" and considers more carefully how such "stressors" are emotionally articulated.

The role of language is addressed by Redley (2003), who argued that the use of *emotional* language may serve as a rhetorical device, as part of an account about a life that is not going 'as desired', as hoped for. The use of shame – or related terms – can be understood as a way of accounting for a situation, and for an act – that is understood to run counter to collectively held values. One of Redley's interviewees – all of whom lived in an area of socioeconomic disadvantage, and had been treated in hospital for self-harm – provides an illustration of this, talking of the importance of being able to "look yourself in the eye" – an inability to do so being associated with suicide ("the end").

> "if you can't look yourself square in the eye at the end of the day and see that you've done the best that you can do . . . if you can look and say that this is the best that I can possible do. And it is not worked for you. Then the end is, is the best thing"
>
> (Mr Prospect, in Redley, 2003, p. 359)

Mr Prospect's account speaks to a shared understanding of "standing on your own two feet" as a valued attribute and as such he indicates a "failure" of self here rather than a "failure" of circumstances. Redley argues that the *articulation* of this experience, identifies a "gap" between "desired" (valued) and "actual" (lived) reality. Redley's analysis diverged from many of the other studies included in the review in treating accounts of self-harm as partial, situated, and as social artefacts in and of themselves. This resonates with wider writing on shame, which similarly emphasises the importance of cultural narratives in shaping social action. Ray (2014), for instance, when discussing the role of shame in understanding the London 2011 riots emphasises the importance of "linguistically and culturally embedded norms" (p. 125) in mediating the translation of shame into action. As such, when considering accounts of self-harm and suicide, and their emotional content, these should not be treated as mere descriptors of "what happened", but narratives themselves might be understood as driving and informing social action.

Shame and the "Failure" of Self-Determination

Connecting individual and interactional accounts of emotions in relation to suicide and self-harm with broader structural conditions is a significant challenge. A more subtle way in which shame was present in the reviewed papers was the theme of self-determination, raised often by analysts, but in quite different ways. For instance, Huey et al. (2014) interviewed women experiencing homelessness, examining reporting of "stressors" and the extent to which these related to reporting self-injury. Despite the socioeconomic disadvantage and marginalisation of the women interviewed, and that several appeared to have also been migrants (from e.g. Afghanistan, Angola), Huey et al.'s (2014) analysis focuses narrowly on individual interpersonal stressors – physical and sexual abuse, bereavement and family break-up. They noted that participants indicated:

> a sense of helplessness, or conversely, the belief that one must maintain constant vigilance and control over situations in order to prevent bad things from happening . . . [which] can consequently lead to negative self-evaluations, as well as feelings of shame and guilt, when the individual is unable to control external factors.
>
> (p. 154)

This analysis curiously avoided engaging with the role of structural factors, experiences of stigmatisation, difficulty accessing material resources, or housing, and how these may have further shaped women's experiences and accounts. Instead, Huey et al. concluded that experience of childhood (interpersonal) trauma was the most significant predictor of later self-injury. Experiences of childhood trauma, while almost undoubtedly important, were described as occurring outside of any discussion of social, economic, or political contexts. This approach facilitated an analysis which framed "failures" of self-determination – or the inability to control, or prevent "bad things from happening" – as individual deficits, rather than embedded in structural, cultural or political contexts.

In contrast, Simone Fullagar's (2003) study of understandings of youth suicide in two contrasting rural and urban areas of Australia incorporated a more direct examination of the subtle ways in which structural, political conditions can shape the ways in which suicide is articulated and understood; making death an understandable option in the face of "failures" (or "stressors") which are framed as utterly individual. Fullagar argues that suicide prevention policies, with a focus on individual mental illness and treatment, may actually serve to contribute to processes which encourage individuals to "'see' their own self as pathological and hence shameful" (p. 301).

Fullagar's arguments resonate across the accounts reviewed, which frequently focused on individual failures (and related 'shame') when accounting for acts of suicide or self-harm:

> I didn't want to be alive . . . I couldn't handle the everyday stress of waking up and doing the mundane things, not being at work . . . I'd had enough, I just wanted to bail out of this world, I'd just had enough, I couldn't handle the phone calls, I just couldn't handle the rejections for jobs.
>
> (Byng et al., 2015, p. 941)

Studies which included people who had self-harmed in contexts of economic adversity also featured accounts which individualised these experiences, even where contributing social and political structures were acknowledged. Elliott et al. (2014) noted that "All 16 participants reported economic hardship that *they tended to blame upon themselves*" (p. 3, italics added), while respondents in Barnes et al.'s study referred to their "failure" to get or keep jobs. However, another key theme in Barnes et al.'s study was the role of punitive austerity policies enacted by the UK government around the time of the interviews (2014). This study came closer than many others to engaging with the political contexts in which suicide or self-harm may take place. Some participants did appear to attempt to deflect "self-blame", pointing to the role of welfare policies in creating the challenging economic conditions they found themselves in.

> Apparently I was fit enough for work even though I was absolutely falling apart, couldn't breathe, couldn't do nothing, my head was teetered and just gone and I wasn't there really and yeah, went to a tribunal, me money got squashed, got threw off and everything, no money for about six weeks and then I just snapped one day and ended up trying to overdose.
>
> (Joe, 31, in Barnes et al., 2016, p. 4)

However, while these accounts implicated broader political factors, they were provided in order to explain an instance of hospital treated self-harm. This raises questions as to why, if the "blame" for a difficult economic situation is directed externally, individuals nevertheless respond through an act of harm against the self. Fullagar's (2003) analysis, as well as recent literature on shame, stigma and neoliberalism, provides a partial answer to this: contemporary politics in the UK and US individualises blame (and shame) for economic problems in insidious, difficult to resist, ways. Thus, even where individuals may be able to name structural, economic, or political conditions as causing misfortune, cultural narratives about individual responsibility may still shape how people *feel*, and – relatedly – how they act. A recent paper by Scambler goes further, arguing that stigma is *weaponised* in contemporary austerity politics – reflected in, for instance, the "bedroom tax" and increasingly intrusive and punitive "testing" carried out on people claiming disability benefits, each of which are singled out by Barnes et al.'s respondents (Scambler, 2018). Scambler argues (echoing Fullagar) that such policies contribute to individuals feeling shamed and responsible for "failures", even where these can be located in structural conditions. These arguments can be related to Mills' recent excoriating analysis of media coverage of "austerity suicides", where she argues that "stigmatisation is key in crafting a hostile environment for welfare claimants – a context against which suicide makes sense" (2018, p. 316). Here, I suggest that a consideration of emotions, particularly shame, can contribute to making further sense of suicides in these contexts.

Conclusion

In this chapter, I have highlighted two ways in which accounts of shame among those who have self-harmed or died by suicide can be tied to broader social, cultural and political contexts: shame as a rhetorical device, explaining and justifying acts of suicide or self-harm; and shame in relation to "failures" in self-determination. In doing so, I have begun to sketch out the importance of attending to qualitative accounts, and to emotions, in developing an understanding of suicide as an issue of social justice. I have sought to tentatively build on these insights and suggest some further ways of thinking about these issues whilst going beyond a *description* of the shaming aspects of living with socioeconomic disadvantage and marginalisation. This discussion, I suggest, can be related to Fricker's (2007) concept of epistemic injustice, showing how social contexts may impact on experience, and on accounts of experience, including how they are "heard" by researchers (LeBlanc & Kinsella, 2016).

Going forward, the analysis developed in this chapter advocates greater, critical, use of the accounts of those who have self-harmed, or died by suicide. Such work would contribute greatly to existing theoretical endeavours which have tended to focus more on cultural texts, as in Mills' (2018) psychopolitics of austerity suicides. I suggest that engaging critically with accounts of those who have self-harmed or died by suicide provides partial, but nevertheless vitally important, insights into emotional aspects of these practices. Shame is one such emotional aspect, and while I have foregrounded it here, this should not foreclose engagement with other emotions and their role in shaping or giving meaning to suicide or self-harm. In particular, consideration of the role of anger (also a key feature of the original review) is warranted, particularly given the close association between anger, shame and violence in Scheff's work (Scheff & Retzinger, 2001).

The critical approach that I have sketched out in this chapter emphasises the importance of attending to accounts of those who have died by suicide, or self-harmed. Doing so can, I suggest, provide important explanatory insights into the relationship between these practices and broader structural conditions. However, I have also shown the limitations of approaches to qualitative analysis which merely describe or reproduce the "voices" that are more often neglected in suicide research. While in many ways a positive move, I suggest that qualitative research can in some cases reproduce the epistemic injustice identified in quantitative approaches, by objectifying the "subject" of research (LeBlanc & Kinsella, 2016). Further, without care, qualitative research may fail to attend to the hermeneutic injustice experienced by marginalised groups: individuals may not have the language or knowledge to name structural disadvantage, drawing instead on more readily available, politically supported cultural narratives which privilege individual responsibility, self-blame and shame (Mills, 2018; Tyler & Slater, 2018). As such, I argue that qualitative work in this area must engage critically and reflexively with the situated nature of accounts, and seek to cultivate awareness of the ways in which broader structures, contexts or ideologies – of colonialism, oppression, neoliberalism – may shape these accounts.

Notes

1 Since completing the original review, I have refined the original analysis, and identified one new publication (McDermott and Roen, 2016). As such there are some minor differences between the review discussed here and that reported in the original report for Samaritans.
2 The choice of the phrase "mechanisms" was driven by the research and policy team at Samaritans, and reflects an epistemological approach that sits uneasily with the qualitative studies and theoretical approaches I drew on.

References

Abrams, L. and Gordon, A. (2003) Self-harm narratives of urban and suburban young women *Affilia*, 18, 4, 429–444.

Abrutyn, S. (2017) What Hindu Sati can teach us about the sociocultural and social psychological dynamics of suicide. *Journal for the Theory of Social Behaviour*, 4, 4, 522–539.

Abrutyn, S. and Mueller, A.S. (2014) The socioemotional foundations of suicide: A microsociological view of Durkheim's suicide. *Sociological Theory*, 32, 4, 327–351.
Ahmed, S. (2014) *The Cultural Politics of Emotion*, Edinburgh: Edinburgh University Press.
Atkinson, P. (2009) Illness narratives revisited: The failure of narrative reductionism, *Sociological Research Online*, 14, 5.
Atkinson, P. (2010) The contested terrain of narrative analysis – an appreciative response, *Sociology of Health & Illness*, 32, 4, 661–662.
Barbalet, J.M. (2001) *Emotion, Social Theory and Social Structure: A Macrosociological Approach*, Cambridge: Cambridge University Press.
Barnes, M.C., Gunnell, D., Davies, R., Hawton, K., Kapur, N., Potokar, J. and Donovan, J.L. (2016) Understanding vulnerability to self-harm in times of economic hardship and austerity: A qualitative study, *BMJ Open*, 6, 2.
Boden, Z.V.R., Gibson, S., Owen, G.J. and Benson, O. (2016) Feelings and intersubjectivity in qualitative suicide research, *Qualitative Health Research*, 26, 8, 1078–1090.
Burkitt, I. (2014) *Emotions and Social Relations*, London: Sage.
Button, M.E. (2016) Suicide and social justice, *Political Research Quarterly*, 69, 2, 270–280.
Byng, R., Howerton, A., Owens, C.V. and J. Campbell (2015) Pathways to suicide attempts among male offenders: the role of agency. *Sociology of Health & Illness*, 37, 936–951.
Carel, H. and Kidd, I.J. (2014) Epistemic injustice in healthcare: A philosophical analysis, *Medicine, Health Care and Philosophy*, 17, 4, 529–540.
Case, A. and Deaton, A. (2015) Rising morbidity and mortality in midlife among white non-Hispanic Americans in the 21st century, *Proceedings of the National Academy of Sciences*, 112, 49, 15078–15083.
Chandler, A. (2016) *Self-injury, Medicine and Society: Authentic Bodies*, Basingstoke: Palgrave Macmillan.
Chandler, A. (2017) Explaining the relationship between socioeconomic disadvantage, self-harm and suicide: a qualitative synthesis of the accounts of those who have self-harmed, *Socioeconomic Disadvantage and Suicidal Behaviour*, London: Samaritans.
Chandler, A. (in press) Socioeconomic inequalities of suicide: sociological and psychological interventions, *European Journal of Social Theory*.
Chandler, A., King, C., Burton, C. and Platt, S. (2016) General practitioners' accounts of patients who have self-harmed: A qualitative, observational study, *Crisis: The Journal of Crisis Intervention and Suicide Prevention*, 37, 42–50.
Chandler, A., Myers, F. and Platt, S. (2011) The construction of self-injury in the clinical literature: a sociological exploration, *Suicide and Life Threatening Behavior*, 41, 1, 98–109.
Cleary, A. (2012) Suicidal action, emotional expression, and the performance of masculinities, *Social Science & Medicine*, 74, 498–505.
Cleaver, K., Meerabeau, L. and Maras, P. (2014) Attitudes towards young people who self-harm: Age, an influencing factor, *Journal of Advanced Nursing*, 70, 12, 2884–2896.
Cobb, M.C. (2018) Casualties of debate: A critique of the sociology of emotion, *Sociology Compass*, 0, 0, e12643.

Cover, R. (2012) *Queer Youth Suicide, Culture and Identity: Unlivable Lives?* London: Routledge.

Denzin, N.K. (2016) Critical qualitative inquiry, *Qualitative Inquiry*, 23, 1, 8–16.

Dolezal, L. (2015) *The Body and Shame: Phenomenology, Feminism and The Socially Shaped Body*, Lanham: Lexington Books.

Douglas, J. (1967) *The Social Meanings of Suicide*, Princeton: Princeton University Press.

Elliott, M., Naphan, D.E. and Kohlenberg, B.L. (2014) Suicidal behavior during economic hard times, *International Journal of Social Psychiatry*, 61, 5, 492–497.

Everall, R.D., Bostik, K.E. and Paulson, B.L. (2006) Being in the safety zone: Emotional experiences of suicidal adolescents and emerging adults. *Journal of Adolescent Research*, 21, 4, 370–392.

Fitzpatrick, S. (2011) Looking beyond the qualitative and quantitative divide: Narrative, ethics and representation in suicidology, *Suicidology Online*, 2, 29–37.

Fricker, M. (2007) *Epistemic Injustice: Power and the Ethics of Knowing*, Oxford: Oxford University Press.

Fullagar, S. (2003) Wasted lives: The social dynamics of shame and youth suicide, *Journal of Sociology*, 39, 3, 291–307.

Goffman, E. (1968) *Stigma: Notes on the Management of Spoiled Identity*, London: Penguin.

Goffman, E. (1973) *The Presentation of Self in Everyday Life*, Woodstock: Overlook Press.

Haw, C., Hawton, K., Gunnell, D. and Platt, S. (2015) Economic recession and suicidal behaviour: Possible mechanisms and ameliorating factors, *International Journal of Social Psychiatry*, 61, 1, 73–81.

Hjelmeland, H. (2016) A critical look at current suicide research, In White, J., Marsh, I., Kral, M.J. and Morris, J. (eds) *Critical Suicidology: Transforming Suicide Research and Prevention for the 21st Century*, Vancouver: UBC Press.

Hjelmeland, H. and Knizek, B.L. (2010) Why We Need Qualitative Research in Suicidology, *Suicide and Life-Threatening Behavior*, 40, 1, 74–80.

Hjelmeland, H. and Knizek, B.L. (2016) Time to change direction in suicide research, In O'Connor, R. and Pirkis, J. (eds) *The International Handbook of Suicide Prevention*, Chichester: John Wiley & Sons. pp. 696–709.

Huey, L., Hryniewicz, D. and Fthenos, G. (2014) "I had a lot of anger and that's what kind of led me to cutting myself": Employing a social stress framework to explain why some homeless women self-injure, *Health Sociology Review*, 23, 2, 3864–3890.

Jaworski, K. (2014) *The Gender of Suicide*, Aldershot: Ashgate.

Kidd, S.A. (2004) "The walls were closing in, and we were trapped": A qualitative analysis of street youth suicide, *Youth & Society*, 36, 1, 30–55.

LeBlanc, S. and Kinsella, E.A. (2016) Toward epistemic justice: A critically reflexive examination of "sanism" and implications for knowledge creation, *Studies in Social Justice*, 19, 1, 59–78.

Lester, D. (1997) The role of shame in suicide. *Suicide and Life-Threatening Behavior*, 27, 4, 352–361.

Lupton, D. (1998) *The Emotional Self: A Sociocultural Exploration*, London: Sage.

McDermott, E. and Roen, K. (2016) *Queer Youth, Suicide and Self-Harm – Troubled Subjects, Troubling Norms*, Basingstoke: Palgrave Macmillan.
Mills, C. (2018) "Dead people don't claim": A psychopolitical autopsy of UK austerity suicides, *Critical Social Policy*, 38, 2, 302–322.
Mok, P.L.H., Kapur, N., Windfuhr, K., Leyland, A.H., Appleby, L., Platt, S. and Webb, R.T. (2012) Trends in national suicide rates for Scotland and for England & Wales, 1960–2008, *The British Journal of Psychiatry*, 200, 3, 245–251.
Munt, S.R. (2007) *Queer Attachments: The Cultural Politics of Shame*, London: Routledge.
O'Connor, R.C. (2011) The integrated motivational-volitional model of suicidal behavior. *Crisis*, 32, 6, 295–298.
Platt, S. (2011) Inequalities and Suicidal Behaviour, In O'Connor, R.C., Platt, S. and Gordon, J. (eds) *International Handbook of Suicide Prevention: Research, Policy and Practice*, Oxford: Wiley-Blackwell. pp. 211–234.
Probyn, E. (2005) *Blush: Faces of Shame*, Minneapolis: University of Minnesota Press.
Ray, L. (2014) Shame and the city – "looting", emotions and social structure, *The Sociological Review*, 62, 1, 117–136.
Redley, M. (2003) Towards a new perspective on deliberate self-harm in an area of multiple deprivation, *Sociology of Health and Illness*, 25, 4, 348–373.
Redley, M. (2010) The clinical assessment of patients admitted to hospital following an episode of self-harm: A qualitative study, *Sociology of Health & Illness*, 32, 3, 470–485.
Retzinger, S.M. (1995) Identifying shame and anger in discourse, *The American Behavioral Scientist*, 38, 8, 1104.
Reynders, A., Kerkhof, A.J.F.M., Molenberghs, G. and Van Audenhove, C. (2016) Stigma, Attitudes, and Help-Seeking Intentions for Psychological Problems in Relation to Regional Suicide Rates, *Suicide and Life-Threatening Behavior*, 46, 1, 67–78.
Rhodes, T. and Treloar, C. (2008) The social production of hepatitis C risk among injecting drug users: a qualitative synthesis, *Addiction*, 103, 10, 1593–1603.
Riessman, C.K. (2008) *Narrative Methods for the Human Sciences*, Thousand Oaks: Sage.
Samaritans (2017) *Socioeconomic Disadvantage and Suicidal Behaviour*, London: Samaritans.
Saunders, K.E.A., Hawton, K., Fortune, S. and Farrell, S. (2012) Attitudes and knowledge of clinical staff regarding people who self-harm: A systematic review, *Journal of Affective Disorders*, 139, 3, 205–216.
Sayer, A. (2005) Class, moral worth and recognition, *Sociology*, 39, 5, 947–963.
Scambler, G. (2018) Heaping blame on shame: "Weaponising stigma" for neoliberal times, *The Sociological Review*, 66, 4, 766–782.
Scheff, T.J. (1990) *Microsociology: Discourse, Emotion, and Social Structure*, Chicago: University of Chicago Press.
Scheff, T.J. (2006) Aggression, hypermasculine emotions and relations: the silence/violence pattern, *Irish Journal of Sociology*, 15, 1, 24–39.
Scheff, T.J. (2014) The ubiquity of hidden shame in modernity, *Cultural Sociology*, 8, 2, 129–141.
Scheff, T.J. and Retzinger, S.M. (2001) *Emotions and Violence: Shame and Rage in Destructive Conflicts*, Lincoln: iUniverse inc.

Scott, M.B. and Lyman, S.M. (1968) Accounts, *American Sociological Review*, 33, 1, 46–62.
Sedgwick, E.K. and Frank, A. (1995) Shame in the Cybernetic Fold: Reading Silvan Tomkins, *Critical Inquiry*, 21, 2, 496–522.
Shiner, M., Scourfield, J., Fincham, B. and Langer, S. (2009) When things fall apart: Gender and suicide across the life-course, *Social Science & Medicine*, 69, 5, 738–746.
Stack, S. and Wasserman, I. (2007) Economic Strain and Suicide Risk: A Qualitative Analysis, *Suicide and Life-Threatening Behavior*, 37, 1, 103–112.
Turner, J.H. and Stets, J.E. (2006) Sociological Theories of Human Emotions, *Annual Review of Sociology*, 32, 25–52.
Tyler, I. and Slater, T. (2018) Rethinking the sociology of stigma, *The Sociological Review*, 66, 4, 721–743.
White, J., Marsh, I., Kral, M.J. and Morris, J. (2016) *Critical Suicidology: Transforming Suicide Research and Prevention for the 21st Century*, Vancouver: UBC Press.
Wiklander, M., Samuelsson, M. and Åsberg, M. (2003) Shame reactions after suicide attempt, *Scandinavian Journal of Caring Sciences*, 17, 3, 293–300.
Williams, M. (1997) *Cry of Pain: Understanding Suicide and Self-harm*, London: Penguin.
Wray, M., Colen, C. and Pescosolido, B. (2011) The Sociology of Suicide, *Annual Review of Sociology*, 37, 1, 505–528.

Part II

3 Cultural Continuity and Indigenous Youth Suicide

Michael J. Chandler and Christopher E. Lalonde

Introduction

This chapter—a partial reprise of previously reported evidence (e.g., Chandler and Lalonde, 1998, 2009; Chandler, Lalonde, Sokol and Hallett, 2003; Chandler and Proulx, 2008, 2010) concerning the suicides of Indigenous youth—unfolds in three sections. Section I is largely about matters of aggregation, and the rudimentary mathematics involved in arriving at some culturally fair way of computing the suicide rates characteristic of various Indigenous groups. Skipping ahead, Section III details a range of social determinants shown to successfully distinguish between Indigenous communities with heart-stoppingly high and surprisingly low to absent suicide rates. Sandwiched in between, Section II sidesteps such surrounding empirical considerations, by taking up the challenging conceptual task of anticipating what might reasonably count as such potential community-level factors predictive of Indigenous youth suicide. Here, attention will be focused on the many ills of *dualistic thought*—the familiar false dichotomy between selves and societies—and the "cult of the self-contained individual" (Cushman, 1990) that has arisen as a result of what Nietzsche (1988, 1880) summed up as:

> The general imprecise way of observing everywhere in nature opposites . . . where there are not opposites, but differences in degree . . . has led us into . . . an unspeakable amount of pain, arrogance, harshness, estrangement, [and] frigidity . . . because we think we see opposites instead of transitions.
>
> (cited in Gjerde and Onishi, 2000)

Such philosophical inner-workings aside, and in keeping with the foundational premises driving this volume, a convincing case will hopefully be made that what best insulates members of diverse sociocultural groups from suicide are collective efforts to repair ongoing social injustices.

Section I

This chapter draws upon a three decade-long program of research aimed at better understanding two deeply puzzling matters. The first of these concerns how it could possibly be that so many young persons—youth with all of life's potential sweetness not yet full on their lips—can and do so regularly choose to end their own lives. Relatedly, the second puzzle focuses special attention on Indigenous youth, and the "epidemics" of youth suicide alleged to characterize such special populations. The US Centers for Disease Control and Prevention (2010), for example, report that American Indian and Alaskan Native youth (ages 10–24) have the highest suicide rates of all ethno-racial groups within the US, at 31.27 suicides per 100,000 (Leavitt, Ertl, Sheats, Petrosky, Ivey-Stephenson and Fowler, 2018). Available Canadian data are little different (Chandler et al., 2003).

Few would be surprised by such grizzly facts. The appropriate adjectives, or so we have been taught, to properly modify the mythical term *Indian* are, in no particular order, both *drunken* and *suicidal*. Having been caught (so to speak) *red-handed*, by clinching first place in the race to the top of the suicide charts, Indigenous persons are frequently thought of as suffering some racial stigmata or genetic fault, while the rest of us are encouraged to happily imagine that we (their colonizers) are somehow better insulated against alcohol poisoning, hopelessness, and self-appointed death—a perfect cover-story for all those who wish to believe that nothing can or should be done.

Obviously, little about this is even minimally satisfactory, including the suspect prospect of compacting more than two decades of empirical research into one slim chapter. Give or take the several meta-theoretic flights reserved for Section II, what is selectively written here will, consequently, attempt to mirror those social justice themes that broadly steer this volume; focusing primary attention on the many forms of social *in*justice commonly suffered by Indigenous groups. Still, more particularly, the task to be taken up will focus primarily on finding alternative explanations for the widely reputed *claim* that, when painted with the same broad but indiscriminate brush, Indigenous populations of every stripe are regularly said to have markedly elevated suicide rates (Chandler and Lalonde, 1998, 2009), arguably the highest suicide levels in the world.

As pains will be taken here to show, all such over-arching evidentiary claims to the effect that Indigenous persons are somehow more suicidal than their non-Indigenous counterparts likely come down to this or that unschooled form of sloppy book-keeping. As has been shown (see, for example Hodgkenson, 1990), while making up only approximately three percent of North America's total population, Indigenous groups have been found to be responsible for more than half of the continent's cultural diversity. This is clearly in the running for truth. Across Canada there exist, for instance, 634 distinct First Nations (called Bands in Canada and tribes in the US) that speak more than 60 distinct languages, each with their own unique cultural traditions, art forms, stories, songs, etc. In the province of British Columbia alone, where much of the research to be reported here was conducted, there exist some 203 distinctive Bands, speaking some 43 different languages and 60 different dialects. Some of these groups live in the mountains, or pocket deserts, or on the sea shore, or prairies. To wrongly imagine that all of these groups are somehow as alike as any two peas in a pod needs to be counted as a mistake of enormous arrogance. BC alone is larger than most of Western Europe, only with more languages and distinctive cultural ways. Who could imagine lumping all of the diverse peoples of Europe into one indiscriminate stew? Certainly Durkheim (1897/2002), the progenitor of modern epidemiologic research into matters of suicide, did not. Rather, he was convinced, as this chapter means to convince its readers, that all attempts to paint diverse cultural groups with the same broad brush is a fools-errand. What needs to be done instead is to seek out some level of aggregation (or sorting) that makes cultural, as well as conceptual, sense.

With questions about what constitutes proper levels of aggregation on the table, it is important to begin by first getting clear about what constitutes a sensible strategy for dividing up Canada's or North America's various Indigenous populations. For the suspect purpose of various political sound bites (e.g., for public talk of national suicide rates) it has often been thought sufficient to merely lump anyone and everyone with some claim for "Aboriginal Status" (*sic*) into a single fuzzy, unwashed conglomerate, before simply counting up that proportion of this total that actually attempted or completed suicide. Such figures—numbers that typically hover at a rate more or less double that of the general population—often make the headlines, or figure importantly into dubious government documents. At best, however, these statistical artifacts only succeed in wrongly convincing the unwary that something important is being said. Adding up apples and oranges hardly begins to cover it. Rather, simply summing across all of Canada's more than 600 Bands, or the 200-plus First Nations living in BC, is not only demeaning and racist, but ultimately squanders already scarce resources by allocating them evenly and thus thinly across all communities without regard to actual need.

As a possible alternative to simply summing across the Indigenous peoples of an entire country or continent, one might imagine instead lumping everyone into their respective language groups, or "mother tongues." Although something like this is potentially more defensible, on cultural grounds, than merely throwing everyone into the same indiscriminate melting pot, awkwardly, no one has yet tried this on. If they did, such efforts would likely fail, at least in North America where Indigenous mother tongues are quickly approaching extinction (Chandler et al., 2003), and typically depend on matters of accidental geography.

A better alternative, it is argued, would be to cluster Indigenous persons by *Band* or tribe. Because BC is the only Canadian province where deaths by suicide are routinely recorded by Band, such data served as the source of the evidence reported here. Figure 3.1 displays the Band-Level youth suicide rate for each of BC's distinctive 203 Bands. What is immediately obvious is just how jagged or saw-toothed this portrait of BC's Band-level suicide rates actually proved to be.

Figure 3.2 reports the same data, this time portrayed by Band ordered from lowest to highest youth suicide rates. Again, what is perhaps most compelling about this figure is that more than half of these Bands suffered no youth suicides during a 6- and then 15-year reporting window (Chandler and Lalonde, 2009), while many others experienced youth suicide rates more than a hundred times that of non-Indigenous youth.

Clearly, what inquiring minds want to know is what distinguishes those Bands with low or absent youth suicide rates from other Indigenous communities where youth suicides are epidemic? Why do some 90% of the youth suicides that happen among the First Nations Bands of Western Canada happen in only 10% of these Indigenous communities? Section III that follows is meant to provide some answers to such questions. Before turning to these matters, however, it will prove useful to first explore some of the implications that the findings just reported have for what has become a highly suspect, but hugely expensive and rapidly expanding suicide prevention industry.

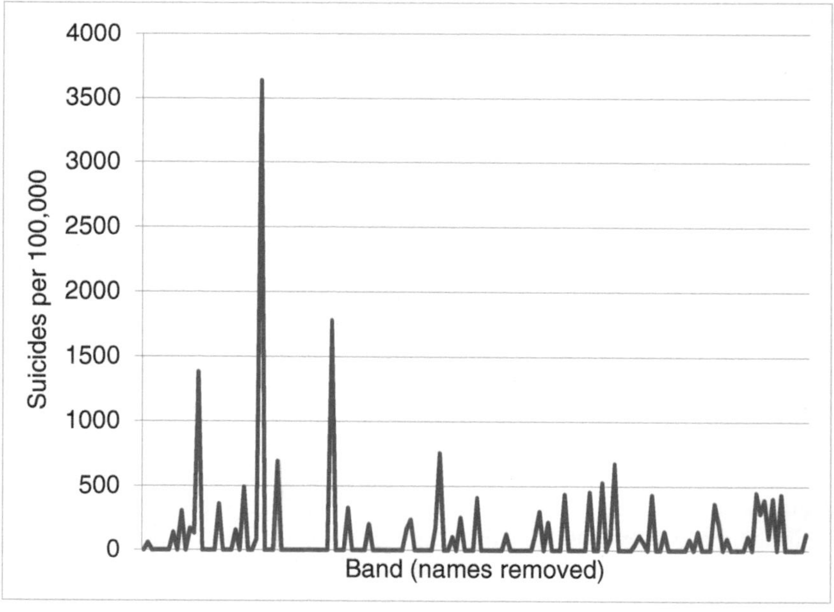

Figure 3.1 Youth Suicide Rate by Band (BC, 1987–1992)

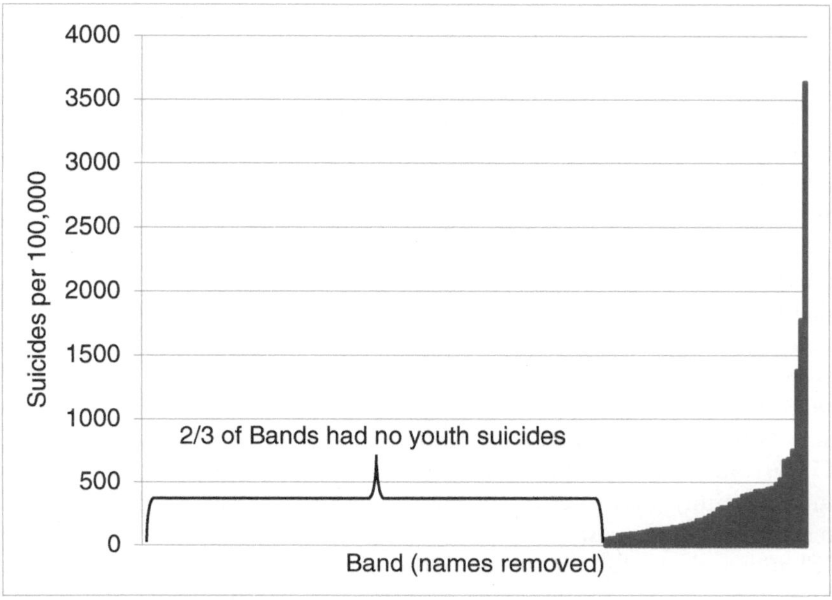

Figure 3.2 Youth Suicide Rate by Band (BC, 1987–1992)

Predicting Individual Suicides from Existing Epidemiological Data

The data just rehearsed not only make it plain that any and all omnibus claims concerning the suicidality of the whole of Canada's, or anyone else's, Indigenous youth are wrong and prejudicial. Given the evidence in hand, it is hard to imagine, for example, how the private mental lives of half of BC's Indigenous youth have somehow escaped the hopelessness and depression thought to vex everyone else, or how parachuting in teams of counselors meant to patch up those remaining might change this picture.

Here is the rub. Things that occur regularly tend to be easy to predict. Tomorrow the sun will rise as it ordinarily does. By contrast, predicting rare occurrences typically proves difficult or impossible. Youth suicides, however heart breaking they may prove to be, are extremely rare. By convention, suicides are customarily reported as deaths per 100,000. As earlier reviewed, the generic suicide rate across the whole of North America hovers around 10 per 100,000; typically double that for youth and presumably 10 times that number for Indigenous youth (Chandler et al., 2003). The evident conclusion is that, however long such tragedies may remain in our hearts and minds, suicides are statistically rare, and can almost never be anticipated. If such odds were taken to your local bookmaker, the best bet would obviously be to predict that no one would ever commit suicide, a wager that, even under dire circumstances, would prove to be correct on more than 99,950 times out of every 100,000 occasions.

Hypothetically, it might appear possible to improve one's odds of making correct predictions about individual suicides by concentrating attention only on those judged to display so-called *early warning* signs or symptoms. Perhaps so-called *gatekeepers* could do this for us. Candidate markers such as depressed mood, suicidal ideation, and even previous failed suicide attempts might potentially be used for such predictive purposes There are, however, insurmountable problems with all such speculative culling approaches. Manifest depression, for example, is as common as clay among young people (Chandler et al., 2003), and the rate of suicidal ideation among even ordinary adolescents has been shown to be around at least 50 percent (Meehan, Lamb, Saltzmen and O'Carroll, 1992). Even locking in on groups of those who have already unsuccessfully made serious suicide attempts will not help. The vast majority of such *unsuccessful* (*sic*) suicide attempters do so only once (Chandler et al., 2003). One could, in desperation, potentially hold out hope for some as yet un-invented survey or psychological assessment tool. If suicide rates were closer to 20 (or 40 or even 80) per 100, then such hopes might prove reasonable. As it is, where known suicides are set against base-rates of 100,000, for example, all reasonable hopes of finding efficient predictors are automatically doomed to failure.

Imagine somehow attempting to build an assessment tool that, when appropriate cut-offs had been established, could successfully pick out truly suicidal youth from a group of 100 candidates. Even then, when confronted with real-world base-rates of 10–100 per 100,000, such identical cut-off scores would automatically generate many thousands of so-called *false positives*—wrongly identified young persons whose belts, sharps, shoelaces and other freedoms would be taken away on the strength of no more than a simple statistical misunderstanding.

What is true about prediction is also true of prevention. Who could we convincingly imagine might possess the skills required to make such life altering judgments? How many days or weeks have such *gatekeepers* been trained for this seemingly impossible task, and what are they trained to be on the look-out for? In short, successfully picking out from a sea of others, how are those rare individuals who will actually end up taking their own lives to be identified? All this is a hopeless enterprise, not unlike trying to catch lightning in a bottle.

Notwithstanding this statistical impasse—the utter impossibility of anticipating the deaths by suicide of single individuals—our collective conscience and potential public outrage do not allow turning a blind eye and simply doing nothing. Faced with this conundrum, the US, along with Canada and much of the rest of the once United Kingdom, has opted for the usual responsibility-shifting strategy of encouraging separate groups, including Indigenous communities, to invent their own *home-grown* suicide prevention plans. When such efforts fail, as there is every indication that they have, then responsibility can naturally be off-loaded onto unwary participating communities.

Given this win-win wager, the Canadian government, along with many other post-colonial remnants, has undertaken what, most generously, could be described as a failed *natural experiment*—a kind of multiple pronged free-for-all in which separate groups, including Indigenous communities, are encouraged to invent their own *home-grown, made from scratch* suicide prevention strategy. The overarching *plan*, if there is one, appears to have been to throw a lot of unbridled money on the table, all in the hopes that some as yet unimagined intervention strategy will somehow mysteriously disclose itself.

The closest thing to a common thread running through what has emerged from these diverse community-oriented efforts is what have come to be known as "gatekeeper" strategies. The kernel idea driving most of these otherwise homespun efforts is that somehow, within troubled communities, there already exist certain individuals or groups (coaches, priests, bartenders, elders, etc.) that already have the trust, or, failing that, at least an insider's ear, concerning who might be at special risk to suicide (Wexler, White and Trainor, 2015).

The potential fault with all such potential *gatekeeper* approaches is that there is no one to tell such designated informers what does and does not actually count as an early warning sign of suicide. *Watch out for signs of depression*, they are told, without having any way of knowing that everyone they happen to know has every right to be depressed. At least in the case of most Indigenous communities, their past is regularly seen as a cultural joke, just as any hope for a realistic future is automatically dismissed as joke number two. How could anyone living in the more run-down and forgotten of such Indigenous communities *not* be hopeless and depressed?

In the absence of better guidance, the usual interim protocol adopted by such programs has commonly been to encourage separate groups, including Indigenous individual communities, to simply make it up as they go. Although such a free-for-all strategy is perhaps consistent with new-found commitments to eclecticism and *community control*, most such enterprises remain unwittingly devoted to the usual individualistic prospect that, behind whatever idiosyncrasies of circumstance might mark each such separately conceived individual, there, nevertheless, continues to remain some false hope for the existence of some common, wide-spectrum, suicide prevention elixir—some set of common practices equally suitable as a purge against suicide in every quarter. All such hoped-for prospects aside, there exists, for the moment, unsurprisingly, little (read *no*) evidence to corroborate such hopes.

Nevertheless, such *gatekeeper* programs typically continue to be very big businesses, globally costing taxpayers hundreds and hundreds of millions of dollars each year. The open question is how such gatekeeper programs are meant to work?

The answer, unsurprisingly, depends on who you ask. Because they tend to be home grown, such programs often enjoy a measure of popularity in the communities in which they operate, providing some modest income and some suspect status to front-line workers. Such popularity notwithstanding, such gatekeeper programs typically provide only minimal training about the supposed *early warning signs* of suicide—signs that seemingly have no legitimacy in fact—and rely on imagined referral networks that often do not exist (Wexler, White and Trainor, 2015). Nor is it at all clear what it supposedly is it about such programs that might count as evidence of success. For some, simply educating a larger public about suicide is thought to be sufficient justification for their continuing existence. That is, there appears to be no real evidence that such programs actually work. Kirmayer and colleagues (2010), for example, end their exhaustive review of such suicide prevention programs by concluding that, despite the untold millions invested, there is not a single shred of confidence-inspiring evidence that any of these projects have actually 'worked' to prevent a single death. The stark conclusion, then, to which all such evidence leads is that we appear to have all been fishing in the wrong pond; somehow mistakenly imagining that the causes and cures of suicide are all secreted away within individual hearts and minds. How so many have come to harbor such misguided thoughts, and what one might do to exorcise them, involves a detour into the mysteries of so-called *substance dualism* (Chandler and Dunlop, 2015)—the subject of Section II to follow.

Section II: Let No Man (*sic*) Rend Asunder what God has Joined Together

The allegorical "pond" eluded to earlier (the one where nothing is ever caught), is perhaps best understood as that entire pool of beliefs and intuitions that together make up what Rorty (1987) has labeled the West's 2,000-year-old "Judeo-Graeco-Roman-Christian-Renaissance-Enlightenment-Romanticist" perspective. Although there is no hope of entirely slipping the leash on this intellectual heritage, some of its nastiest bits could well be done without. High on the list of such matters is, according to Nietzsche (1988, 1880):

> The general imprecise way of observing everywhere in nature opposites . . . where there are not opposites, but differences in degree . . . has led us into wanting to comprehend and analyze the inner world, also the spiritual-moral world, in terms of such

> opposites. An unspeakable amount of pain, arrogance, harshness, estrangement, (&) frigidity has entered into human feelings because we think we see opposites instead of transitions.

What all these words amount to is the broad claim that any talk about this or that dichotomy, and especially the dichotomy between self and society, is a colossal mistake, responsible for the blood-thick silence that has settled over much of the life sciences, leaving everyone imprisoned within their own sub-disciplinary cells. Nowhere has this been truer than within those professional circles concerned with human suffering. Here the so-called "cult of the individual" (Cushman, 1990) operates at full throttle, regularly dismissing as incomplete any proposed explanation that mistakenly attempts to locate sources of trouble outside of the skins of supposedly self-contained individuals. The rudely chosen name for such mistakes is what Achen and Shively (1995) have called the *psychologist's fallacy* (i.e., any misguided attempt to drag individualistic constructs across the border into collectivist territory; an intended slight only matched by the similarly derisive "ecological fallacy" (Piantadosi, Byar, and Green, 1988), a proposed contrapuntal error committed by wrongly imagining that it is possible to infer the nature of individuals through the study of social aggregates). Such boundary violations should not be thought of as fallacious. Rather, they are ideas in need of repair.

One key manifestation of the false dichotomies erected between selves and societies has been the divisive claim that single individuals and whole cultures are not only cut from different bolts of cloth, but need to be studied using concepts and methods that have real currency only within the confines of their own disciplinary perimeters (Sani, 2008). Worse still, the standard approach to managing such antinomies has been to elevate one pole of the pair to a privileged position, while treating the other as a sort of epiphenomena or shadow of the machine (Overton, 1997). All such *tit for tat* bickering is mirrored in the burlesque afforded by the fact that, prior to the fall of the Berlin Wall, and on crossing the underground border between East and West, the German tram conductors of the day were required to stop the train and change their uniforms to match the politics of the governments above. The wall is of course long since gone, but it sadly remains the case that transiting social science barriers still ordinarily requires a complete change of ideological uniforms.

One could, perhaps, be forgiven for wrongly imagining that suicide is somehow a paradigm case for troubles that are assumed to begin and end within the skin of single individuals. Someone dies, usually in private, there typically are no accomplices, outsiders shake their heads, and death has no extra-personal finger to point. Notwithstanding Durkheim and a newer breed of scattered public health officials, most treat such deaths as cases closed, and view attempts to drag in this or that socio-cultural matter as unnecessarily intrusive and beside the point. Were it not for the fact that such "monistic" approaches typically predict nothing and explain nothing, we might remain free to imagine that, given a light salting of studies exploring this or that socio-cultural matter, we are all free to turn our attention elsewhere.

At a more generic level, Dewey (1917, 1925) echoed many of the same concerns being voiced here, stating that "dualism [e.g., self *vs.* society dualisms] appears to me only two monisms stuck loosely together, so that all the difficulties of monisms are multiplied by two" (p. 491). Similarly, Geertz (1973) cautions us that

> the thing to ask about [artificially divided selves and societies, and] a burlesqued wink or a mock sheep raid is not what their ontological status is. It is the same as that of rocks on the one hand and dreams on the other—they are things in this world.
>
> (p. 10)

What is needed in the place of such divisive notions are concepts that can be made to work in both such epistemic worlds.

Self- and Cultural Continuity as Bridges over Troubled Waters

Although interpretive changes of the sort to be promoted here remain the exception rather than the rule, there are grounds for hope that change is in the wind. Of late, the majority of evolutionary biologists, for example, have worked to dissolve many old dichotomies (e.g., inherited *vs.* acquired attributes), however much they may remain parts of our common vernacular (Ingold, 2000). With respect to self/society dichotomies, however, such good news remains relatively thin on the ground.

More importantly, and of special relevance to the purposes of this chapter, one of the most stubborn of all of these false dichotomies appears to be the one dividing selves from societies. According to Boesch (1991), any bridge-building efforts between these apparent solitudes are doomed before they begin, simply because there are no footholds allowing us to move between such impenetrable conceptual worlds. Boesch may not, however, have been entirely right about this. Rather, by drawing on solution strategies introduced by recent generations of post–Kuhnian scholars such as Lakatos (1978), Laudan (1977), Witherington, (2011), and Overton (2013), all of whom intend to provide just such footholds. The common conviction generally shared by these and other like-minded scholars is that, notwithstanding a common obligation on those subscribing to a given paradigm to defend their own core concepts against all possible incursions, such paradigmatic notions are nonetheless surrounded by what have been described as *belts* of so-called *satellite-like* concepts—concepts that, after the fashion of overlapping Venn diagrams, can be made to successfully compute within more than one paradigmatic horizon. In short, the best hope for successfully promoting commerce between warring paradigms that feature either selves or societies would appear to begin by capitalizing on whatever overlapping conceptual machinery they might hold in common, and to employ such shared coinage as bargaining chips in ultimately negotiating some *rapprochement*; in this case between working concepts simultaneously relevant to both single individuals and whole cultural groups.

Although there are, perhaps, other candidate concepts that hold out the promise of serving as Boesch's missing footholds, and of fitting together all those things we have been told could never be joined, the focus of attention in Section III that follows will be the concept of *continuity*—the stuff out of which both personal and cultural identities are arguably constructed, and the loss of which opens the door to individual and community level suicides.

Section III: Deconstructing the Person–Culture Dichotomy: A Case Study of Indigenous Youth Suicide

Several pages ago, Section I of this chapter ended with an open question: what distinguishes Indigenous communities in which youth suicide is effectively missing, from others where such suicides are epidemic? Speculatively, the answer being groped for in Section II was that both individual and collective suicides are best understood as the consequence of the collapse of self-or cultural *continuity*—whatever that turns out to be. The balance of this chapter, and all of Section III, is given over to clarifying what is meant by these notions of continuity, and demonstrating their efficacy in sorting the suicidal from the non-suicidal. Such an account needs to begin by first laying out certain of the so-called *constitutive conditions* of both personhood and culture.

The Paradox of Sameness and Change

If they are to remain recognizable instances of what individual selves and whole cultures are ordinarily taken to be, then both, it will be argued, must satisfy at least two *constitutive conditions*. First, both are forced by the temporally vectored nature of our public and private lives to constantly *change*—like sharks, gill-less and awash in the temporal stream, if the living quit moving, they die. Second, inevitable change notwithstanding, both individuals and whole cultures must be understood to somehow remain recognizably the same, lest the very notions of persistent individuals and enduring cultures cease to have any interpretable meaning (Luckman, 1979).

The claim that the earlier and later manifestations of a given person or particular culture must necessarily count as belonging timelessly to one and the same *continuant* (Strawson, 1999) is true for at least two reasons, one of which is quintessentially historical and *backwards referring*, the other *forward anticipating*, and so all about securing one's own or one's community's future. As William James (cited in Flanagan, 1996) put it: *Life is like a skiff moving through time with a bow as well as a stern*—a stern traced by the ripples of its passing, and a bow bearing down on its own as yet unrealized future. Try to imagine an individual with no access to or ownership of her or his own past, or a culture denuded of all its historical ways. What you would end up with is either: a) some former individual stripped of both past responsibilities and future entitlements; or the mere ghost of some former cultural group now reduced to nothing more than a milling crowd. Imagine, for example, St. Peter's now impossible task of guarding the Pearly Gates if, every time someone turned over some new leaf, he or she became a new soul in the world. Imagine further the anguish of *Plenty Coups*, the last great Chief of the Crow Nation, who, shortly before his death in 1932, recounted:

> I can think back and tell you much more of war and horse-stealing. But when the buffalo went away the hearts of my people fell to the ground, and they could not lift them up again. After this nothing happened.
>
> (Lear, 2008, p. 2)

In short, if both sameness and change did not lie at the heart of human existence, and if self- and cultural continuity did not operate to bridge our earlier and later ways of being, then, as Unger (1975) points out, past promises would have no claim upon us, and the experience of novelty and innovation in the flow of collective history would be lost (Chandler, 2001). As such, the concepts of both personal and cultural identity hinge on achieving some measure of individual and cultural continuity. The anticipated penalties for breakdowns in such identity preserving processes include increases in the numbers of individual suicides and elevated community-based suicide rates.

Putting temporarily aside, the question of how self- and cultural continuity might actually be measured or related to matters of suicide, the idea that sameness and change must somehow be held together in an awkward embrace is among the oldest of our old ideas. Aristotle (cited in Wiggins, 1980, pp. 88–89), for example, stated that *animals differ from what is not naturally constituted in that each . . . has within it a principle of change and remaining the same.* Centuries later, and in close agreement with almost everyone in between, Locke (1694/1956) emphasized that it is necessary to consider one's self (or culture) as the same thing in different times and places. Without attempting some *tour de force* of quotations all saying more or less the same thing, it remains worthy of note that among somewhat more contemporary theorists such as

Cassirer (1923), who spoke of *temporal unity*, Chisholm (1971) of *intact persistence*, and Strawson (1999) of *diachronic singleness* many more (e.g., Harré, 1979; MacIntyre, 1977; Parfit, 1971; Rorty, 1976; Taylor, 1992; Wiggins, 1980; etc.) have all worked to make the common point that continuity is a prerequisite for being any sort of coherent self or culture whatsoever. What none of these theorists attempted to demonstrate, however, is just how continuity, in its varied manifestations, might actually be measured or studied. These neglected matters are the business of the remainder of this chapter.

Measuring Self- and Cultural Continuity

The present program of research focused on Indigenous youth suicide was almost equally divided into work that featured the study of self-continuity, on the one hand, and cultural continuity on the other. Had we but world enough and time (Marvell, 1681), equal space would have been given over to both of these related matters. Given the intended focus of this volume, however, primary emphasis will be centered here almost exclusively on how those continuities present in whole cultural groups can and have been measured. Potential readers interested in learning more about the assessment strategies developed for use in exploring the self-continuity warranting strategies employed by both Indigenous and non-Indigenous youth are referred to the 2003 SRCD Monograph published by Chandler and colleagues.

As detailed in Section I, some 15 years of complete population data on youth suicide was made available for the whole of British Columbia's 203 First Nations Bands that, as documented earlier, varied dramatically in their rates of youth suicide. Pointedly, half of these 200-plus communities experienced no youth suicides during this study period, whereas 90 percent of the recorded suicides occurred in only 10 percent of these Indigenous communities. The task that these findings set was that of identifying potential cultural continuity markers that could discriminate between Bands with low and high suicide rates.

What is perhaps the most common epidemiologic strategy for attacking such problems is to randomly fish out each and every conceivable, ready-to-hand potential predictor at one's disposal, and to set some omnibus computer program the task of sorting possible wheat from chaff—a selection strategy the scope of which is limited only by available processing capacity, and one's tolerance for the resulting deluge of often uninterpretable findings. The theory driven socio-cultural research reported here proceeded quite differently, by focusing exclusively on candidate markers that met the criteria of indexing the efforts of individual Indigenous communities to introduce changes meant to restore or rehabilitate their own cultural past, or to better insure community control of their own civic future. Efforts to designate physical spaces for carrying out traditional cultural practices, efforts to preserve Indigenous languages, and to restore women to positions of political authority are examples of such *backward-referring* activities theorized to help maintain or restore cultural continuity. Other candidate markers were chosen because they describe *forward-anticipating* community efforts aimed at improving local control over present and future civic life. Efforts to wrestle from government control matters of policing, child protection services and health delivery are examples. Finally, it proved possible to identify two more potential cultural continuity factors that seemed particularly pertinent to both resurrecting a cultural past, and securing community ownership of the future. Achieving a measure of self-government, and control over school curricula are instances of such double-barreled cultural continuity markers.

Perhaps the most straight forward means of taking the measure of these cultural continuity markers is to simply count up the raw number of such predictor variables present in each tribal community. Utilizing the original 6 cultural continuity factors available in 1998, Figure 3.3 depicts data for the period between 1987 and 1992.

These findings were closely replicated in a second wave of data collection covering the period between 1993 and 2000, and involving three additional cultural continuity markers—traditional language use, control of child and family services, and level of participation of women in local governance—evidence reported here in Figure 3.4 (Chandler and Lalonde, 2009). As can be seen from an examination of these figures,

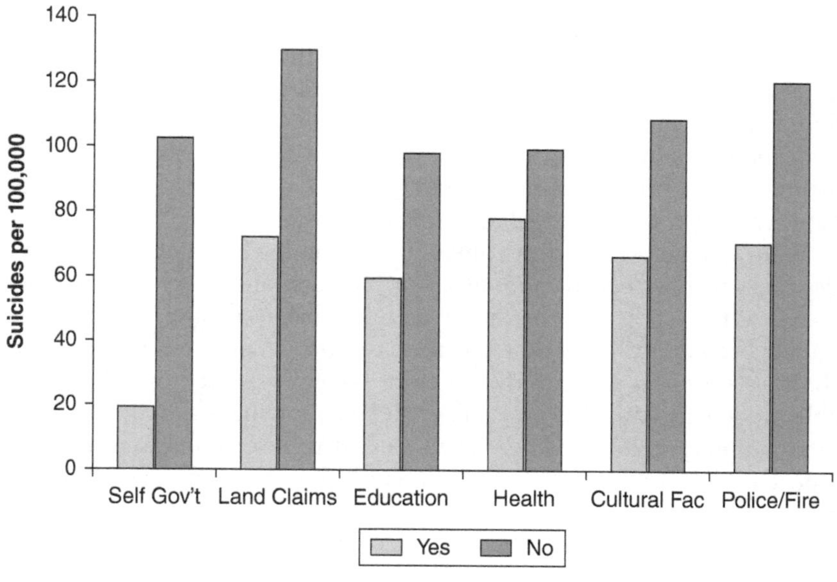

Figure 3.3 Community youth suicide rates by presence or absence of indicator

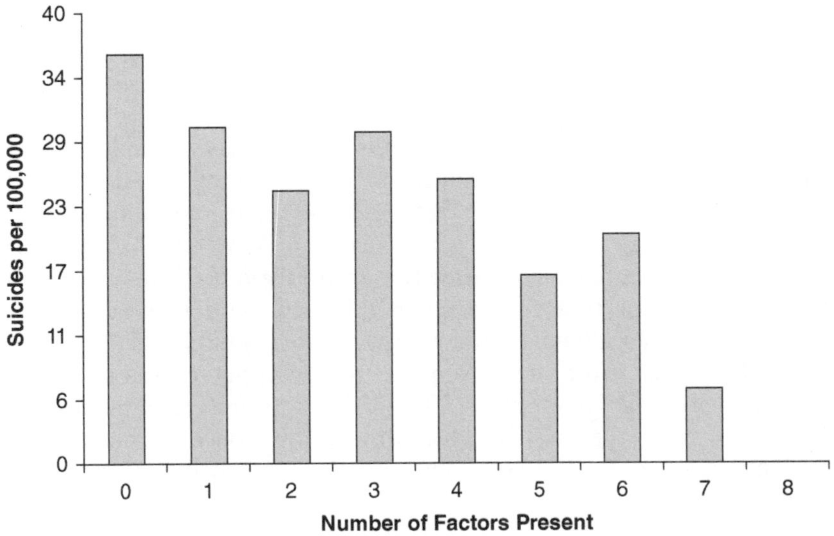

Figure 3.4 Youth suicide rate by number of factors present (1993–2000)

every Band characterized by all available cultural continuity markers experienced no youth suicides during the now 15-year study period, whereas those communities lacking any of these protective factors suffered youth suicide rates often orders of magnitude higher than the national average. Taken together, these data are credited with making a very strong case that the wellbeing of Western Canada's First Nations youth is strongly associated with the extent to which their cultural community is hard at work, both rebuilding endangered connections to its cultural past, struggling to regain control of its own civic future. Put somewhat differently, the menace of Indigenous youth suicide is clearly shown here to be reduced or eliminated by efforts on the part of Indigenous communities to address and reduce the social injustices imposed on them in the wake of colonization.

Conclusion

Without meaning to over-rehearse what has already been said, all or most of the foregoing boils down to three take-home messages. The first of these is that, because suicide is so statistically rare, any and all efforts to pick out in advance those uncommon individuals who do go on to actually take their own life is statistically doomed to failure. What also goes down with the sinking of this same ship is any hope of fashioning some workable suicide prevention program that relies on the vanished prospect of identifying and putting to use *early warning signs* of suicide in the making. No predictive or prevention enterprise that sets out to somehow beat a base-rate of 10 or 40 or even 80 per 100,000 deserves to be taken seriously. Kirmayer and colleagues (2010) drive this point home with their sobering conclusion that there is no credible evidence that such undertakings have saved a single life.

The second proposed take-home point is that much of the blame for what amounts to a litany of failures to properly understand any and everything situated on the cusp between individual and cultural matters, is best laid at the door of what Cushman (1990) has labeled our historical allegiance to what he termed *the cult of the individual*—the quasi-religious conviction that there is some unbreachable divide between all things concerning individuals and everything socio-cultural. The bulk of Section II of this chapter was given over to conceptual efforts to undermine these presumptive solitudes. The partial fix promoted here involved working to make the case that, by trafficking in concepts that occupy overlapping spaces in a common interpretive framework (concepts such as self- and cultural continuity) individual and cultural identity could be better understood and studied, not as things of a different kind, but as different levels of description of the same thing. All of this was taken as a license to attempt a series of empirical studies into individual and cultural continuity, and their relation to Indigenous youth suicide.

Finally, as detailed in Section III, attention was focused on the measurement of so-called cultural continuity, and the demonstration that Indigenous groups hard at work in attempting to reverse the ramped social injustices of post-colonial politics commonly succeeded in effectively eliminating youth suicide in their communities. Data of the sort presented provides, it was argued, strong evidence for abandoning individually based approaches to suicide, and adopting instead more promising social justice approaches.

References

Achen, C. H., and Shively, W. P. (1995). *Cross-level inference*. Chicago, IL: University of Chicago Press.

Boesch, E. E. (1991). *Symbolic action theory and cultural psychology*. Berlin, Germany: Springer-Verlag.

Cassirer, E. (1923). *Substance and function*. Chicago, IL: Open Court.

Chandler, M. J. (2001). The time of our lives: Self-continuity in native and non-native youth. In H. W. Reese (Ed.), *Advances in child development and behavior* (Vol. 28, pp. 175–221). New York: Academic Press.

Chandler, M. J., and Dunlop, W. L. (2015). Identity development, crises, and continuity: Death defying leaps in the lives of indigenous and non-indigenous youth. In B. Hewlett (Ed.), *Adolescent identity: Evolutionary, developmental, and cultural perspectives* (pp. 105–134). New York: Routledge, Taylor & Francis.

Chandler, M. J., and Lalonde, C. E. (1998). Cultural continuity as a hedge against suicide in Canada's First Nations. *Transcultural Psychiatry*, 35, 191–219.

Chandler, M. J., and Lalonde, C. E. (2009). Cultural continuity as a moderator of suicide risk among Canada's First Nations. In L. J. Kirmayer and G. G. Valaskakis (Eds.), *Healing traditions: The mental health of aboriginal peoples in Canada* (pp. 221–248). Vancouver, Canada: UBC Press.

Chandler, M. J., and Proulx, T. (2008). Personal persistence and persistent peoples: Continuities in the lives of individual and whole cultural communities. In F. Sani (Ed.), *Self continuity: Individual and collective perspectives* (pp. 213–226). New York Psychology Press.

Chandler, M. J., and Proulx, T. (2010). Stalking young persons' changing beliefs about belief: Theory, research and implications for practice. In L. D. Bendixen and F. C. Fwuxh (Eds.), *Personal epistemology in the classroom* (pp. 197–219). Cambridge: Cambridge University Press.

Chandler, M. J., Lalonde, C. E., Sokol, B. W., and Hallett, D. (2003). Personal persistence, identity development, and suicide. *Monographs of the Society for Research in Child Development*, 68(2, Serial No. 273).

Chisholm, R. M. (1971). On the logic of intentional action. In R. Binkley, R. Bronaugh, and A. Marras (Eds.), *Agent, action, and reason* (pp. 38–80). Toronto: University of Toronto Press.

Cushman, P. (1990). Why the self is empty: Towards a historically situated psychology. *American Psychologist*, 45, 599–611.

Dewey, J. (1917). Duality and dualism. *Journal of Philosophy, Psychology, and Scientific Methods*, 14, 491–493.

Dewey, J. (1925). *Experience and nature*. Chicago, IL: Open Court.

Durkheim, É. (1897/2002). *Suicide – A study in sociology*. London: Routledge.

Flanagan, O. (1996). *Self expressions: Mind, morals and the meaning of life*. New York: Oxford University Press.

Geertz, C. (1973). *The interpretation of cultures: Selected essays*. New York: Basic Books.

Gjerde, P. F., and Onishi, M. (2000). Selves, cultures, and nations: The psychological imagination of the Japanese in the era of globalization. *Human Development*, 43, 216–226.

Harré, R. (1979). *Social being: A theory for social psychology*. Oxford: Blackwell.

Hodgkenson, H.L. (1990). *The demographics of American Indians: One percent of the people, fifty percent of the diversity*. Washington, DC: Institute for Educational Leadership and Center for Demographic Policy.

Ingold, T. (2000). Evolving skills. In H. Rose and S. Rose (Eds.), *Alas poor Darwin: Arguments against evolutionary psychology* (pp. 273–297). New York: Harmony Books.

Kirmayer, L., Fraser, S., Fauras, V. and Whitley, R. (2010, working paper 14). *Current Approaches to Aboriginal Youth Suicide Prevention*.

Lakatos, I. (1978). *The methodology of scientific research programmes: Philosophical papers (Vol. 1)*. New York: Cambridge University Press.

Laudan, L. (1977). *Progress and its problems: Towards a theory of scientific growth*. Berkeley, CA: University of California Press.

Lear, J. (2008) *Radical hope: Ethics in the face of cultural devastation*. Cambridge, MA: Harvard University Press.

Leavitt R. A., Ertl A., Sheats K., Petrosky E., Ivey-Stephenson A., and Fowler K. A. (2018). Suicides among American Indian/Alaska Natives — National Violent Death Reporting System, 18 States, 2003–2014. *MMWR Morbidity and Mortality Weekly Report* 2018, 67, 237–242.

Locke, J. (1956). *Essay concerning human understanding*. Oxford: Clarendon Press. (Original work published 1694).

Luckman, T. (1979). Personal identity as an evolutionary and historical problem. In M. V. Cranach (Ed.), *Human ethology*. Cambridge: Cambridge University Press.

MacIntyre, A. (1977). Epistemological crisis, dramatic narrative, and the philosophy of science. *The Monist*, 60, 453–472.

Marvell, A. (1681/1919). "To his coy mistress." Poem published posthumously. Arthur Quiller-Couch, ed. 1919. *The Oxford book of English verse: 1250–1900.*

Meehan, P., Lamb, J., Saltzmen, L. and O'Carroll, P. (1992). Attempted suicide among young adults: Progress toward a meaningful estimate of prevalence. *American Journal of Psychiatry*, 149, 41–44.

Nietzsche, F. (1988, 1880). The wanderer and his shadow. In R. J. Hollingdale (Ed.), *A Nietzsche Reader*. London: Penguin. (Original work was published in 1880).

Overton, W. F. (1997). Beyond dichotomy: An embodied active agent for cultural psychology. *Culture and Psychology*, 3, 315–334.

Overton, W. F. (2013). A new paradigm for developmental science: Relationism and relational-developmental-systems. *Applied Developmental Science*, 17, 2, 94–107.

Parfit, D. (1971). Personal identity. *Philosophical Review*, 80, 3–27.

Piantadosi, S., Byar, D. P., and Green, S. B. (1988). The ecological fallacy. *American Journal of Epidemiology*, 127, 893–904.

Rorty, A. O. (1976). *The identities of persons*. Berkeley, CA: University of California Press.

Sani, F. (2008). *Self-continuity: Individual and collective perspectives*. New York: Psychology Press.

Strawson, G. (1999). Self and body: Self, body, and experience. *Supplement to the Proceedings of the Aristotelian Society*, 73, 307–322.

Taylor, C. (1992). *Sources of the self: The making of the modern identity*. Cambridge, MA: Harvard University Press.

Unger, R. (1975). *Knowledge and politics*. New York: Free Press.

Wexler, L., White, J., and Trainor, B. (2015). Why an alternative to suicide prevention gatekeeper training is needed for rural Indigenous communities: Presenting an empowering community storytelling approach. *Critical Public Health*, 25, 2, 205–217.

Wiggins, D. (1980). *Sameness and substance*. Cambridge, MA: Harvard University Press.

Witherington, D. C. (2011). Taking emergence seriously: The centrality of circular causality for dynamic systems approaches to development. *Human Development*, 54, 66–92.

4 Strengthening Borders and Toughening Up on Welfare

Deaths by Suicide in the UK's Hostile Environment

China Mills

Introduction

In post-recession austerity Britain, governmental appeals to strengthen UK borders occur alongside calls to 'toughen up' on welfare provision. These measures are part of a web of tightening immigration controls that constitute what the UK Home Office calls a 'hostile environment' – a set of policies designed to both deter migrants and to create conditions so hostile that people voluntarily leave. A number of disabled people's activist groups have pointed out that the UK is also a hostile environment for disabled people, and particularly for those who claim welfare, given the landscape of punitive welfare reform. The crafting of a 'hostile environment' for migrants and disabled people includes punitive measures based on disentitlement, deterrence, surveillance, hostility, overwhelming bureaucracy, and administrative violence that aim to get people to stop claiming welfare and/or leave the UK.

This chapter takes seriously the need 'to structure into our analysis of a person's death the context of social injustice in which they lived' (Reynolds, 2016, 170). It aims to understand how the crafting of a hostile environment creates conditions that make life, for some, unliveable and that incite, elicit, and invite suicidality. By using this language, I am trying to get at the fact that hostile environments are crafted and designed with intention, which means that even if policy makers don't intend for suicide in response to these policies, the system is designed to produce certain conditions of hostility and these conditions invite suicidality. These are conditions that are lethal (Povinelli, 2011), that constitute and produce debility (Puar, 2017), and that are affective – they make people *feel* particular ways (such as ashamed, exhausted and hopeless). Thus, the chapter looks at some of the ways that welfare and immigration detention 'practices' kill people (Stevenson, 2012), perpetrating a lethality that is often not spectacular and that is administrative, proctological and seemingly banal. The starting point for the chapter is that suicide is inseparable from the wider background of bordering practices, state violence, hierarchisation and coloniality that make up everyday life in the UK. These processes are often assumed to be normal, necessary, and rational because they are constitutive of modernity and modern nation state-making.

Focus throughout this chapter is on an assemblage of bordering practices evident in political speeches, newspaper reports, and reports from NGOs and activist groups, as well as research literature, that features the voices of those who have experienced immigration detention and/or welfare reform first-hand. After setting out contemporary 'hostile environment' policies, the chapter details the relevance of bordering practices to thinking about suicide. It then explores the ways some individuals and groups move away from psychocentric, individualising and depoliticising agendas by making visible the ways detention and welfare reform exacerbate and cause distress and suicide. Bordering and hierarchisation and their historical links to eugenics and racialised enslavement, and the constitutive centrality of colonial logic, are then detailed. Groups of people positioned outside of (though constitutive to) the categorisation systems of modern western humanity have long experienced governmental policy as largely hostile, and suicide has also long been a response to violent bordering practices. Thus, this chapter concludes that hostile environment policies are not new nor singular, and nor can they be 'fixed' by tweaking policy, given that the pervasive underlying logic of these policies intersects with other systems to create conditions that kill people, sometimes through suicide.

Hostile Environments

In 2013, before becoming UK Prime Minister, Theresa May, as part of the Conservative-Liberal Democrats coalition government, introduced a new Immigration Bill (UK Government, 2014), which she explained, in an interview with *The Telegraph* newspaper, aims to 'create a really hostile environment for illegal migrants' (Travis, 2013). According to May, 'What we don't want is a situation where people think that they can come here and overstay because they're able to access everything they need'.

'Hostile environment' policies (as set out in the 2014 and 2016 Immigration Bills) were the result of the 2012 Hostile Environment Working Group, created under the Coalition Government of 2010–2015. This group was later renamed the 'Inter-Ministerial Group on Migrants' Access to Benefits and Public Services' (Liberty, 2018). Since June 2013, the Interventions and Sanctions Directorate (ISD) has been responsible for enforcing 'hostile environment' policies. In a Freedom of Information (FoI) request filed in 2013, which asked about the purpose of the Unit (cited in Yeo, 2017), the Home Office stated that:

> The unit has overall responsibility for removing incentives for people to stay illegally and encourage those who are in the country unlawfully to regularize their stay or leave the UK. This is achieved by

> ensuring a range of interventions and sanctions are systematically applied to deny access to services and benefits for those who are unlawfully in the UK. The unit works closely with government departments and a range of other partners across the public and private sectors to identify those migrants accessing such services and benefits to which they are not entitled.
>
> (Yeo, 2017)

'Hostile environment' policies included a switch to a 'deport first, appeal later' policy, and a reduction in the number of grounds for appeal. A further key move in making it 'as inconvenient and unpleasant as possible to live in Britain without documents' (MacDonald, 2017) was the dispersal of surveillance in checking immigration status throughout civil society and the public sector (UK Government, 2014), evidence of the ways immigration controls are now 'embedded in everyday interactions' (Liberty, 2018, 5) and performed at street level. Arguably one of the most hostile environments in the UK – immigration detention – is not the result of new policies, although it is impacted by them. The 'UK detains more migrants than any European country except Greece'; is the only country in Europe to have indefinite detention (i.e. detention with no time limit); and routinely detains migrants in prisons, which is considered unlawful throughout the European Union (Detention Action, 2014, 5).

Frances Ryan (a journalist for *The Guardian* newspaper who has played a key role in raising awareness about the impact of austerity measures on disabled people), wrote an article in 2018 titled: "The hostile environment? Britain's disabled people live there too" (Ryan, 2018). Ryan points out that Britain's social security system is 'itself defined by an increasingly "hostile environment"', where changes to immigration policy that aim to 'deport first, appeal later', 'sound terrifyingly familiar to anyone going through the benefits assessment system – a system marked by "remove people's income first, appeal later"' (Ryan, 2018). Key components of this hostile welfare environment are a range of welfare deterrence technologies, including welfare conditionality, punitive sanctions, and intrusive Work Capability Assessments (Fletcher and Wright, 2017).[1]

The crafting of hostility towards welfare claimants has for some years now been framed as toughening up on welfare. In 2011, then Prime Minister, David Cameron, gave a speech after a series of riots following protests in Tottenham, London, over the death of Mark Duggan, a Black British man who was killed by police on 4th August. According to Cameron:

> For years we've had a system that encourages the worst in people – that incites laziness, that excuses bad behaviour, that erodes self-discipline, that discourages hard work . . . above all that drains responsibility

> away from people . . . this is moral hazard in our welfare system – people thinking they can be as irresponsible as they like because the state will always bail them out . . . I want us to look at toughening up the conditions for those who are out of work and receiving benefits.
> (Cameron, 2011)

Here we see a now familiar reconfiguring of welfare entitlement into a 'moral hazard' that demands a 'toughening up' in regards to those receiving benefits. This mobilises discursive repertoires of the 'scrounger', and divisive classifications of skivers versus strivers, which enact mass stigmatisation of people who claim benefits, creating a punitive anti-welfare common-sense (Jensen, 2014; Tyler, 2013), used to justify the creation of a 'vast web of disentitlement strategies' (Wacquant, 2009, 91), of which 'surveillance, sanctions and deterrence' are key (Fletcher and Wright, 2017, 323).

Thus, it apparent that political discourse to strengthen borders occurs alongside calls to toughen up on welfare – and that both coalesce around questions of 'entitlement' to benefits (including, financial assistance and healthcare) and ideas about what constitutes fitness. These discourses share much in common: both imply moral economies of worthiness that ascribe market 'value' to forms of life that create some lives as worthless; both create the 'degradation of the recipient self and glorification of the working self' (Wacquant, 2009, 101); both mobilise discursive framings of migrants and welfare claimants (especially disabled people) as economic burdens used to stigmatise recipients and craft an environment hostile to those who require state support; individualise and decontextualise the reasons a person might claim benefits, locating it inside 'lazy' or deviant minds; both mobilise these framings to craft a punitive anti-welfare and anti-immigration common-sense (Tyler, 2013), based on disentitlement, deterrence, surveillance, and hostility; and both involve criminalisation of those deemed 'illegal', 'undocumented', or 'cheating' the system.

The intersections between welfare, distress, disability and immigration are not 'new' (and are related to but different from the linkages between disablement and migration, see Burns, 2017; Pisani and Grech, 2015). Mirza (2014, 226) shows how the intersections of ableism with racial capitalism and colonialism are foundational to the nation state and its deployment of 'disabling processes', including the 'systematic vilification' of asylum seekers as 'dangerous, fraudulent, manipulative, and most of all welfare-seeking' (Mirza, 2014, 226). Controlling immigration, then, has long been linked to and justified through protecting welfare provision/the welfare state, while immigration policies in many countries discriminate against disabled people based on their categorisation as an economic 'burden' (Mirza, 2014). For example, the exclusion of migrants thought to be potential 'wards of the state' at Ellis Island in the 1920s – a site through which millions of migrants to the US passed, and whose numerical quotas and administrative practices created racial categories closely tied to the creation and maintenance of borders (Ngai, 2014).

Bordering Practices

Bordering practices have long connected to practices of categorisation and hierarchisation of human/non-human – used to justify both slow and spectacular violence in the name of 'welfare'.

Bordering performs a classificatory politics in both welfare and migration, i.e. marking the borders of entitlement through binaries of migrant/citizen; and skivers/strivers. It is also at work within these categories, constructing divisive borders within marginalised groups, for example, between those deemed deserving and undeserving; and is internalised and affectively experienced (Mills, 2017). Here construction of the 'bogus' asylum-seeker and 'illegal immigrant' as a 'burden on the taxpayer' (Jones et al., 2017, 125), is set against the 'model migrant' who is portrayed as hyper-productive (Yukich, 2013). Similarly, Briant et al. (2013, 880), in a content analysis of media representations of disability in the UK, found that those claiming benefits due to mental health were framed as 'faking it', alongside an overall increase (post-Recession) in use of words like 'workshy', 'skiver' and 'drain on the economy' to describe claimants of disability benefits.

Bordering is made possible by and makes possible hierarchised moral economies of value and worth (Fortier, 2017), where 'worth' is conceptualised through an economistic framing of productivity and value is reduced to market value (Povinelli, 2011). Bordering confers legitimacy through these hierarchies – meaning that people use hierarchies to differentiate themselves and/or their families from the 'undeserving' category, and bordering practices are internalised and affectively experienced (Mills, 2017). 'Burden' discourse also hinges on a moral economy linking to early eugenicist conceptualisations of fitness/unfitness and calculations of the economic cost of certain groups of people deemed inferior. These formulations have long been used to argue for the systematic eradication, compulsory sterilisation, institutionalisation, and policing of immigration, of racialised (and) disabled people. Indeed, there is a historical link between financial depressions and eugenic policies (such as sterilisation laws) (Kühl, 2013, 76) that would seem to be repeating under current austerity. Eugenics is a technology used to strengthen nation-states while also 'bettering' the (usually) white race (Kühl, 2013, 6). Many eugenic policies saw individuals as responsible for making 'good' choices for the 'betterment of the race', ideas that were seen as compatible with welfare states (Kühl, 2013). For example, John Maynard-Keynes, usually thought of as the Father of Britain's welfare state was also director of the (British) Eugenics Society between 1937 to 1944. Eugenics today is often enacted under the guise of self-determination and freedom of choice (Kühl, 2013, 185), something that chimes with the demonisation of welfare claimants in the UK as 'skivers', making poor lifestyle choices.

Scholarship and activism around borders analyse 'border*ing* as a social practice' that is not only associated with the territorial boundaries of nation-states, meaning that 'borders should not be associated exclusively with migrants: borders do not "produce" only migrants, but are fundamental to any differentiation and exclusionary mechanisms of identity-production' (Belcher, Martin and Tazzioli, 2015). Bordering is relational in that it is about the 'creation and maintenance of systems of domination' and 'dispossession, criminalisation, expropriation, exploitation and violence that are predicated upon hierarchies of racialized, gendered, sexualized, economized, and nationalized social existence' (Weheliye, 2014, 1). Bordering is also at work in the categorisation of multiple kinds of self-death into one category called 'suicide' (Marsh, 2010), and in psychiatric classificatory politics more broadly, as they both create borders of ab/normality and as classifications travel across geographical borders (Rose, 2006).

Borders require repetition (as well as enforcement and disruption) (Belcher, Martin and Tazzioli, 2015), which, in the UK, range from theatrically staged street level performances, such as the 2011 anti-immigration vehicles driven around the streets of targeted areas and branded with – 'In the UK illegally? Go Home or Face Arrest'; and the inclusion of journalists on immigration enforcement raids to document and publicise the action (Jones et al., 2017). In 2007, the Department for Work and Pensions started the 'No Ifs, No Buts' campaign – a series of posters in public spaces, such as on billboards and phone boxes, with headlines in red, such as 'Benefit thieves, do you know who's following you?'; and 'Benefit thieves, someone, somewhere, could be reporting you now'. These campaigns are designed to actively craft suspicion between people, and of what others might be saying about you. Less spectacular, though no less deadly, is the mundane everyday administration of welfare and immigration: long battles with the system, appeals processes, letters written to the DWP and the Home office, (re)assessments, phone calls, trying to decipher forms, and on and on. Here hostility is performed through paperwork – filling it in, not having it, navigating it, trying to understand it – an administrative violence. This is what Povinelli (2011) calls cruddy, everyday suffering that is cumulative and durative, and that is key to crafting conditions of lethality for certain groups.

While also used within bordering practices, statistics have played a significant role in exposing the scale of suicide in relation to immigration detention and welfare reform. For example, information about the deaths of both welfare claimants and detained people can be found online, with websites maintained by The Black Triangle Campaign, Calum's List and Inquest.[2] A much-cited study (prompted by disabled activists' concerns, and then much used by activist groups once published) looking at available data between 2010–2013, found that reassessment of disability benefits through the WCA was 'independently associated with an increase in suicides (an additional 590 suicides [5% of the total number]), self-reported mental health problems' (2,700 cases per 10,000) and prescribing of an additional 7,020 antidepressants (Barr et al., 2016, 339).

In a similar way to welfare reform related deaths, numerical information about experiences of detention have had to be fought for – coaxed out of the Home Office through Freedom of Information (FoI) requests and activism. One of the most cited of these is an FoI filed by the NGO No Deportations (and the data of which is available online at www.no-deportations.org.uk/Media-2014/Self-Harm2015.html), which showed that in 2015 there had been 393 recorded suicide attempts (up 11% from the previous year); with 2,957 detainees, including 11 children, on suicide watch. Some, such as the UK Government, have been quick to point out that such statistics show correlation not cause and effect, while simultaneously drawing on the psy-disciplines to frame suicide as the outcome of individual psychological pathology (Mills, 2017).

Psychocentrism and Psychopolitics

In much of the global North, suicide is understood through appeals to psy-expertise that predominantly sees suicide as an outcome of 'mental illness' (Marsh, 2014). This is a psychocentric register (Rimke and Brock, 2012) that frames suicide as the outcome of an individual problem that can be 'treated' through psychological and behavioural modification. The extensive use of deterrence in crafting hostile welfare and immigration environments shows how deeply psychocentrism operates. Deterrence (a psychological theory used to inform welfare and war) is a coercive strategy 'concerned with deliberate attempts to manipulate the behaviour of others through conditional threats' (Freedman, 2004, 6). Deterrence operates by making something so awful that people supposedly 'will' themselves to work, earn, be productive, be ascribed market value, leave the country and 'go home' – based on an assumption of cultures of entitlement and laziness, where state dependency is seen as a cross-generational pathology, like a virus (Fraser and Gordon, 1994). Those who cannot or will not 'will' themselves into paid work or voluntarily leave the country are seen as the truly pathological and when some of these people can no longer bear to endure, when they die by suicide or poor health that comes from poverty and state neglect, this assumption of pathology is confirmed. Because if they killed themselves, so this way of thinking goes, then they must have been 'mentally ill'. At most, the ethical lesson learned from this approach is that we should get better at identifying 'mental illness' early. This makes evident how psychocentrism works to mask 'daily conditions of suffering and immiserisation' and to normalise 'social contexts marked by stigma, exclusion and hate', preventing us from understanding how indifference and 'hate kills' (Reynolds, 2016, 170).

While important existing scholarship details the problems of psychocentrism, this chapter will now turn to attempts by some organisations and research projects to frame mental illness/distress as being both *exacerbated* and *caused by* welfare reform and detention. Here mental distress is used politically to draw attention to the way environments and systems can be designed to induce suicidality. This speaks to my longstanding interest in using the analytic frame of *psychopolitics* to better understand the anxious entanglements of structural and political phenomena with psychic life (Mills, 2017). By psychopolitical, I mean taking seriously the psychic life of border practices and classificatory systems (internalisation, shame, anxiety), and embedding this 'psychic distress in a context of social dis-ease' (Orr, 2006, 29). As an analytic framework, psychopolitics can illuminate the lived affective realities of practices and assemblages of hierarchisation, particularly attending to the dominant narrative framing of negative affect and suicide through psy-categorisation as being symptoms of 'mental illness'. I'm interested in the psychic life (Hook, 2005) of hierarchisation and bordering practices in relation to welfare and immigration - as a way to understand how these practices make people feel, while never losing sight of the structural neo-colonial landscape that is productive of these feelings.

In their report on the 'State of Detention' (2014), the charity Detention Action interviewed a number of people who have experienced UK detention first-hand, and which give a sense of the psychic life of being detained. Souleymane, detained for three and a half years, said:

> Lots of people around me collapsed mentally. They cut their wrists or hung themselves. They couldn't take the endless not knowing. They couldn't take the sense of hopelessness that is the younger brother of indefinite detention – it's always following it around, the two come together.
>
> (Detention Action, 2014, 7)

Another detainee, Abdal, talked about detention as a 'death warrant', a 'question of hopelessness, exhaustion and the shame', a whole process that

> is just one part of a much wider system designed to break you mentally and physically. The terrible thing is that it often works. I saw many people self-harm in there. I saw people hang themselves. I tried to commit suicide a number of times.
>
> (Detention Action, 2014, 11–13)

In research by Jones et al. (2017) one woman reported feeling so scared at being stopped by the UK Border Agency that she wondered if 'perhaps suicide is better' (Jones et al., 2017, 37). In their interviews with 46 women seeking asylum and detained in Yarl's Wood Immigration Removal Centre, Women for Refugee Women (Girma et al., 2014, 4) found that: all of the women said that detention made them unhappy, '93% felt depressed, 85% felt scared, and more than half thought about killing themselves. Ten women, more than one in five, had tried to kill themselves. One third had been on suicide watch in detention'. One woman explained that 'Living is not worthwhile anymore. Being dead would be much better' (Girma et al., 2014, 4). When asked about their mental health, 37% of the women interviewed said they had mental health problems, including psychosis, post-traumatic stress disorder, depression, insomnia and flashbacks (Girma et al., 2014, 5). Examining the cases of 50 torture survivors held in immigration detention, Medical Justice (2012) found that 34% of those detained experienced suicidal intent/ ideation or actual self-harm; and 16% attempted suicide.

Welfare reforms have also been linked to suicide (Mills, 2017). Much of the research, including extensive interviews from the Welfare Conditionality project (2013–2018), points to the distressing impact of conditionality and sanctions, including an embodied fear of the possibility of sanctions (Welfare Conditionality Project, 2018). A 2014, adult psychiatric morbidity survey found that 66.4% of Employment and Support Allowance (ESA) recipients had suicidal thoughts; and 43.2% had attempted suicide (compared to 21.7 and 6.7 of general population) (McManus et al., 2016, 3). An article in the Manchester Evening News in April 2018, tells the story of Amy – a 21-year-old woman and mother in Lancashire – who killed herself because she felt '"pressurised" to find work under new rules for [benefits] claimants' (Halle-Richards, 2018). At an inquest into her death, a coroner said that 'the risk of losing benefits would "play massively on a young woman's mind with a young child and history of illness"' Amy's mental health nurse said: 'Her anxiety seemed more focused on financial matters. Since the government has been putting pressure on people going back to work, we have seen a rise in patients coming through presenting similar symptoms of feeling pressured'.

These accounts show that the claim that detention and welfare reform worsen mental health or exacerbate existing distress doesn't have to serve a psychocentric, individualising or depoliticising agenda. Even more psychopolitical are claims that detention and welfare reform *cause* mental distress and directly lead to suicide. Detention Action recount the story of a woman from Guinea who despite having a valid visa spent seventeen months detained in Yarl's Wood Immigration Removal Centre and had six 'episodes of acutely severe mental distress' involving self-harm and 'was frequently in isolation or handcuffed to prevent her self-harming' (Detention Action, 2014, 16). In 2014, the High Court found MD had been detained unlawfully. According to Detention Action, while not unusual,

> what makes MD's case unique is that it is the first time that a judge, presented with irrefutable evidence from medical specialists, has found that detention caused the onset of a mental disorder . . . For MD, detention did not exacerbate a pre-existing mental disorder – it caused the disintegration of her mental health.
>
> (Detention Action, 2014, 17)

Similar landmark occurrences have occurred within welfare reform, particularly from Coroners verdicts that welfare reform leads to suicide. Mary Hassell's (a senior coroner for inner North London) verdict that the suicide of Michael O'Sullivan, a disabled man who hanged himself, had been a 'direct result of being ruled "fit to work"' (McVeigh, 2015; Pring, 2015). At the time, this was 'thought by campaigners to be the first official link of WCAs to suicide' (Chakelian, 2015).

This shows a sustained attempt by diverse actors to move away from a psychocentric framing of suicide, by showing how suicide and mental distress can be responses to welfare reform and detention. Important political work is done here, yet using psychiatric classifications and diagnostic tools – themselves bordering practices productive of hierarchies and key to individualisation – to show the negative impact of hostile environment policies is also problematic (Mills, 2015). Discussing the intersectional health impact of oppression and injustice for women, McGibbon and MacPherson (2013) point out 'an inherent paradox when one is gathering evidence to expose the mental health impacts of oppression: in order to make a case for the impact of oppression, one must consider evidence related to psychiatric diagnostic categories' (72), when for many women, including low-income racialised women in many global north contexts, 'these categories play a central role in locating the "problem" in individual women, rather than in misogynist social systems' (72). Furthermore, where mental health is used as a framing device to signify what's wrong with detention or welfare reform and to highlight injustices, it risks becoming a 'stand in' that doesn't address the devaluation of distressed and mad people's lives within a global hierarchy of mobility (Mirza, 2014, 231). Similarly, Puar (2017) shows how liberal frameworks of disability, including psychiatric classifications, may work to obscure *debilitation* as a profitable process that marks certain bodies out as available for injury. This can lead to 'paradoxical efforts to humanize the essentially inhumane practice of mass confinement' (Mirza, 2014, 224) potentially legitimising 'practices that are inherently unjust' (231).

The Colony as Hostile Environment

Frances Ryan's (2018) article in *The Guardian* (mentioned at the beginning of this chapter) was key in making the link between hostile immigration environments and hostile welfare environments. The article was written in response to the Windrush scandal, where Caribbean migrants who arrived in the UK in and after 1948 as Commonwealth Citizens, were violently impacted by changes to immigration law in 2012, which questioned their right to live in the UK. Some people were threatened with deportation, while others were deported, and access to free healthcare was stopped. Ryan (2018) writes that:

> It's noticeable that, while every part of the media is now covering Windrush, stories about disabled people dying after losing their benefits are continually ignored . . . The same politicians and newspaper editors rushing to show solidarity for Windrush citizens being treated appallingly by the Home Office are strangely silent when the benefit system is doing the same to disabled people.

Ryan isn't saying one kind of injustice is worse than another here. She instead seems to be asking why public capacity for outrage and mourning have been enabled for one set of people in a particular circumstance, and not for another. The significance of Windrush goes deeper than the fact that Britain's 'hostile environment' policies became more publicly visible through their impact on the Windrush generation. For the 'Caribbean as the primal scene of the protracted modern colonization of the Americas'– shows how 'racialisation remains vital' to current ways of being (Weheliye, 2014, 29) – vital to and constitutive of bordering practices, racialising assemblages and hierarchisation through differentiation. Britain's dominance of the Atlantic slave trade was a key constitutive moment in modernity (Hall, 2017). The transformation of humans into property involved 'perpetual, systematic and violent struggle', hence the plethora of codes, statues, bureaucracy and administration of colonialism (Hall, 2017, 70). The founding violence of the so-called 'discovery' of the Caribbean was/is constantly repeated in the battles fought over it by colonial powers, the violence of racialised slavery, the everyday violence of plantation life, and the postcolonial after lives of these violent repetitions (Hall, 2017).

Suicide was central to slavery and also to abolitionist narratives in British North America and the USA, where suicides of enslaved people during the Middle Passage created tensions in how the fundamental conceptions of slavery – property and personhood - were understood (Pierson, 1988; Snyder, 2015). Indigenous First Nations people writing from settler colonies (long established hostile environments) have pointed out the link between colonialism and suicide (Chrisjohn, McKay and Smith, 2017). Furthermore, suicides of disabled people in the UK related to welfare reform must be understood within a context of the deaths that occur through wider indifference towards disabled people (Mencap, 2007) and disability hate crime. Just as suicides in immigration detention occur against widespread deaths in search of asylum.

While I don't think the violence of colonialism can be compared to or transposed to understanding the UK's current hostile environment policies, there seems to be a linkage between Britain's long history of violent colonial administration (the making of hostile environments in and through the colonies) and current UK 'hostile environment' policies. This is especially so if we take seriously that colonialism is central to modernity and was/is a condition of possibility for current day bordering practices. The technologies and practices of differentiation and hierarchisation honed during racialised enslavement and colonialism, were underscored by capital and run for a profit. Today, private companies, such as Maxiumus,[3] bid for government contracts to carry out Work Capability Assessments on disabled welfare claimants (attempting to differentiate those 'fit' for work); while companies such as Mitie[4] hold contracts to run Immigration Removal Centres.

The colonial history of crafting hostile conditions that incite distress and suicidality makes the psychopolitics of anti-colonial revolutionary and psychiatrist Frantz Fanon highly relevant. In his critique of the psychopathology of colonialism, Fanon, who worked in French colonised Algeria, critiques colonial psychiatry for framing resistance to colonialism as a mental pathology. Weheliye (2014) extends this to examine how those deemed 'aberrations from the ethnoclass of Man' (including racialised, poor, incarcerated, mad, and disabled people) are made subjects through and of (subjected to) 'racializing assemblages' that aim to establish differences and hierarchies as 'natural' (28). Weheliye (2014, 28) points out that,

> even though racializing assemblages commonly rely on phenotypical differences, their primary function is to create and maintain distinctions between different members of the Homo sapiens species that lend a suprahuman explanatory ground (religious or biological, for example) to these hierarchies.

Here, bordering practices and racialising assemblages produce differentiation in entitlement – using psychological, pathological and behavioral explanations to justify disentitlement or lack of recognition to entitlement completely. Differently from this colonial logic, Fanon shows how distress is not always the result of biology or character but can be 'the direct product of the colonial situation' (Fanon, 1963, 250). If applied to suicide, Fanon's work widens the analytic frame – enabling us to see that suicidality and self-harm in the context of welfare reform and immigration detention are not (or not always) linked to 'mental illness' (which often functions as a code word for biology or character) but a direct product of border practices (categorisation, hierarchisation, moral economies of worth). Yet the very nature of the lethal cumulative debilitating conditions (Povinelli, 2011; Puar, 2017) traced here as eliciting suicidality, is that they evade simplistic formulations of cause and effect, obscuring how suicide is a 'direct product' of hostile environments.

Conclusion

Focusing on the constitutive linkages between immigration and welfare, and framing these as two examples of a much wider global assemblage of border practices, has served two key purposes within this chapter. One is to understand suicide as linked to ongoing repetitive border struggles, including systems of categorisation and administration that are violent in both banal and spectacular ways. Important work has been done to resist a psychocentric gaze and to frame suicide as a response to hostile policies, yet, this can be problematic where it reifies invdiualising and pathologising psychiatric diagnoses. This suggests i.e. a key move may be to delink distress and suicide from mental health categorisation, while simultaneously interrogating how we understand cause and effect when presented with forms of everyday, cumulative hostility. The second related point has been to see that suicide is inseparable from the wider background of state violence, racialising assemblages, hierarchisation and coloniality that are often defined as normal, necessary, and rational and that are foundational to modern nation-states. Ware, Ruzsa and Dias show that (2014) 'these systems are not broken' and 'can't be fixed or reformed' (178), instead they function as extensions of racist and genocidal policies and practices' (164), that intersect with other systems (health, education, etc) and thus require revolution rather than only policy change. This highlights the pervasiveness of border practices to immigration, welfare, disability and distress, meaning that tweaks and fixes in one part of the system might never be enough because the underlying logic of these systems create conditions that devalue certain lives, and kill people, partly through inciting them to kill themselves.

Notes

1 Work Capability Assessments are used to reassess recipients of out of work disability benefits (Employment and Support Allowance [ESA]). They were originally introduced by the Labour Government in 2008, and subsequently rolled out by the Conservatives, and were used to reassess over one million people between 2010–2013.
2 www.inquest.org.uk/deaths-of-immigration-detainees; http://calumslist.org/; https://blacktrianglecampaign.org/
3 www.maximusuk.co.uk/health-programmes/independent-health-assessments
4 www.mitie.com/services/custody/immigration-services/

References

Barr, B., Taylor-Robinson, D., Stuckler, D., Loopstra, R., Reeves, A. and Whitehead, M. (2016). 'First, do no harm': Are disability assessments associated with adverse trends in mental health? A longitudinal ecological study. *Journal of Epidemiology and Community Health*, 2016(70): 339–345.

Baumberg, B., Bell, K. and Gaffney, D. (2012). *Benefits Stigma in Britain*. London: Turn2Us.

Belcher, O., Martin, L. and Tazzioli, M. (2015). Border struggles: Epistemologies, ontologies, and politics. *Dark Matter: In the Ruins of Imperial Culture*, 12. Online: www.darkmatter101.org/site/category/issues/12-border-struggles/
Briant, E., Watson, N. and Philo, G. (2013). Reporting disability in the age of austerity: the changing face of media representation of disability and disabled people in the United Kingdom and the creation of new 'folk devils'. *Disability and Society*, 28(6): 874–889.
Burns, N. (2017). The human right to health: Exploring disability, migration and health. *Disability & Society*, 32(10): 1463–1484.
Cameron, D. (2011). PM's speech on the fightback after the riots. August 15. www.gov.uk/government/speeches/pms-speech-on-the-fightback-after-the-riots
Chakelian, A. (2015). Disabled man killed himself over benefit cut, Coroner rules. *New Statesman*, 21 September. Online: www.newstatesman.com/politics/welfare/2015/09/disabled-man-killed-himself-over-benefit-cut-coroner-rules
Chrisjohn, R.D., McKay, S.M. and Smith, A.O. (2017). *Dying to Please You: Indigenous Suicide in Contemporary Canada*. Pentictona: Theytus Books.
Detention Action. (2014). The State of Detention: Immigration Detention in the UK in 2014. London: Detention Action. Online: http://detentionaction.org.uk/wordpress/wpcontent/uploads/2014/10/The.State_.of_.Detention.pdf
Fanon, F. (1963). *The Wretched of the Earth*. (C. Farrington, Trans.). New York: Grove Weidenfeld.
Fletcher, D.R. and Wright, S. (2017). A hand up or a slap down? Criminalising benefit claimants in Britain via strategies of surveillance, sanctions and deterrence. *Critical Social Policy*, 8(2): 323–344.
Fortier, A. (2017). The psychic life of policy: Desire, anxiety and 'citizenisation' in Britain. *Critical Social Policy*, 37(1): 3–21.
Fraser, N. and Gordon, L. (1994). A genealogy of dependency: Tracing a keyword of the U.S. welfare state. *Signs*, 19(2): 309–336.
Freedman, L. (2004). *Deterrence*. Cambridge: Polity Press.
Girma, M., Radice, S., Tsangarides, N. and Walter, N. (2014). Detained: Women Asylum Seekers Locked up in the UK. Online: www.refugeewomen.co.uk/2016/wp-content/uploads/2016/07/WRWDetained.pdf
Hall, S. (2017). *Familiar Stranger: A Life between Two Islands*. London: Penguin.
Halle-Richards, S. (2018). Struggling young mum took her own life after fearing she would lose benefits under Universal Credit scheme. Manchester Evening News, April 18. Online: www.manchestereveningnews.co.uk/news/greater-manchester-news/universal-credit-benefit-mum-suicide-14544736
Hook, D. (2005). A critical psychology of the post-colonial. *Theory and Psychology*, 15(4): 475–503.
Hull Daily Mail (2011). Woman who drowned in drain was upset about health check. *Hull Daily Mail*, 12 July.
Jensen, T. (2014). Welfare commonsense, poverty porn and doxosophy. *Sociological Research Online* 19(3): 3.
Jones, H., Gunaratnam, Y., Bhattacharyya, G., Davies, W., Dhaliwal, S., Forkert, K., Jackson, E., and Saltus, R. (2017). *Go Home: The Politics of Immigration Controversies*. Manchester: Manchester University Press.
Kühl, S. (2013). *For the Betterment of the Race: The Rise and Fall of the International Movement for Eugenics and Racial Hygiene*. London: Palgrave MacMillan.

Liberty (2018). A Guide to the Hostile Environment. London: Liberty.

MacDonald, K. (2017). What is Hostile Environment, Theresa May's policy that led to the Windrush scandal and other problems? I-News, April 17. Online: https://inews.co.uk/news/politics/what-is-hostile-environment-theresa-may-windrush-eu-citizens-legal-immigrants/

Marsh, I. (2010). *Suicide: Foucault, History, Truth*. Cambridge: Cambridge University Press.

McManus, S., Bebbington, P., Jenkins, R., and Brugha, T. (eds.) (2016). *Mental health and wellbeing in England: Adult Psychiatric Morbidity Survey 2014*. Leeds: NHS Digital.

McGibbon, E. & MacPherson, C. (2013). Stress, oppression & womens mental health: A discussion of the health consequences of injustice. *Women's Health and Urban Life*, 12(2), 63–81.

McVeigh, K. (2015). Fit for work assessment was trigger for suicide, coroner says. *The Guardian*, 21 September. Online: www.theguardian.com/politics/2015/sep/21/fit-for-work-assessment-was-trigger-for-suicide-coroner-says?CMP=share_btn_link

Medical Justice (2012). 'The Second Torture': The immigration detention of torture survivors. Online: www.medicaljustice.org.uk/images/stories/reports/secondtorturesummaryreport.pdf

Mencap (2007). Death by Indifference. London: Mencap. www.mencap.org.uk/sites/default/files/2016-06/DBIreport.pdf

Mills, C. (2017). 'Dead people don't claim': A psychopolitical autopsy of UK austerity suicides. *Critical Social Policy*, 38(2), 302–322.

Mills, C. (2015). The Psychiatrization of Poverty: Rethinking the mental health-poverty nexus. *Social and Personality Psychology Compass*, 9(5), 213–222.

Mirza, M. (2014). Refugee Camps, asylum detention, and the geopolitics of transnational migration: Disability and its intersections with humanitarian confinement. In Ben-Moshe, L., Chapman, C., and Carey, A.C. (Eds) *Disability Incarcerated: Imprisonment and Disability in the United States and Canada*. New York: Palgrave MacMillan. pp. 217–236.

Ngai, M. M. (2014). *Impossible Subjects: Illegal Aliens and the Making of Modern America*. Princeton, NJ: Princeton University Press.

Orr, J. (2006). *Panic Diaries: A Genealogy of Panic Disorder*. Durham, NC and London: Duke University Press.

Pierson, W. (1988). *Black Yankees: The Development of an Afro-American Subculture in 18th Century New England*. Amherst, MA: University of Massachusetts.

Pisani, M. and Grech, S. (2015). Disability and forced migration: Critical intersectionalities. *Disability and the Global South*, 2(1): 421–441.

Povinelli, E. (2011). *Economies of Abandonment*. Durham, NC: Duke University Press.

Pring, J. (2015). Coroner's 'ground-breaking' verdict: Suicide was 'triggered' by 'fit for work' test. Disability News Service, 18 September. Online: www.disabilitynewsservice.com/coroners-ground-breaking-verdict-suicide-was-triggered-by-fit-for-work-test/

Puar, J. (2017). *The Right to Maim: Debility, Capacity, Disability*. Durham, NC: Duke University Press.

Reynolds, V. (2016). Hate kills: A social justice response to suicide. In White J., Marsh, I., Kral, M. J. and Morris, J. (eds.) *Critical Suicidology: Transforming Suicide Research and Prevention for the 21st Century*. Vancouver: UBC Press, pp. 169–187.

Rimke, H. and Brock, D. (2012). The culture of therapy: Psychocentrism in everyday life. In Thomas, M., Raby, R. and Brock, D. (eds.) *Power and Everyday Practices*. Toronto: Nelson, pp. 182–202.

Rose, N. (2006). Disorders without borders? The expanding scope of psychiatric practice. *Biosocieties*, 1(4), 465–484.

Ryan, F. (2018). The hostile environment? Britain's disabled people live there too. *The Guardian*, April 26. Online: www.theguardian.com/commentisfree/2018/apr/26/hostile-environment-britain-disabled-people-windrush-benefits

Snyder, T. L. (2015). *The Power to Die: Slavery and Suicide in British North America*. Chicago, IL, and London: University of Chicago Press.

Stevenson, L. (2012). The psychic life of biopolitics: Survival, cooperation, and Inuit community. *American Ethnologist*, 39 (3): 592–613.

Travis, A. (2013). Immigration bill: Theresa May defends plans to create 'hostile environment'. *The Guardian*, October 10. Online: www.theguardian.com/politics/2013/oct/10/immigration-bill-theresa-may-hostile-environment

Tyler, I. (2013). *Revolting Subjects: Social Abjection and Resistance in Neoliberal Britain*. London and New York: Zed Books.

UK Government (2014). Immigration Act. London: UK Government.

Wacquant, L. (2009). *Punishing the Poor: The Neoliberal Government of Social Insecurity*. Durham, NC: Duke University Press.

Ware, S., Ruzsa, J. and Dias, G. (2014). It can't be fixed because its not broken: Racism and disability in the prison industrial complex. In Ben-Moshe, L., Chapman, C. and Carey, A. C. (Eds.) *Disability Incarcerated: Imprisonment and Disability in the United States and Canada*. New York: Palgrave MacMillan, pp. 163–184.

Weheliye, A. G. (2014). *Habeas Viscus: Racializing Assemblages, Biopolitics, and Black Feminist Theories of the Human*. Durham, NC: Duke University Press.

Welfare Conditionality project. Final findings report. 2013–2018. Online: www.welfareconditionality.ac.uk

Yeo, C. (2017). The hostile environment: What is it and who does it affect? New Europeans, June 3. Online: https://neweuropeans.net/article/1927/hostile-environment-what-it-and-who-does-it-affect

Yukich, G. (2013). Constructing the model immigrant. *Social Problems*, 60(3), 302–20.

5 Suicidal Regimes

Public Policy and the Formation of Vulnerability to Suicide

Mark E. Button

Introduction

In the context of steadily increasing rates of suicide within the United States, everyone seems to agree that suicide is a public health crisis. However, the recognition of a public health problem does not seem to entail the idea that suicide is a *political* problem that reaches into the background conditions of life for citizens and does so in ways that are differentiated by social, economic, and political standing. While states properly spend critical resources to help respond and intervene with individuals who manifest risks for suicide, states have not shown a willingness to see the patterns and concentrations of suicidal persons within their jurisdictions as a feature of their political, ethical, and legal responsibility. Vulnerability to suicide is essentially thought to reside within the mind and complex personal and emotional life of individuals. In this respect, state leaders merely follow the lead of most of the psychological and psychiatric professionals who work in the field of suicidology today.

This chapter advances the argument that this is a mistake, or at least an approach in need of political and structural supplementation. Our understanding and approach to suicide must advance further "upstream"; that is, citizens and leaders must assess and intervene on the formation of vulnerability to suicide much "earlier" than is usually the case today. In accordance with the view that this chapter advances, the risk factors for suicide do not simply refer to individuals in cognitive, emotional, and behavioral distress; the risk factors for suicide also refer to the structural conditions in which people live, especially conditions that are marked by the intersections of poverty and various forms of social and political marginalization (by race, class, age, sexuality, rurality, and veteran status). Since these structural conditions are powerfully influenced by a unique constellation of policy regimes and policy effects, a structural assessment of suicide risk will point us in the direction of a political-institutional approach to the prevention of suicide whose primary aim is to help end the formation of vulnerability to suicide through these policy regimes. The specific purpose of this chapter is to marshal at least some of the initial evidence upon which a political-institutional approach to suicide might be grounded; the necessary work of translating this perspective into political practice will require that citizens hold states and public officials at various levels of government accountable for contributing to and sustaining "suicidal regimes."

(Re)Integrating City and Soul in the Study of Suicide

A false bifurcation dominates our understanding of suicide and frames our approach to it. This bifurcation is one that separates and decontextualizes the individual from the structural-political conditions of human life and then seeks to treat the suicidal subject through various psychological/therapeutic/pharmacological means. While many scholars across a host of diverse fields of inquiry recognize that there are an array of social-environmental factors that shape the personal-psychological lives of individuals (see Allen, Balfour, Bell and Marmot, 2014; Compton and Shim, 2015; Coyne and Downey, 1991), this recognition alone does not generate political or institutional considerations for the specific public policy actions (and inactions) that structure the constitutive and unequal conditions of human existence. This is especially true in the case of the study of suicide and suicide prevention (see also Jaworski, 2016; Kral, 1994; Marsh, 2010; Marsh, 2016; Reynolds, 2016; White et al., 2016; White, 2017).

For example, in a recent sociological study, researchers were able to shed important empirical light on the question of whether the characteristics of where one lives has independent and statistically significant influence on rates of suicide, after controlling for individual-level variables like socioeconomic status, marital status, etc. (Denney et al., 2015). These scholars find that "above and beyond the influence of area composition from individual characteristics, context matters" (324). Specifically, the socioeconomic conditions of the region in which one lives and the number of families living together in an area are associated with statistically significant changes in risks of suicide (with socioeconomic disadvantage playing the more powerful role). But like so many other sociological studies that seek to confirm elements of Durkheim's thesis regarding the role of social forces in rates of suicide, the authors do not attempt to track these artifacts of community life to the political and policy decisions that both make them possible and sustain them over time. These scholars helpfully and effectively dispose of the ecological or "contextual fallacy" that seems to hound sociologists, but they leave us with a deeper political quandary: what accounts for the structural conditions of disadvantage bearing on rates of suicide?

A related problem effects another recent sociological study that seeks to relate Wilson's deindustrialization thesis (1987; 1996) to suicide among black youth in American inner cities (Kurbin et al., 2006). The authors show that cities with greater levels of concentrated disadvantage among blacks – comprised of joblessness, low family income, poverty, limited educational attainment and single female households –experience greater numbers of young black male suicides (Kurbin et al., 2006, 1568). These structural characteristics of cities also have similar effects for whites with the same characteristics of joblessness, low income, low levels of education, etc. In seeking to account for the connections between systemic disadvantage and higher relative rates of suicide, the authors speculate once again along strictly Durkheimian lines that "a lack of social integration may be at the root of these social pathologies" (1573).

Of course, there is little doubt that the absence of economic and educational opportunities over several generations will have important, negative effects on social integration and things like "age-appropriate pro-social roles and positions." Yet, when it comes to assessing and preventing suicide, social integration/social disintegration is not itself a sufficient or exhaustive explanation because these dimensions (as Wilson himself recognized) have upstream *political* sources in public policies related to economic development, job training, income support, affordable housing, family medical leave, adequate education, access to comprehensive health care, and much else besides. Sociologists (still following Durkheim after all these years) are certainly right to point to the social forces that undermine human well-being, but until these social forces are traced to the political structures and agents that bear partial responsibility for them, and until citizens and leaders close the door on willful blindness and bad faith about the relationship between policy regimes and the distribution of vulnerability to suicide, suicide will remain a public health crisis without an adequate *political* level of analysis and response. Under these conditions (as feminist and critical race scholars would point out), a form of political consciousness about suicide that could help to mobilize a sense of shared responsibility for addressing it will have difficulty coming to life in our discourse or in our approach to democratic self-governance.

Throughout the behavioral and medical sciences the city (*polis*) and the soul (*psyche*) have been separated in practice, even though everyone seems to know that this is false ontologically. The consequence – more a product of disciplinary sorting and academic framing-effects than malicious neglect – is that suicide is substantially viewed as the act of an unwell individual within a condition of social and political normativity. If we reject this false bifurcation and emphasize the reciprocal constitution of persons and social-political institutions, then it becomes possible for us to at least consider the hypothesis that suicide (and "suicidality" more broadly) might also reflect the reality of individuals struggling within conditions of systematic disadvantage, marginalization, and structural injustice that are subject to political analysis and alternative political responses. To be sure, one's position in relation to suicidality is bound to be a complex mix of personal and structural-institutional conditions.

But since the latter conditions so rarely figure within the practical assessment and prevention of suicide, we need to ask: what evidence is there to lend support to the idea that vulnerability to suicide is also constituted by policy regimes?

Psycho-Structural Distress and the Making of Vulnerability to Suicide

The annual age-adjusted suicide rate in the United States (2015) is 13.26 (per 100,000) (CDC, 2015). The annual suicide rate has been steadily climbing, with 20.87% increase since 2006 (10.97/100,000); from 1999 to the present, the greatest increase in the suicide rate – over 40% – has occurred in rural areas of the U.S. According to the most recent data available, from 1999 through 2014, the percent increase in the age-adjusted suicide rate was greater for females (45% increase) than males (16% increase), resulting in a narrowing of the gender gap in suicide rates (CDC, 2016).[1]

In 2015, the following ten states (see Table 5.1) had the highest rates of suicide in the U.S. Nevada, Arizona, and Oregon are frequently in the top ten as well, depending on the year. Why do these states – nearly all located in the western part of the U.S. – have such high rates of suicide? What is different about these states relative to the rest of the country? What points of evidence might help us unravel these questions? The following table and subsequent analysis offers at least a few possible clues.[2]

Mapping Suicide and Poverty

Utilizing U.S. Census Bureau data for "Small Area Income and Poverty Estimates for all ages in poverty" (2014) and the Centers for Disease Control and Prevention WISQARS (Web-based Injury Statistics Query and Reporting System), we can compare rates of poverty and suicide on a county-level basis. Comparing those counties with the highest rates of suicide with county-level poverty information shows that while there is not a strict one-to-one relationship between high levels of poverty and high rates of suicide in all cases, there is nonetheless a significant relationship in these variables across many states and counties. As the Table 5.2 further illustrates, high suicide rates (relative to both the in-state and annualized national suicide rate) do not depend on conditions of poverty, but in almost all cases, high rates of poverty and rurality correlate with significantly higher rates of suicide. In 31 counties analyzed within six states (Wyoming, Alaska, Montana, New Mexico, Utah, and South Dakota), 17 counties with rates of poverty (≥19.5%) also had significantly higher rates of suicide than the rest of the state. Twenty counties with poverty rates ≥19.5% had suicide rates higher than the annualized U.S rate for the relevant time period (2008–2014). Another way to view

Table 5.1 Highest Age-Adjusted Suicide Rates by State (U.S. 2015)

State and Rank	*2015 Age-Adjusted Suicide Rate[1] (per 100,000) 2015*	*Multiple Counties with High Levels of Poverty (20% or more)*	*Firearm Regulations[2] Score, Gun Death Rate (per 100,000) and Rank (out of 50)*	*Adult Ranking Mental Health[3] (prevalence and access)*	*Youth Ranking Mental Health[4] (prevalence and access)*	*State Party Control*
Wyoming (1)	28.24	No	F (45/50) 19.5 (4/50)	34/51	38/41	Rep
Alaska (2)	26.83	Yes	F (44/50) 23.4 (1/50)	13/51	7/51	Rep
Montana (3)	25.25	Yes	F (38/50) 19.3 (6/50)	35/51	48/51	Split
New Mexico (4)	23.53	Yes	F (29/50) 18.5 (7/50)	33/51	40/51	Split
Utah (5)	22.42	Yes	F (29/50) 12.8 (19/50)	51/51	27/51	Rep
Idaho (6)	22.19	Yes	F (46/50) 14.8 (15/50)	43/51	42/51	Rep
South Dakota (7)	20.57	Yes	F (40/50) 11.2 (33/50)	12/51	4/51	Rep
Oklahoma (8)	20.42	Yes	F (27/50) 18.0 (8/50)	40/51	33/51	Rep
Colorado (9)	19.46	Yes	C (14/50) 12.5 (22/50)	22/51	19/51	Split
Arkansas (10)	19.11	Yes	F (38/50) 16.9 (11/50)	31/51	50/51	Rep

[1]American Foundation for Suicide Prevention (2015). *AFSP's latest data on suicide are taken from the Centers for Disease Control and Prevention (CDC) Data & Statistics Fatal Injury Report for 2015. Suicide rates listed are Age-Adjusted Rates.*
[2]Law Center to Prevent Gun Violence (2016).
[3]Mental Health America, 2016 State of Mental Health in America: Ranking the States.
[4]Ibid.

these data is that a sizable portion of the high suicide rate in these states is concentrated in counties with high levels of poverty. It is also important to point out that those counties and states with strong correlations between poverty and suicide are counties in which American Indians and Alaskan Natives constitute the majority of suicides.

The data in Table 5.2 supports other recent research that has found that a population's risk for suicide is most clearly associated with county-level poverty rates (Kerr et al., 2017). Kerr and colleagues have found that previous associations of unemployment with suicide rates disappeared when poverty was included in the relevant models, suggesting that the effects of unemployment (especially long-term unemployment) were mediated through poverty (2017, 473). This clearly points in the direction of a need for greater state and county-level involvement in establishing and sustaining programs that address localized pockets of poverty – especially in rural areas – as a public policy means of helping to reduce suicide (see also Rehkopf and Buka, 2006).

Unemployment benefits on their own appear to only have a marginal positive affect on rates of suicide (Cylus, Glymour and Avendano, 2014); however, overall per capita spending by states have a significant impact on suicide rates (Flavin and Radcliff, 2009). At the time of Flavin and Radcliff's important (and singular study) connecting public policy decisions to rates of suicide nation-wide, the estimated "cost" of reducing a state's suicide rate by a full point was $45 in per capita public assistance funding (2009, 203). While the dollar amount has certainly increased over the intervening years, the broader point remains: public policy regimes have a dramatic impact on state and national rates of suicide. As Table 5.2 also shows, those counties with the highest rates of suicide relative to the rest of the state population are those counties that are more rural in character. The correlations of high poverty and rurality with higher rates of suicide points to the importance of targeted suicide prevention resources and services for those living in rural America, starting with (but not restricted to) multi-pronged anti-poverty measures.

Access to Firearms

Nine out of the ten states with the highest rates of suicide in the U.S. have received a failing score by the Law Center to Prevent Gun Violence for having weak gun laws and correspondingly high rates of gun death. Firearms are used in approximately 50% of all suicides in the U.S. and the presence of a gun in a home is highly predictive of its use for completed suicide, by both men and women, but especially by youth, 15–24 years old (Brent and Bridge, 2003). It is important to recognize that guns in a home generates an independent, increased risk for suicide in those with no apparent psychopathology. According to one study, guns in the home produced a three-fold elevated risk for suicide in those with

Table 5.2 Poverty Rate/Suicide Rate by County in Six States

County (State)	*2014 All Ages Poverty Rate by County.[5] U.S. Rate = 13.5% (2015)*	*Age-Adjusted Suicide Rate by County[6] (with rates for American Indian/Alaskan Native where available)*	*Annualized Age-Adjusted Suicide Rate by State (2008–14). U.S. Rate = 12.26%.*	*County-level Suicide Rate Difference with State Suicide Rate (2008–14)*	*2010 Census Percent Rural*
Albany (Wyoming)	**24%**	14.96%	22.90%	−7.33	11.9
Freemont (Wyoming)	14%	**28.84%**		+5.94	51.4
Converse (Wyoming)	9.3%	**31.70%**		+8.8	55.4
Wade Hampton (Alaska)	**35.7%**	**85.09%** (89.97% AI/AK)	21.98%	+63.11	NA
Nome (Alaska)	**26.1%**	**72.27%** (86.07% AI/AK)		+50.29	66.1
Yukon-Koyukuk (Alaska)	**25.7%**	**79.82%** (95.13% AI/AK)		+57.84	100
Bethel (Alaska)	**23.8%**	**46.93%** (49.33% AI/AK)		+24.95	73.9
NW Arctic (Alaska)	**23.2%**	**48.91%** (62.32% AI/AK)		+26.93	57.5
Lake (Montana)	**22.7%**	**29.4%**	22.29%	+7.11	83.4

[5] U.S. Census Bureau, Small Area Income and Poverty Estimates (2014)
[6] CDC, WISQARS (2008–2014)

psychiatric disorder but a nearly 33-fold increased risk for completed suicide in those without apparent psychopathology (Kellermann et al., 1992; Miller and Hemenway, 1999; Brent and Bridge, 2003).

The type of laws that are utilized to assess a state's overall score relative to the regulation of firearms include the following: Whether states require background checks for the private sale of firearms, require mental health records to be submitted to the National Instant Criminal Background Check System, impose liability on people who negligently store firearms (reducing access for minors), or allow family members or law enforcement to petition to disarm persons who are deemed a threat to themselves or others. Consistent with the scholarship that shows an inverse relationship between the restrictiveness of firearm regulations and overall suicide rates, the six states with the highest scores relative to these type of gun control measures are also the states with some of the lowest rates of suicide in the U.S.: California (10.48), Connecticut (9.7); New Jersey (7.7); Massachusetts (8.63); Maryland (9.49); New York (8.15).

State-wide gun safe storage laws would be an especially effective means of helping to reduce suicide rates among young people (see Anestis, 2018). Given the lethality of firearms, states with high levels of suicide and high levels of suicide by firearms would also be well advised to consider adopting extreme risk protective orders, or "red flag" laws, that enable a family member or law enforcement official to ask a court to restrain a person from possessing any firearms for a specified length of time.

Mental Health

Table 5.1 also utilizes survey data from Mental Health America to measure a community's mental health needs, access to care, and outcomes. States with high rankings have lower prevalence of mental illness and higher rates of access to care for adults. Lower rankings indicate that adults and youth have higher prevalence of mental illness and lower rates of access to care.[3] Seven out of ten states with the highest rates of suicide in the United States were in the bottom third of all states for higher prevalence of mental illness and lower access to care for adults – with Utah ranked last. Six out of the ten states were in the bottom third for youth with a higher prevalence of mental illness and lower access to care – with Arkansas next to last.[4] Improving access to mental health care resources – especially for low-income urban and rural areas – through a combination of incentives for mental health care professionals and the use of communication technologies should be a priority for states that seek to reduce the rate of suicide in their population.

In four of the states listed in Table 5.1, suicide is the leading cause of death among 10–24-year-olds (Alaska, Utah, South Dakota, and Colorado); in New Mexico, suicide is the second leading causes of death for this age group. Another population made vulnerable to suicide nationally and in these states is veterans. After adjusting for differences in age and sex, the risk for suicide was 22% higher among Veterans compared with U.S. civilian adults (VA, 2016). There is an especially high burden of suicide among middle-aged and older Veterans: In 2014, about 65 percent of all Veterans who died by suicide were ages 50 and older, although rates of suicide were highest among younger Veterans (ages 18–29) and lowest among older Veterans (ages 60 and older). Suicide resulting from firearm injuries remains high: In 2014, about 67 percent of all Veteran deaths by suicide were the result of firearm injuries. Data related to veterans in the states that are the focus of this chapter is provided in Table 5.3.[5]

Suicide under Conservative Party Control

Political leaders across all partisan divisions care deeply about preventing suicide. Six out of ten states with the highest rates for suicide in the U.S. are controlled by the Republican Party (in two additional states – Colorado and Alaska – Republicans control the State Senate),[6] and many of these states have long histories of Republican control. What potential relevance might this fact have for the prospect of reducing suicide in these states? The majority of these states are regimes whose political and philosophical center of gravity is a combination of federalism (emphasizing local

Table 5.3 Veteran Suicide Rate by State/Nation and % Firearm

State	*2015 State Age-Adjusted Suicide Rate (per 100,000)*	*State Veteran Suicide Rate (2014)*	*State Veteran Suicide Rate compared to National Veteran Rate of 38.4 (2014)*	*Method: % Firearm by State Veterans*
Wyoming	28.24	55.0	Not Significantly different	**N/A**
Alaska	26.83	54.4	Not Significantly different	N/A
Montana	25.25	68.6	**Significantly Higher**	**63.8%**
New Mexico	23.53	59.8	**Significantly Higher**	**67%**
Utah	22.42	62.4	**Significantly Higher**	**65.9%**
Idaho	22.19	46.6	Not Significantly different	**74.1%**
South Dakota	20.57	47.9	N/A	N/A
Oklahoma	20.42	53.8	**Significantly Higher**	**63.8%**
Colorado	19.46	47.1	Not Significantly different	**66.9%**
Arkansas	19.11	48.1	**Significantly Higher**	**72%**

and state control) and a diffuse mixture libertarianism and neoliberalism committed to rolling back the state in many areas of society and the economy. This broad philosophy of governance is also embedded within a wider western political ecosystem that is anchored by the mythos of individual autonomy, self-reliance, and personal responsibility for one's place in the social scheme of things. In light of these ideological and social currents – not all of which are reducible to party identification – suicide prevention will also require working on the social norms and cultural scripts that facilitate and encourage individuals – especially men, but increasingly also women – to cope autonomously or suffer privately in response to diminished economic prospects, relative inequality and poverty, ill health, and social isolation/marginalization.

How might this kind of social norm agenda come about? To the degree that a political-institutional approach to suicide can begin to uncover the extent to which suicide is not a problem for or within individual minds alone, but one that also implicates states, policy choices, and policy effects, than it becomes conceivable to imagine citizens rewarding with elected office those leaders who are willing to take-on some of the "psychache" (Shneidman, 1993) of their citizens and craft public policies (especially fiscal and health policies) that will help lift this burden for those stuck in poverty and marginalized and devalued by society. Translating the index provided in Table 5.1 (or something like it) into a legislative score card for the purposes of educating and mobilizing electoral votes could easily be imagined. Of course, this electoral strategy requires seeing government as a co-agent and ally of social good and one with moral and political responsibilities to help secure substantive equal life chances of human flourishing for all. Since these commitments to social justice often run counter to dominant political and economic forces in these states (and elsewhere), additional lines of norm entrepreneurship should be explored.

Here is one such possibility. We might imagine a response to suicide that takes seriously and works from within the religious (Christian) orientation of many of those who strongly identify with the Republican Party in the west and throughout the U.S. While these states have high rates of suicide, six out of ten have explicit laws rendering physician-assisted aid-in-dying illegal (two additional states – Utah and Wyoming – do not have any explicit legal code on this issue).[7] The active role that the majority of these states play in preventing people with terminal illness from acquiring the legally approved means to end their suffering under medical supervision suggests that state governments view themselves as possessing ultimate dominion over the life and death of their subjects. Within Christian theology (going back to St. Augustine and St. Thomas Aquinas) the belief that life is given by God and hence not something that can be disposed of by the receiver was the essential idea that made suicide sinful and hence immoral and illegal for centuries. As Simon Critchley has recently noted: "The implicit moral judgment on suicide that comes down to us from Christian theology remains intact and in force" (2015, 12). If a state sees itself as ultimately responsible for upholding the sanctity of God-given life – carrying out a spiritual commission in secular time – then, working within these philosophical and legal views, what additional steps should states take to prevent further assaults on the sanctity and dignity of life?

This question matters because the number of people seeking physician-assisted aid-in-dying is dwarfed by the number of people who die by suicide. In Oregon, the first state to legally permit physician-assisted aid-in-dying, the greatest number of people to die under the State's Death with Dignity Act was 135 (2015).[8] Seven hundred and seventy-two people died by suicide in Oregon in 2016.[9] The same philosophical/religious commitments that speak *against* physician aid-in-dying also tell in *favor* of preventing the formation of suicidality in the first place and they do so regardless of one's policy preference on aid-in-dying laws (or capital punishment) because they both seek to preserve the sacredness and dignity of life. In light of these commitments, perhaps conservative citizens (and others) might help empower and reward their elected leaders for acting in accord with their deeply-held beliefs regarding the sanctity of life (in utero and post utero) by looking further upstream in the policy process for ways that they can use their temporal powers to prevent suicide. That these public officials would also be serving the poor, marginalized, and under-valued among us would be an added social-political-theological bonus for all.

Integrating Theory and Practice

How should we conceptualize the contribution that a political-institutional approach can make to the prevention of suicide? One way to do so is to supplement an influential existing account of suicide in the form of "fluid vulnerability theory" (Rudd, 2006). This theory (itself an elaboration of Beck's modal theory of psychopathology) examines temporal fluctuations and interactions of thoughts, feelings, behaviors, and physiology over time to identify periods of increased risk of suicide. The starting point for this account is the idea that individuals have a "baseline" risk of suicide that is comprised of various cognitive vulnerabilities (Rudd, 2000) and personal characteristics, such as propensity for mental illness, personality factors, interpersonal problem solving skills, personal and family history, etc. Individuals with multiple risk factors for suicide have a higher "baseline" risk for suicide and as a consequence of this, an acute life stressor or time-sensitive "perturbation" can precipitate suicidal conduct (or activate the "suicidal mode") for these persons. "Individuals with many historical and developmental vulnerabilities are at increased risk for suicide because they tend to have a higher set point around which their risk fluctuates on a moment-to-moment basis" (Wolfe-Clark and Bryan, 2017, 11).

A political-institutional perspective on this valuable account would add the following considerations to the theory and practice of suicide prevention.

The individual baseline risk for suicide is not an individual characteristic alone but is shaped by the complex interactions of social-economic determinants with personal-psychological characteristics, and these interactions have powerful, upstream *political* determinants. The baseline risk for suicide will vary by individual, yet the baseline risk for some socially-structured groups of people (some American Indians and Alaskan Natives; LGBT youth; urban black children; poor rural whites; the elderly; military personnel) is both higher in relative (aggregate) terms and also subject to more relentless inflationary pressures than others. Both of these features – higher socially-structured baseline risk and augmented inflationary pressures – are partially the product of public policy action and inaction in domains like poverty alleviation, income support, family support services, access to mental health services, gun control measures, and much else besides.

As a consequence of this structurally differentiated variability in the baseline risk for suicide, the acute life stressors that prompt an active suicidal mode should be subject to political-institutional investigation and political mobilization. For example, economic recessions and unemployment rates are tied to the actions of governments in numerous areas of macroeconomic policy from trade policy, market regulations, to job training programs. Internationally, the soaring rates of suicide and suicide attempts by Myanmar refugees on the Thai border, and among Afghan and Syrian refugees in Greece implicate multiple governments in conflict, the production of asylum-seekers, and the lengthy and dignity-stripping conditions in which refugees are compelled to wait for political asylum. In all of these cases (and many others that could be listed) the time dimension of "acute risk perturbation" looks very different depending upon one's social and political standing in an economic or global political order, but the very existence and duration of these crises are a product of political action or (more often) inaction on the part of policy regimes and their leaders.

Limits and Conclusion

There are important limitations to the broad approach and data points introduced in this chapter. The kind of general risk and vulnerability to suicide that has been located in specific policy regimes will not be relevant at the individual level in all cases. Correlation does not establish causation and this chapter does not attempt to offer a predictive or explanatory model of suicide. Additionally, a political-institutional orientation to suicide is unlikely to have any direct bearing upon clinical applications. This is consistent with recent meta-analyses that indicate that the overall effects of demographic factors in shaping risk for suicide are statistically but not clinically relevant (Huang et al., 2017). However, this does not mean that the approach outlined here cannot have relevance for practice. The level of analysis and intervention will instead turn to the intersection of our primary political institutions and the specific experiences of diverse groups of citizens within them. More broadly speaking, states that are politically serious about suicide prevention will take steps to act on the ways that they act upon persons: materially/economically; coercively though laws and regulations; and discursively through norms and the perpetuation of shared social scripts. Citizens who adopt this framework will hold their elected officials at all levels of public policy making and public leadership accountable to this vital task.

Notes

1 Prior to going to press, the latest CDC data became available and tells a worsening story about suicide mortality in the United States: From 1999 through 2017, the age-adjusted suicide rate increased 33% from 10.5 to 14.0 per 100,000. The age-adjusted suicide rate for the most urban counties in 2017 was 16% higher than in 1999 and was 53% higher in the most rural counties (20.0 per 100,000) (CDC, 2018).

2 An alternative hypothesis for observed regional variations in suicide in the United States posits that increases in altitude (and low blood oxygen) contributes to major depressive disorder and suicide. See Kious, Brent, Kondo, Douglas, Renshaw and Perry (2018).

3 The seven measures that make up the adult ranking include: adults with any mental illness (AMI); adults with dependence or abuse of illicit drugs or alcohol; adults with serious thoughts of suicide; adults with any AMI who did not receive treatment; adults with AMI reporting unmet need; adults with AMI who are uninsured; adults with disability who could not see a doctor due to cost.

4 The seven measure that make up the youth ranking include: youth with at least one past year of past major depressive episode (MDE); youth with dependence or abuse of illicit drugs or alcohol; youth with severe MDE; youth with MDE who did not receive mental health services; children with private insurance that did not cover mental or emotional problems; students identified with emotional disturbance for an individualized educational program.

5 Data is drawn from U.S. Department of Veteran Affairs, "Veteran Suicide Data Sheets" (2016).

6 As a result of the 2018 election, Colorado is now controlled by Democrats.

7 In 2017 the American Association of Suicidology approved a statement entitled: "Suicide isn't the same as physician aid-in-dying." There are many points of difference between the practice of physician aid in dying and the behavior that has traditionally been described and medically recorded as suicide. For a helpful discussion see Battin 2017.

8 Oregon Health Authority, Public Health Division: "Oregon Death with Dignity Act, Data Summary" (2016).

9 CDC Statistics of the State of Oregon 2016.

References

Allen, J., Balfour, R., Bell, R. and Marmot, M. (2014). "Social Determinants of Mental Health." *International Review of Psychiatry* 26 (4): 392–407.

Anestis, M. (2018). *Guns and Suicide: An American Epidemic.* New York: Oxford University Press.

Brent, D.A. and Bridge, J. (2003). "Firearms Availability and Suicide: Evidence, Interventions, and Future Directions." *American Behavioral Scientist* 46 (9): 1192–1210.

CDC. (2015). Web-based Injury Statistics Query and Reporting System (WISQARS). Atlanta, GA: US Department of Health and Human Services.

CDC. (2016). Web-based Injury Statistics Query and Reporting System (WISQARS). Atlanta, GA: US Department of Health and Human Services.

Compton, M. and Shim, R.S. (2015). "The Social Determinants of Mental Health." *Focus* 13 (4): 419–425.

Coyne J. and Downey, G. (1991). "Social Factors and Psychopathology: Stress, Social Support, and Coping Processes." *Annual Review of Psychology* 42: 401–425.

Critchley, S. (2015). *Notes on Suicide.* London: Fitzcarraldo Editions.

Cylus, J., Glymour, M. and Avendano, M. (2014). "Do Generous Unemployment Benefit Programs Reduce Suicide Rates? A State Fixed-Effect Analysis Covering 1968–2008." *American Journal of Epidemiology* 180 (1): 45–52.

Denney J., Wadsworth T., Rogers R. and Pampel F. (2015). "Suicide in the City: Do Characteristics of Place Really Influence Risk?" *Social Science Quarterly* 96 (2): 313–329.

Flavin, P. and Radcliff, B. (2009). "Public Policies and Suicide Rates in the American States." *Social Indicators Research* 90 (2): 195–209.

Hedegaard, H., Curtin, S.C. and Warner, M. (2018). Suicide mortality in the United States, 1999–2017. NCHS Data Brief, no 330. Hyattsville, MD: National Center for Health Statistics.

Huang, X., Ribeiro J.D., Musacchio K.M. and Franklin J.C. (2017) "Demographics as Predictors of Suicidal Thoughts and Behaviors: A Meta-analysis." PLOS ONE 12 (7): e0180793.

Jaworski, K. (2016). *The Gender of Suicide: Knowledge Production, Theory and Suicidology.* London: Routledge.

Kegler, S.R., Stone, D.M. and Holland, K.M. (2017). "Trends in Suicide by Level of Urbanization—United States, 1999–2015." *MMWR Morbidity and Mortality Weekly Report 2017* 66: 270–273.

Kellermann, A., Rivara, F., Somes, G., Reay, D., Fancisco, J., Banton, J., Prodzinski, J., Flinger, C. and Hackman, B. (1992). "Suicide in the Home in Relation to Gun Ownership." *New England Journal of Medicine* 327: 467–472.

Kerr, W.C., Huguet, N., Caetano, R., Giesbrecht, N. and McFarland, B. (2017). "Economic Recession, Alcohol, and Suicide Rates: Comparative Effects of Poverty, Foreclosure, and Job Loss." *American Journal of Preventive Medicine* 52 (4): 469–475.

Kious, B.M., Kondo, Douglas, G. and Renshaw, Perry, F. (2018). "Living High and Feeling Low: Altitude, Suicide, and Depression." *Harvard Review of Psychiatry* 26 (2): 43–56.

Kral, M. (1994). "Suicide as Social Logic." *Suicide and Life-Threatening Behavior* 24 (3): 245–255.

Kurbin, C., Wadsworth T. and DiPietro S. (2006). "Deindustrialization, Disadvantage and Suicide among Young Black Males." *Social Forces* 84 (3): 1559–1579.

Marsh, I. (2010). *Suicide: Foucault, History and Truth*. Cambridge: Cambridge University Press.

Marsh, I. (2016). "Critiquing Contemporary Suicidology." In J. White, I. Marsh, M. Kral and J. Morris (Eds.), *Critical Suicidology: Transforming Suicide Research and Prevention for the 21st Century* (pp. 15–30). Vancouver: University of British Columbia Press.

Miller, M. and Hemenway, D. (1999). "The Relationship between Firearms and Suicide: A Review of the Literature." *Aggression and Violent Behavior* 4 (1): 59–75.

Rehkopf, R. and Buka, S. (2006). "The association between suicide and the socio-economic characteristics of geographical areas: a systematic review." *Psychological Medicine* 36: 145–157.

Reynolds, V. (2016). "Hate kills: A social justice response to suicide." In J. White, I. Marsh, M. Kral and J. Morris (Eds.), *Critical Suicidology: Transforming Suicide Research and Prevention for the 21st Century* (pp. 169–187). Vancouver: University of British Columbia Press.

Rudd, M.D. (2000). "The Suicidal Mode: A Cognitive-Behavioral Model of Suicidality." *Suicide and Life-Threatening Behavior* 3 (1): 18–33.

Rudd, M.D. (2006). "Fluid Vulnerability Theory: A Cognitive Approach to Understanding the Process of Acute and Chronic Suicide Risk." In T.E. Ellis (Ed.), *Cognition and Suicide: Theory, Research, and Therapy* (pp. 355–368). Washington, DC: American Psychological Association.

Shneidman, E. (1993). *Suicide as Psychache: A Clinical Approach to Self-Destructive Behavior*. Northvale, NJ: J. Aronson.

White, J., Marsh, I., Kral, M. and Morris, J. (Eds.) (2016). *Critical Suicidology: Transforming Suicide Research and Prevention for the 21st Century*. Vancouver: University of British Columbia Press.

White, J. (2017). "What Can Critical Suicidology Do?" *Death Studies* 41 (8): 472–480.

Wilson, W.J. (1987). *The Truly Disadvantaged: The Inner City, the Underclass, and Public Policy*. Chicago, IL: University of Chicago Press.

Wilson, W.J. (1996). *When Work Disappears: The World of the New Urban Poor*. New York: Vintage Books.

Wolfe-Clark, A. and Bryan, C. (2017). "Integrating Two Theoretical Models to Understand and Prevent Military and Veteran Suicide." *Armed Forces and Society* 43 (3): 478–499.

6 Protest Suicide among Muslim Women

A Human Rights Perspective

Silvia Sara Canetto and Mohsen Rezaeian

Suicidality is a significant issue for women in Muslim-majority communities and countries. Not only are rates of nonfatal suicidal behavior and suicidal ideation higher among women than among men in these communities and countries (see Canetto, 2015b); women's mortality by suicide is also unusually high there, relative to men's. Five (Afghanistan, Bangladesh, Indonesia, Iraq, and Pakistan) of the six countries where women's suicide rates are higher than men's rates are Muslim-majority (World Health Organization, 2014).

In this chapter, we document a female suicidal behavior script that recurs in Muslim-majority communities and countries. It is a script of suicide as a protest against, and as a way to escape, the institutionalized oppression and abuse women experience in their families and communities.[1] Uneducated and poor young women living in rural areas are especially likely to engage in protest suicide. In this chapter, we also discuss the implications of women's protest suicide for suicide theory, research, and prevention. We argue that women's protest suicide challenges dominant, male-centered (and mostly U.S.-origin) theory that women are protected from suicide, especially during their reproductive years, or when they have extensive family ties, for example, via marriage. We also argue that women's protest suicide challenges dominant male- and U.S.-centered theory that suicide is caused by a combination of a frustrated need to belong and feelings of being a burden, and that it is a symptom of a mental disorder (Joiner, Hom, Hagan, & Silva, 2016). As a desperate response to human rights abuses, women's protest suicide compels us to move beyond dominant frameworks, and to adopt a human rights perspective to suicide theory, research, and prevention.

Language

Prior to entering into the substance of this chapter, we address issues of terminology. An examination of language is important because language reflects and reinforces values. Consistent with trends in the field (e.g., Canetto, 1992, 1997) in this chapter we do not use terms such as "completed suicide," "suicide attempt," or "failed suicide." One reason is that these terms confound outcome with intent. Studies indicate that, independent of the outcome of the suicidal act, most suicidal people have some ambivalence about killing themselves. Studies also show that the outcome of the suicidal act is influenced by circumstantial factors (such as proximity to a hospital), not just by intent (Canetto, 2008; World Health Organization, 2014). Another reason for our terminology choice is that terms like "attempted suicide" imply that surviving a suicidal act is a failure, and that dying of suicide is a success. It is interesting, in this regard, that in Anglophone countries where the language of successful and failed suicide is used, men typically "succeed" while women "fail" at suicide (see Canetto, 1992, 1997; Canetto & Lester, 1995, 1998, for a discussion). In light of these issues, in this chapter we use the term *nonfatal suicidal behavior* to refer to suicidal behavior that did not result in death, the term *suicide* to refer to suicidal behavior that resulted in death, and the term *suicidality* to refer to suicidal ideation, nonfatal, and/or fatal suicidal behavior. At the same time, in this chapter, we use the expression *protest suicide* to refer to nonfatal and fatal acts of protest suicidal behavior (instead of *protest suicidal behavior*) to connect with the literature about protest suicide as a political act—a literature that mostly focuses on men (Ben Cheikh, Rousseau, & Mekki-Berrada, 2011; Spehr & Dixon, 2013). Protest suicide is the expression used in this literature for suicidal behavior as a "purposive political act intended to change oppressive political policies or practices" (Spehr & Dixon, 2013, p. 368).

This chapter focuses on protest suicide among women living in Muslim-majority communities and countries. The term "Muslim" here refers to Muslim heritage, not to individual religiosity. We recognize that Muslim heritage encompasses a broad range of beliefs and practices. This variability depends, among other things, on the traditions that were in place in a community or country prior to when Islam took hold (Ahmed, 1992). At the same time, we think that there are enough commonalities in beliefs and practices across Muslim-majority communities and countries to make Muslim-heritage a meaningful framework of analysis.

Suicide and Islam

In Muslim-majority communities and countries, suicide is *haram*, that is, forbidden. Islam's prohibition of suicide is related to the view that life belongs to God. Suicide is viewed negatively also because it implies giving up hope in God (Dabbagh, 2012; Okasha & Okasha, 2009; Rezaeian, 2008; Sachedina, 2005). For example, in the *Qur'ān* (4:29) it is stated: "You should not kill yourself because God has been merciful to you." In many Muslim-majority countries, suicidal behavior is also a crime. For example, under Pakistani law, suicidal behavior is punishable with fines, and even a jail term. Most commonly, suicidal behavior results in stigma and harassment of suicidal individuals and their family (Khan, Naqvi, Thaver, & Prince, 2008).

Women's Suicidality in Muslim-Majority Communities and Countries: Who, Where, How, and Why

In this section, we examine a female suicide-script observed in Muslim-majority communities and countries. We describe the typical characteristics of suicidal women in these communities and countries. We also describe where their suicidal behavior tends to occur, by what method, and in response to what events. In other words, we address a common who, how, where, and why of female suicidality in Muslim-majority communities and countries.

Who: In Muslim-majority communities and countries, women have higher rates of suicidal ideation and nonfatal suicidal behavior than men—though there is significant rates-variability across communities and countries (see Canetto, 2015b). Female suicide mortality is also high in several Muslim-majority communities and countries, with five (Afghanistan, Bangladesh, Indonesia, Iraq, and Pakistan) of the six countries[2] where women's suicide rates are higher than men's being Muslim-majority (World Health Organization, 2014). Also, the male to female ratio of age-standardized suicide rates is 1.4[3] in low- and middle-income countries located in the Eastern Mediterranean region, that is, in a region that includes only Muslim-majority countries (World Health Organization, 2014).

Due to underreporting, Muslim-majority countries both women's and men's rates of suicidal ideation and suicidal behavior are likely higher than official rates indicate (Pritchard & Amanullah, 2007). Cultural norms, including suicidal behavior being considered a sin and/or a crime, are believed to contribute to the underreporting (Khan, Naqvi, Thaver, & Prince, 2008). There are also indications that at least in some communities, women's suicidal behavior is more underreported than men's. For example, a West Bank, hospital-based study found that suicidal behavior by women was almost never reported to the police, while suicidal behavior by single men often was. For context, women arrived at the hospital accompanied by a male family member, while single men usually went alone. Hospital staff said that they did not report women's suicidal behavior to protect women from harassment (Dabbagh, 2012). The researchers who did this work however challenged this narrative. They argued that reporting of female suicidal behavior is avoided to protect the suicidal woman's male family members. They noted that the agency implicit in a suicidal act is perceived as a challenge to male authority. Through a suicidal act, a woman makes her discontent visible—a behavior that violates expectations that women be silent, especially about their unhappiness (Billaud, 2012; Dabbagh, 2012; Rasool & Payton, 2014).

There are indications that women's suicide rates in Muslim-majority communities and countries may be unreliable also in the opposite direction, with a portion of women's recorded suicides being indirect or direct homicides (Campbell & Guiao, 2004, for the Middle East and Central Asia; Coskun et al., 2012, in Turkey; Dabbagh, 2012, in Palestine). For example, in some communities, women who are accused of locally-defined moral improprieties (e.g., speaking with a man who is not a close relative) or who have *experienced sexual abuse by men* (including rape) may be forced to kill themselves or murdered, with their death reported as a suicide (see Canetto, 2015b, for a review).[4]

Suicidal ideation, nonfatal suicidal behavior, and suicide are most common in women who are young, married, uneducated or under-educated, poor, and/or living in rural areas (see Canetto, 2015b, for a review).[5] For example, an Iranian study (Aliverdinia & Pridemore, 2009) found that female suicide rates were highest in provinces with low levels of urbanization, female education, and female labor-force participation.

Where: Where information about location is provided, the home is a common site of women's suicidal behavior in Muslim-majority communities and countries (Boostani et al., 2013; Rasool & Payton, 2014). A likely reason is that women in these communities and countries are often confined to the home. Home is also the place where women experience the abuse that triggers the protest suicide. Enacting the protest suicide in the home may be a way of pointing to the family as the instigator. Engaging in a suicidal act at home also forces the family to be the "audience for the [desperate protest] 'performance'" (Rasool & Payton, 2014, p. 248).

How: Women's suicide methods vary by region. In the region encompassing Afghanistan, Iraq, and Iran, women's suicidal behavior typically involves self-burning (see Canetto, 2015b, for a review).[6] In this region, suicidal behavior by self-burning is significantly more common in women than in men. For example, suicide rates by self-burning in Iraqi Kurdistan were estimated at 15.5 per 100,000 in women, and 1.2 in men (Othman 2011). In other regions, for example, in Southeastern Turkey, hanging is women's typical suicide method (Altindag et al., 2005). In yet other locations, for example, in Pakistani cities, ingestion of organophosphate insecticides is a common suicide method among women (Khan & Reza, 2000). The method's local meaning plays a role in its being chosen. In the regions of Iran and Iraq where self-burning is the typical female suicide method, "I will burn myself" is a statement that women make when dealing with stress (Othman, 2011, for Iraq; Rezaie et al., 2011, p. 162, for Iran). In Iran, setting oneself ablaze is also viewed as a way for a woman to prove herself "sinless" when she is accused of moral improprieties, which locally, includes being the *target* of sexual harassment or abuse (Rezaie et al., 2014, p. 323). In Kurdish areas, self-burning is said to be connected with the "Zoroastrian fire imagery [that] pervades Sufi poetry"—fire being perceived as a way to "transcendent annihilation"

(Billaud, 2012; Rasool & Payton, 2012, pp. 247–248). According to Rasool and Payton, "Kurds are very familiar with the 'weapons of the weak'—self-immolation as a form of political protest . . . [having] been part of Kurdish nationalist fight since the 1990s." Kurdish women may choose self-burning as a way to reclaim their body ("a disputed territory") from male control—through "utter destruction" of their body. Rasool and Payton argued that

> through gendering the pre-existing discourse of self-immolation as political protest . . . [self-burning by women] blurs the boundaries between the personal and the political, through analogizing the collective experience of authoritarian rule shared by the Kurds with the authoritarianism of patriarchal family relations.
>
> (2012, p. 248)

Why: The suicidal ideation and behavior of women who live in Muslim-majority communities and countries are often explained as a response, and even as an impulsive reaction to family problems.[7] These family problems may be described as a "quarrel" (Lari et al., 2009, p. 98), a "disruption" (Altindag et al., 2005, p. 480), or a "conflict" (Alaghenhbandan et al., 2011, p. 164)—making it look like women overreact to minor difficulties. Upon close inspection of the evidence, however, it becomes clear that the family problems that are the context of women's suicidality are anything but trivial. They often involve institutionalized violations of human rights (e.g., the right to education, paid work, choice in marriage and divorce, and being safe from sexual, physical and emotional abuse), and with women having no options for recourse. Specifically, according to studies, the family problems that precede Muslim women's suicidality include: forced withdrawal from school; being prohibited from paid work; confinement to the house; being prohibited from living alone, including after divorce or widowhood; close surveillance of their every behavior by family members; being forbidden to marry someone of their own choosing; forced marriage, including to settle a dispute between families or tribes; polygamy by the husband; addiction of the husband; bearing and raising a large number of children; blame and harassment for not having children or for not producing male children; having to literally serve the husband and his extended family; difficulties or inability to obtain a divorce; social (e.g., shunning) and economic problems following a divorce; and emotional, physical and/or sexual abuse by family members (see Canetto, 2015b, for a review).[8] Many of these problems are based on the Muslim practice of male guardianship, with women's every major life decision (e.g., education; marriage) being the purview of their father, husband, brother, or son (Eltahawy, 2015).

Interview studies with women who survived a suicidal act have documented the ways women describe their desperate attempt to escape a life of misery through suicide. In these studies, women articulate a sense of not having socially acceptable "means of self-expression and self-determination" (Rasool & Payton, 2012, p. 250). For example, an Afghani woman "with self-inflicted burns over 90 percent of her body" said that she did not know what else to do to avoid being sold into marriage (Nawa, 2002). An Iranian woman stated that she set herself on fire because she had been "accused of being a 'dokhtarza', i.e., a woman . . . [who gives] birth to girls only." *Dokhtarza* is a label that can "ruin the woman's identity and social status since her husband and all members of the family . . . [can] lash . . . [at her by saying]: 'You can't even deliver boys'" (Boostani et al., 2013, pp. 3157–3158). Several women in the same Iranian study said that they did not see a way out of patriarchal oppression except via suicide: "I suffered a lot of hardships. I saw self-burning as the only way of release," said a woman. Another woman stated: "there is no choice but suicide for the person who reaches a deadlock." Yet another woman reported that she had "appealed to suicide to get rid of her patriarch" (p. 3161). The Palestinian women interviewed in a study by Dabbagh (2004) talked about feeling entrapped, in their house, family and community, by patriarchal systems, ideologies and practices; and about wanting to escape, but seeing no way to end the oppression except through suicide. Many described themselves as "suppressed, subdued, suffocated, and pressurized (*makboota, maktooma, makhnooa, madghuta*)," not as depressed (Dabbagh, 2004, p. 211). The story of Aisha, narrated in a study of suicide in Palestine, provides an illustration of this kind of situation (Dabbagh, 2012). Aisha recounted that her younger brother started sexually abusing her when she was 10. At age 12, "[d]istressed by what . . . [he] was doing to her," she overdosed (Dabbagh, 2012, p. 294). Aisha hoped that her suicidal act would mobilize her family. Her suicidal act, however, did not change the situation. No one in the family helped her. In fact, "[h]er brother kept on abusing her" (Dabbagh, 2012, p. 294). At age 15, Aisha left her parents' house following an arranged marriage. This marriage did not bring an end to her maltreatments. Her husband started bringing home other women and sleeping with them. Eventually Aisha obtained a divorce. Around age 20, her family arranged for her to be married again. Her second husband was much older than she was. He also beat her. Desperate to escape this second abusive marriage, she attacked an Israeli soldier in the hope to be put in prison, and that way, have a break from her violent husband. In her interview, she said that she liked life in prison. Being in prison gave her the distance from her family she had long sought. When she was released from prison, however, she was forced again into subjugation to the men of her family. Per patriarchal custom, she had to live with her older brother, and to defer to him authority over her personal decisions. This brother prohibited her from working outside of the home. He also forbade her to marry a man she liked. In desperation, she engaged in two more suicidal acts. At the time of her interview, Aisha was more determined than ever to kill herself—unless she found a way to escape the patriarchal tyranny of her family and community: "I can't live like this," she said. "Either I emigrate or I die. I'll make myself die" (p. 297).

Studies of women's suicide mortality in Muslim-majority communities and countries also provide evidence about the role of patriarchal beliefs, practices and systems in women's suicides (see Canetto, 2015b, for a review).[9] Here are a few examples. A study of women's violent deaths in rural Bangladesh described the case of a woman who hanged herself following "frequent quarrels" with her husband and his family about not having become pregnant after several years of marriage (Ahmed et al., 2004, p. 317). Similarly, in a study of the high suicide rates of young women in Southeastern Turkey, it was reported that suicide for these women was "a means to escape from unbearable lives" (Altindag et al., 2005, p. 480). It was noted that "violence is common in their families" (p. 480). What made these Turkish women's lives unbearable was also that they were confined to the house. "Most of them do not take part into social, economical and cultural activities," wrote the authors of the study (p. 480). Women's "[i]lliteracy and language difficulties make it difficult for women to even go to the doctor," they noted. Similarly, the authors of a study of women who died of self-inflicted burns in Tabriz, Iran, concluded that these women had suffered "degradation in the family, many . . . [having been] subjected to male domination and arrogance" (Maghsoudi et al., 2004, p. 219). Along the same line, Alaghenhbandan and colleagues wrote that self-burning for Iranian young women is "a means of both escaping from [the] intolerable conditions and speaking out against [the patriarchy-based] abuse" they experience in their families and society (2011, p. 168). According to the authors of a study of self-burning in Afghanistan, "women and girls appear to see this horrifying act as a means of both escaping from intolerable conditions and speaking out against abuse, since their actual voices do not bring about changes that would allow them to lead safe and secure lives." A woman whose sister set herself ablaze explained what happened this way: "My 18-year-old sister did not want to marry this man and asked my father several times not to give her to the farmer. But he ignored her pleas. One day I heard that my sister had taken petrol and committed [sic] self-immolation" (Raj et al., 2008, p. 2203).

Discussion

Women's protest suicide in Muslim-majority communities and countries challenges dominant suicide theory. It exposes dominant theory as androcentric and U.S.-centric. Specifically, it makes visible how dominant theory is based on the experience of a narrow range of humanity, that is, the experience of European-descent men living in high-income, and mostly-Anglophone countries (see Canetto, 2008; 2015b).

In this final section, we address some of the cultural and gender biases in dominant theory. For example, we show how women's protest suicide in Muslim-majority communities and countries challenges dominant male- and U.S.-centered theory that women are protected from suicide, especially when they are young and/or married. We also show how women's protest suicide challenges the theory (e.g., Joiner et al., 2016) that suicide is caused by a combination of a thwarted need to belong and perceiving oneself as a burden, as well as suicide capability; and that suicide is a symptom of a mental disorder. We conclude this final section with a discussion of why understanding and preventing women's protest suicide requires moving beyond dominant frameworks, and adopting a human rights perspective.

Being a Woman is not Suicide-Protective

It has long been an axiom of dominant suicidology that, by their very nature, women are averse to suicide, especially during their reproductive years. This idea, which can be traced to assumptions about the natural (e.g., cognitive, moral) inferiority of women, has been framed in various ways, including in evolutionary jargon. Women are presumably protected from suicide because they are driven by self-preservation instincts. By contrast, men are believed to be capable of suicide because, as a superior form of humanity, they can conceive of, and be motivated by higher values than self-preservation. Women are also presumed to be less courageous than men. Because of these assumptions, women are thought to be less capable than men to take their own lives (see Canetto, 1992, 1992–1993, 2008, 2015a, for analyses of gender myths of suicidality). Women's protest suicide adds to the evidence challenging these assumptions. Women's protest suicide clusters in the-life stage, the reproductive years, when, according to dominant canon, women should be least inclined to suicide. Women's protest suicide also involves methods (e.g., self-burning and hanging) that, in the dominant canon, are considered violent and disfiguring, and therefore, presumably unacceptable to women.

For Women, Social Integration and Social Regulation Are often Suicide Risk Factors, not Protectors

It is core to the dominant canon that being embedded in a social network (social integration, as Durkheim (1897/1951) called it), and being subject to the normative demands of a social network (social regulation, as Durkheim termed it) are suicide protectors. For example, being married (a form of social integration) is assumed to be suicide-protective, while being single is assumed to carry suicide risk. In a recent version of social-integration theory, thwarted belongingness (defined as an unmet need for connectedness) is presumed to be an essential condition for suicidality (Joiner et al., 2016).

Women's protest suicide in Muslim-majority communities and countries demonstrates the cultural and gender specificity of these assumptions. As illustrated by research evidence, women's protest suicide is not motivated by a frustrated need for belonging—as interpersonal theory assumes of all suicides. Rather, women's protest suicide appears to be the expression of *a thwarted need for individuation*—a need to be free from suffocating connectedness (Aliverdinia & Pridemore, 2009; Canetto, 2015b; Coskun et al., 2012; Dabbagh, 2004, 2012; Haarr, 2010; Maghsoudi et al., 2004; Rezaie et al., 2014; van Bergen, Smit, van Balko & Saharso, 2009). An example of interpersonal theory's failure to account for the interpersonal experiences and needs of women who engage in protest suicide is the *Interpersonal Needs Questionnaire* (*INQ*), a measure based on interpersonal theory (Van Orden, Cuckrowitz, Witte & Joiner, 2012). The INQ includes items about feeling unwelcome in social situations (e.g., "These days, I often feel like an outsider in social gatherings"), and no items about the need to be safe from physical, sexual, and/or psychological abuse. The absence, in the INQ, of items measuring the need for safety from abuse is striking because abuse is an important predictor of women's suicidality in the United States, not only in Muslim-majority countries. For example, a meta-analysis of longitudinal studies (the majority of which were from the United States) found that a history of intimate-partner violence increases women's risk for suicidal behavior (Devries et al., 2013). In other words, intimate-partner violence is a major predictor of women's suicidality in a diversity of communities and countries, including the United States. Yet, the need to be safe from violence is not measured by an instrument based on the leading interpersonal theory of suicide.

Feeling Like a Burden is not a Central Theme in Women's Suicidality

The interpersonal theory of suicide postulates that feeling like a burden ("an intractable sense of burdensomeness" or "the perseverative misperception that one's death by suicide unburdens others" (Joiner et al., 2016, pp. 240, 245)) is an essential experience in the pathway to suicidality. Research, however, shows that women's protest suicide in Muslim-majority communities and countries is not about feeling like a burden. If anything, women's protest suicide is a response to *being burdened by others* (Canetto, 2015b). As an example of the gender and cultural biases embedded in the interpersonal theory of suicide, the *INQ* (Van Orden et al., 2012) includes items about feeling like a burden (e.g., "These days, the people in my life would be better off if I were gone" and "These days, the people in my life would be happier without me"), and no items about *others being a burden* to the individual.

Suicidality is not First and Foremost about Mental Illness

It is dominant canon that suicide is caused by mental disorders, if not a mental disorder itself (Harris & Barraclough, 1997; Insel & Cuthbert, 2015; Joiner et al., 2016; however, see Hjelmeland & Knizek, 2017, for a critique of the mental illness paradigm). "Our view is that 100% of suicide deaths are spurred by mental disorders" (p. 245); and "[s]uicide is an exemplar of derangement . . . even more so than florid psychosis or mania" (p. 242), wrote Joiner and colleagues (2016). Some U.S.-based authors (e.g., Oquendo & Baca-Garcia, 2014) have argued in favor of adding a suicidal-behavior-disorder category to the *Diagnostic and Statistical Manual of Mental Disorders*.

Women in Muslim-majority communities and countries find themselves in situations of extreme institutionalized oppression (e.g., Douki et al., 2007; Eltahawy, 2015; Hekmat, 1997; Skaff, 2013). "[F]or the great majority of women in Islamic societies, education and work are not yet established rights, while virginity, fertility, and obedience are still duties," noted Douki and colleagues in an article detailing forms of female discrimination and abuse in the Muslim world (p. 182). Therefore, if and when women in these communities and countries develop a mental disorder or become suicidal, it is also because of the oppressive life conditions they experience, not independent of those conditions (e.g., Canetto 2015b; Douki et al., 2007; Rezaeian, 2010). For example, Douki and colleagues stated that

> in many Islamic societies, the experiences of self-worth, competence, autonomy, economic independence as well as physical, sexual and emotional safety and security which are essential to good mental health, are systematically denied to countless women . . . Such gender based discrimination is not only a gross violation of human rights but directly contributes to the growing burden of disability caused by poor mental health.
>
> (pp. 187–188)

Why a Human Rights Framework Matters in Suicide Theory, Research, and Prevention

Across a range of Muslim-majority communities and countries, suicidal behavior, particularly suicidal behavior by self-burning, often is a way for young women to rebel against, and escape the restrictions and abuse they experience in their families and society. In these communities and countries women have limited or no options of self-determination and influence, and also limited or no means to escape institutionalized oppression (Canetto, 2015b; Rezaeian, in press).

For these reasons, women's suicidal behavior in Muslim-majority communities and countries needs first and foremost to be examined from a *human rights perspective*. Framing these women's suicidality as a mental illness obscures the social-injustice context of the behavior. It also medicalizes and discounts rightful distress as insanity (Ahmed et al., 2004; Ali et al., 2013; Aliverdinia & Pridemore, 2009; Campbell & Guiao, 2004; Canetto, 2015b; Dabbagh, 2004, 2012; Groohi et al., 2006; Devries et al., 2011; Haarr, 2010; Hanna & Ahmad, 2013; Maghsoudi et al., 2004; Raj et al., 2008; Rasool & Payton, 2014; Rezaeian, 2010; Rezaie & Schwebel, 2012; Rezaie et al., 2014; van Bergen et al., 2009). Bringing a human rights perspective to Muslim women's protest suicide is particularly important given the tendency, in dominant-discourse *everywhere*, to frame women's distress (whatever its source) as a private matter—and also to blame women for their distress (see Canetto, 1997, for an analysis).

For context, it is noteworthy that when men are suicidal (in Muslim-majority communities and countries, and elsewhere), social and economic injustices are invoked as triggers—with men's potential individual psychopathology typically being overlooked (Canetto, 1991; 1992–1993; 1997; 2008). To illustrate this point, compare how self-burning is interpreted when men engage in it versus when women do it. Consider, for example, the case of Bouazizi, the street vendor who in 2010 set himself ablaze in Tunis. His behavior was interpreted as a response to the socioeconomic and political problems of his country, "a way to confront oppression, felt injustice and social suffering" (Ben Cheikh et al., 2011, p. 495). The media described him a political activist and the instigator of the Arab Spring. In the Arab world as well as outside he was hailed as a hero. A square in Paris and the main square in Tunis were named after him. In 2011, *Time* magazine made him the person of the year (Rezaeian, 2014b). All through this, no questions were asked about his mental status or the impulsivity of his act.

By contrast, consider how cases of women's protest self-burning are presented in the media. To start with, these cases do not receive media attention proportionate to the number of women affected, and the vastness of the region involved. Second, when these cases are covered, questions about the women's mental status, maturity, or judgment are often raised: "They are uneducated women . . . Some have mental issues. They don't think about the results of their actions. In their minds, this is the only solution," said an official interviewed about women's self-burning for a *World Politics Review* article (Motlagh, 2007). Third, negative and passive terms (e.g., "victim," for example, in Maghsoudi et al., 2004; "tragic," for example, in Groohi et al., 2006; Mabrouk et al., 1999; Motlag, 2007; Raj et al., 2008), rather than positive, active terms (e.g., courageous) recur in reports about women who set themselves ablaze in protest against patriarchal systems, ideologies, and practices. Finally, even when the protest aspect of women's self-burning is noted, the act is still linked to private problems (e.g., Boostani et al., 2013), instead of being recognized as signaling public issues and social injustice. As a result, women's protest self-burning does not engender the recognition and empathic response that men's protest self-burning triggers. In this regard, it is to be noted that women's human rights violations are more likely to occur in the context of the family than men's human rights violations. A reason is that patriarchal oppression operates as much in the private as in the public domain. A consequence is that women's human rights violations may be dismissed, and even excused as private matters (see Canetto, 2018).

Many of the researchers who have documented women's protest suicide in Muslim-majority communities and countries have recommended a human rights approach to suicide prevention. They have argued that the prevention of women's protest suicide should aim at institutionalizing and protecting, for example, women's freedom of movement, and women's rights to education, choice in marriage, and properly compensated work.[10] For example, Aliverdinia and Pridemore (2009), Groohi and colleagues (2006), as well as Rad and colleagues (2012), recommended expanding Iranian women's access to education and paid work as a way to prevent their suicidal behavior. Similarly, Rezaeian (2010) urged Muslim societies to commit to educational, economic, and social rights and opportunities for women, as a suicide prevention strategy. This would involve "recognizing the rights of females, tackling illiteracy among both males and females, prohibiting forced child marriage, providing economic and social support especially for young females," he wrote (p. 40).

It is important to note that, for some Muslims, the *Qur'ān* is foundational to their support of women's and men's equality (Rezaeian, 2010). According to them, the Qu'ran makes it clear that the sole basis for superiority of any person over another is piety and righteousness (Belhadj, 1994, cited in Douki et al., 2010, p. 188). Those who take this position may point to Badawi as an example of a theologian who attributed "the subordination of women to misinterpretation of Islam, rather than to Islam itself" (Douki et al., 2010, p. 188). Yet other Muslims use verses of the *Qur'ān*, (e.g., the verse "Men are superior (or protectors, depending on the translation of *kawamouna*) to women because Allah has made some of them to excel others" (4:34)), precisely to justify women's subordination to men.[11]

Conclusions

A human rights perspective is critical to understanding and preventing women's protest suicide in Muslim-majority communities and countries.

A human rights approach has the potential to also reduce suicidality globally, given the evidence (e.g., Canetto, 2015a; Devries et al., 2011; Devries & Seguin, 2013) about the role of abuse and violence in women's suicidality in a diversity of communities and countries. In our view, a human rights perspective is necessary not only because of the evidence linking female suicidality and human rights violations, but also because the protection of human rights is fundamental to social justice.

Notes

1 Women's protest suicide is not unique to Muslim-majority communities and countries. It has also been documented, for example, in Hindu-majority India (Rezaeian, 2017a), in Buddhist-majority Sri Lanka (Marecek, 2000), and in the South African Lowveld (Niehaus, 2012). For the purpose of focusing this chapter, we limit our attention here to women's protest suicide in Muslim-majority communities and countries.

2 China is the other country where suicide rates have been higher in women than in men (World Health Organization, 2014). Between 2002 and 2015, suicide rates in China, however, have significantly declined, and for women more than for men, the result being that women no longer represent the majority of suicides (Jiang, Niu, Hahne, Hu, Fan, Shen, & Xiao, 2018).

3 The countries included in this region by the World Health Organization are Afghanistan, Djibouti, Egypt, Iran, Iraq, Jordan, Lebanon, Libya, Morocco, Pakistan, Somalia, South Sudan, Sudan, the Syrian Arab Republic, Tunisia, and Yemen (World Health Organization, 2014).

4 For studies documenting this pattern see Aliverdinia & Pridemore, 2009, in Iran; Coskun et al., 2012, in Turkey; Dabbagh, 2012, in Palestine; Douki, Ben Zineb, Nacef, & Halbreich, 2007, in Islamic societies; Rasool & Payton, 2014, in the Kurdistan region of Iraq; Skaff, 2013, in the Middle East.

5 For studies documenting this pattern see Ahmadi, 2007, in Iran; Ahmadi et al., 2009, in Iran; Alaghenhbandan, Lari, Joghataei, Islami, & Motavalian, 2011, in Iran; Ali, Mogren, & Krantz, 2013, in Pakistan; Aliverdinia & Pridemore 2009, in Iran; Boostani, Abdinia, & Anaraki, 2013, in Iran; Altindag et al., 2005, in Turkey; Campbell & Guiao, 2004, for the Middle East and Central Asia; Coskun, Zoroglu, & Ghaziuddin, 2012, in Turkey; Dabbagh, 2012, in Palestine; Goren et al., 2004, in Turkey; Groohi, Rossignol, Barrero, & Alaghehbandan, 2006, in Kurdistan, Iran; Hadi, 2005, in Bangladesh; Haarr, 2010, in Tajikistan; Khan & Reza, 1998, in Iran; Khan et al., 2009, in Pakistan; Khlat & Courbage, 1995; Lari, Alaghenhbandan, Panjeshahin, & Joghataei, 2009, in Iran; Mabrouk, Omar, Massoud, Sherif, & El Sayed, 1999, in Egypt; Maghsoudi et al., 2004, in Iran; Nazarzadeh et al., 2013, in Iran; Othman, 2011, in Iraqi Kurdistan; Panjeshahin, Lari, Talei, Shamsnia, & Alaghehbandan, 2001, in Iran; Rad et al., 2012, in Iran; Othman, 2011, in Iraqi Kurdistan; Rasool & Payton, 2014, in the Kurdistan region of Iraq; Rezaie, Khazaie, Soleimani, & Schwebel, 2011, in Iran; Shahid & Hyder, 2008, in Pakistan; Syed & Khan, 2008, in Pakistan; Yasan, Danis, Taman, Ozmen, & Ozkan, 2008, in Turkey.

6 For studies documenting this pattern see Ahmadi, 2007; Ahmadi et al., 2009, in Iran; Alaghenhbandan et al., 2011, in Iran; Billaud, 2012, in Afghanistan; Campbell & Guiao, 2004, for the Middle East and Central Asia; Groohi, Alaghehbandan, & Lari, 2002, in Kurdistan, Iran; Groohi et al., 2006, in Kurdistan, Iran; Hanna & Ahmad, 2013, in Iraqi Kurdistan; Lari et al., 2009, in Iran; Maghsoudi et al., 2004, in Iran; Maghsoudi,

Samnia, Garadaghi, & Kianvar, 2006, in Iran; Othman, 2011, in Iraqi Kurdistan; Panjeshahin et al., 2001, in Iran; Rad, Anvari, Ansarinejad, & Panaghi, 2012, in Iran; Rasool & Payton, 2012, in the Kurdistan region of Iraq; Rastegar, Joghataei, Adli, Zadeh, & Alaghehbandan, 2007; Rezaeian, 2017b, in Iran; Rezaie et al., 2011, in Iran; Rezaie et al., 2014, in Iran; Saadat, Bahaoddini, Mohabatkar, & Noemani, 2004, in Iran.

7 For studies documenting this pattern see Ahmadi, 2007, in Iran; Ahmadi et al., 2009, in Iran; Ahmed, Van Ginneken, Razzaque, & Alam, 2004, in Bangladesh; Ayub et al., 2013, in Pakistan; Alaghenhbandan et al., 2011, in Iran; Ali et al., 2013, in Pakistan; Al-Jahdali et al., 2004, in Saudi Arabia; Aliverdinia & Pridemore, 2009, in Iran; Altindag et al., 2005, in Turkey; Asad et al., 2010, in Pakistan; Bilgin, Cenkseven, & Satar, 2007, in Turkey; Boostani et al., 2013, in Iran; Campbell & Guiao, 2004, for the Middle East and Central Asia; Coskun et al., 2012, in Turkey; Dabbagh, 2004, 2012, in Palestine; ; Goren et al., 2004, in Turkey; Groohi et al., 2002, in Kurdistan, Iran; Groohi et al., 2006, in Kurdistan, Iran; Haarr, 2010, in Tajikistan; Hadi, 2005, in Bangladesh; Hanna & Ahmad, 2013, in Iraqi Kurdistan; Khan & Reza, 1998, in Pakistan; Lari et al., 2009, in Iran; Maghsoudi et al., 2004, in Iran; Naved & Akhtar, 2008, in Bangladesh; Nazarzadeh et al., 2013, in Iran; Oner, Yenilmez, Ayranci, Gunay, & Ozdamar, 2007, in Turkey; Othman, 2011, in Iraqi Kurdistan; Rad et al., 2012, in Iran; Raj, Gomez, & Silverman, 2008, in Afghanistan; Rasool & Payton, 2014, in Kurdistan, Iraq; Rezaeian, 2010, for the Middle East; Rezaie et al., 2011, in Iran; Rezaie et al., 2014, in Iran; Shahid & Hyder, 2008, in Pakistan; Syed & Khan, 2008, in Pakistan; van Bergen, Eikelenboom, Smit, van de Looij-Jansen, & Saharso, 2010, and van Bergen, Smit, van Balko, & Saharso, 2009, for Moroccan and Turkish immigrants to the Netherlands; Yasan et al., 2008, in Turkey; Zaidan et al., 2002, in Oman).

8 For studies documenting this pattern see Ahmed et al., 2004, in Bangladesh; Alaghenhbandan, Lari, Joghataei, Islami, & Motavalian, 2011, in Iran; Aliverdinia & Pridemore, 2009, in Iran; Altindag et al., 2005, in Turkey; Billaud, 2012, in Afghanistan; Boostani, Abdinia, & Anaraki, 2013, in Iran; Rezaeian, 2015, in Afghanistan; Campbell & Guiao, 2004, for the Middle East and Central Asia; Coskun et al., 2012, in Turkey; Dabbagh, 2004, 2012, in Palestine; Groohi et al., 2006, in Kurdistan, Iran; Haarr, 2010, in Tajikistan; Hadi, 2005, in Bangladesh; Lari et al., 2009, in Iran; Maghsoudi et al., 2004, in Iran; Naved & Akhtar, 2008, in Bangladesh; Nazarzadeh et al., 2013, in Iran; Othman, 2011, in Iraqi Kurdistan; Rad et al., 2012, in Iran; Raj et al., 2008, in Afghanistan; Rasool & Payton, 2014, in Kurdistan, Iraq; Rezaeian, 2010, for the Middle East; Rezaie et al., 2011, in Iran; Rezaie et al., 2014, in Iran; Yusuf et al., 2000, in Bangladesh.

9 For studies documenting this pattern see Ahmed et al., 2004; in Bangladesh, Alaghenhbandan et al., 2011, in Iran; Aliverdinia & Pridemore 2009, in Iran; Altindag et al., 2005, in Turkey; Campbell & Guiao, 2004, for the Middle East and Central Asia; Coskun et al., 2012, in Turkey; Groohi et al., 2006, in Kurdistan, Iran; Hadi, 2005, in Bangladesh; Hanna & Ahmad, 2013, in Iraqi Kurdistan; Lari et al., 2009, in Iran; Maghsoudi et al., 2004, in Iran; Othman, 2011, in Iraqi Kurdistan; Raj et al., 2008, in Afghanistan; Rezaeian, 2010, for the Middle East.

10 For a range of statements on this issue, see Ahmed et al., 2004: Alaghehbandan et al., 2011; Ali et al., 2013; Aliverdinia & Pridemore, 2009; Campbell & Guiao, 2004; Devries et al., 2011; Douki et al., 2007; Groohi et al., 2006; Hanna & Ahmad, 2013; Maghsoudi et al., 2004; Raj et al., 2008; Rasool & Payton, 2014; Rezaeian, 2010; Saaiq & Ashraf, 2016.

11 Across religions, what religious texts mean is a matter of interpretation; and there are different interpretations for every verse of every religious text.

References

Ahmadi, A. (2007). Suicide by self-immolation: Comprehensive overview, experiences and suggestions. *Journal of Burn Care & Research*, 28(1), pp.30–41.

Ahmadi, A., Mohammadi, R., Schwebel, D., Yeganeh, N., Soroush, A., & Bazargan-Hejazi, S. (2009). Familial risk factors for self-immolation: A case-control study. *Journal of Women's Health*, 18(7), pp.1025–1031.

Ahmed, L. (1992). *Women and Gender in Islam*. New Haven: Yale University Press.

Ahmed, M. K., Van Ginneken, J., Razzaque, A., & Alam, N. (2004). Violent deaths among women of reproductive age in rural Bangladesh. *Social Science & Medicine*, 59(2), pp.311–319.

Alaghenhbandan, R., Lari, A. R., Joghataei, M-T., Islami, A., & Motavalian, A. (2011). A prospective population-based study of suicidal behavior by burns in the province of Ilam, Iran. *Burns*, 37(1), pp.164–169.

Ali, T. S., Mogren, I., & Krantz, G. (2013). Intimate partner violence and mental health effects: A population-based study among married women in Karachi, Pakistan. *International Journal of Behavioral Medicine*, 20(1), pp.130–139.

Aliverdinia A., & Pridemore, W. A. (2009). Women's fatalistic suicide in Iran: A partial test of Durkheim in an Islamic Republic. *Violence Against Women*, 15(3), pp.307–320.

Al-Jahdali, H., Al-Johani, A., Al-Hakawi, A., Arabi, Y., Ahmed, Q. A., Altowirky, J., et al. (2004). Patterns and risk factors for intentional drug overdose in Saudi Arabia. *Canadian Journal of Psychiatry*, 49(5), pp.331–334.

Altindag, A., Ozkan M., & Oto, R. (2005). Suicide in Batman, Southeastern Turkey. *Suicide and Life-Threatening Behavior*, 35(4), pp.478–482.

Asad, N., Karmaliani, R., Sullaiman, N., Bann, C. M., McClure, E.M., Pasha, O., et al. (2010). Prevalence of suicidal thoughts and attempts among pregnant Pakistani women. *Acta Obstetricia et Gynecologica Scandinavica*, 89(12), pp.1545–1551.

Ayub, M., Mushtaq, I., Mushtaq, S., Hafeez, M. A., Helal, N., Irfan, M., et al. (2013). Domestic violence, mental illness, and suicidal ideation: A study from Lahore, Pakistan. *Journal of Mental Health*, 22(6), pp.474–481.

Ben Cheikh, I., Rousseau, C., & Mekki-Berrada, A. (2011). Suicide as protest against social suffering in the Arab world. *The British Journal of Psychiatry*, 198(6), pp.494–495.

Bilgin M., Cenkseven, F., & Satar, S. (2007). An analysis of parent-female adolescent relationships in female adolescent suicides. *Crisis: The Journal of Crisis Intervention and Suicide Prevention*, 28(4), pp.190–197.

Billaud, J. (2012). Suicidal performances: Voicing discontent in a girls' dormitory in Kabul. *Culture, Medicine & Psychiatry*, 36(2), pp.264–285.

Boostani, D., Abdinia, S., & Anaraki, N. R. (2013). Women victims of self-immolation: A 'Grounded Theory" study in Iran. *Quality & Quantity*, 47(6), pp.3153–3165.

Campbell, E. A., & Guiao, I. Z. (2004). Muslim culture and female self-immolation: Implication for global women's health research and practice. *Health Care for Women International*, 25(9), pp.782–793.

Canetto, S. S. (1991). Gender roles, suicide attempts, and substance abuse. *Journal of Psychology*, 125(6), pp.605–620.

Canetto, S. S. (1992). Gender and suicide in the elderly. *Suicide and Life-Threatening Behavior*, 22(1), pp.80–97.

Canetto, S. S. (1992–1993). She died for love and he for glory: Gender myths of suicidal behavior. *Omega—Journal of Death and Dying*, 26(1), pp.1–17.

Canetto, S. S. (1997). Gender and suicidal behavior: Theories and evidence. In R. W. Maris, M. M. Silverman, & S. S. Canetto (eds.), *Review of Suicidology* (pp.138–167). New York: Guilford Press.

Canetto, S. S. (2008). Women and suicidal behavior: A cultural analysis. *American Journal of Orthopsychiatry*, 78(2), pp.259–266.

Canetto, S. S. (2009). Prevention of suicidal behavior in females: Opportunities and obstacles. In D. Wasserman & C. Wasserman (eds.), *The Oxford Textbook of Suicidology and Suicide Prevention* (pp.241–247). Oxford: Oxford University Press.

Canetto, S. S. (2015a). Suicidal ideation and behaviors in girls and women in the United States and Canada: Cultural and Intersectional Perspectives. In D. A. Lamis & N. J. Kaslow (eds.), *Advancing the Science of Suicidal Behavior: Understanding and Intervention* (pp.215–236). Hauppauge, NY: Nova Science.

Canetto, S. S. (2015b). Suicidal behavior among Muslim women: Patterns, pathways, meanings, and prevention. *Crisis: The Journal of Crisis Intervention and Suicide Prevention*, 36(6), pp.447–458.

Canetto, S. S. (2018). Women and human rights: Concepts, debates, progress and implications. In C. Travis & J. White (eds.), *APA Handbook on the Psychology of Women* (Volume II, pp.521–543). Washington, DC: American Psychological Association.

Canetto, S. S., & Lester, D. (1995). Women and suicidal behavior: Issues and dilemmas. In S. S. Canetto & D. Lester (eds.), *Women and Suicidal Behavior* (pp.3–8). New York: Springer.

Canetto, S. S., & Lester, D. (1998). Gender, culture and suicidal behavior. *Transcultural Psychiatry*, 35(2), pp.163–191.

Coskun, M., Zoroglu, S., & Ghaziuddin, N. (2012). Suicide rates among Turkish and American youth: A cross-cultural comparison. *Archives of Suicide Research*, 16(1), pp.59–72.

Dabbagh, N. T. (2004). Narrative expressions of despair under occupation. *Anthropology & Medicine*, 11(2), pp.201–220.

Dabbagh, N. (2012). Behind the statistics: The ethnography of suicide in Palestine. *Culture, Medicine, & Psychiatry*, 36(2), pp.285–305.

Devries, K., Watts, C., Yoshihama, M., Kiss, L., Schraiber, L. B., Deyessa, N., et al. (2011). Violence against women is strongly associated with suicide attempts: Evidence from the WHO Multi-Country study on women's health and domestic violence against women. *Social Science & Medicine*, 73(1), pp.79–86.

Devries, K. M., Mak, J. K., Bacchus, L. J., Child, J. C., Falder, G., Petzold, M., et al. (2013). Intimate partner violence and incident depressive symptoms and suicide attempts: A systematic review of longitudinal studies. *PLOS Medicine*, 10(5), Article Number: e1001439.

Devries, K. M., & Seguin, M. (2013). Violence against women and suicidality: Does violence cause suicidal behavior? In C. Garcia-Moreno & A. Riecher-Rössler (eds.), *Violence Against Women and Mental Health: Key Issues in Mental Health* (Vol. 178, pp.148–158). Basel: Karger.

Douki, S., Zineb, S. B., Nacef, F., & Halbreich, U. (2007). Women's mental health in the Muslim world: Cultural, religious, and social issues. *Journal of Affective Disorders*, 102(1–3), pp.177–189.
Durkheim, E. (1951). *Suicide: A Study in Sociology*. New York: Free Press. (Original work published in 1897).
Eltahawy, M. (2015). *Headscarves and Hymens: Why the Middle East Needs a Sexual Revolution*. New York: Farrar, Straus & Giroux.
Goren, S., Subasi, M., Tirasci, Y., & Ozen, S. (2004). Female suicides in Diyarbakir, Turkey. *Forensic Sciences*, 49(4), pp.796–798.
Groohi, B., Alaghehbandan, R., & Lari, A. R. (2002). Analysis of 1089 burn patients in province of Kurdistan, Iran. *Burns*, 28(6), pp.569–574.
Groohi, B., Rossignol, A. M., Barrero S. P., & Alaghehbandan, R. (2006). Suicidal behavior by burns among adolescents in Kurdistan, Iran: A social tragedy. *Crisis: The Journal of Crisis Intervention and Suicide Prevention*, 27(1), pp.16–21.
Haarr, R. N. (2010). Suicidality among battered women in Tajikistan. *Violence against Women*, 16(7), pp.764–788.
Hadi, A. (2005). Risk factors of violent death in rural Bangladesh. *Death Studies*, 29(6), pp.559–572.
Hanna, V. N., & Ahmad, A. (2013). Corrected and republished: Suicide in the Kurdistan region of Iraq, state of the art. *Nordic Journal of Psychiatry*, 67(2), pp.140–144.
Harel-Fisch, Y., Abdeen, Z., Walsh, S. D., Radwan, Q., & Fogel-Grinvald, H. (2012). Multiple risk behaviors and suicidal ideation and behavior among Israeli and Palestinian adolescents. *Social Science & Medicine*, 75(1), pp.98–108.
Harris, E. C., & Barraclough, B. (1997). Suicide as an outcome for mental disorders: A meta-analysis. *The British Journal of Psychiatry*, 170(3), pp.205–228.
Hekmat, A. (1997). *Women and the Koran: The Status of Women in Islam*. New York: Prometheus Books.
Hjelmeland, H., & Knizek, B. (2017). Suicide and mental disorders: A discourse of politics, power, and vested interests. *Death Studies* (Special Issue), 41(8), pp.481–492.
Insel, T. R., & Cuthbert, B. N. (2015). Brain disorders? Precisely. *Science*, 348 (6234), pp.499–500.
Jiang, H., Niu, L., Hahne, J., Hu, M., Fang, J., Shen, M., & Xiao, S. (2018). Changing of suicide rates in China, 2002–2015. *Journal of Affective Disorders*, 240, pp.165–170.
Joiner, T. E., Hom, M. A., Hagan, C. R., & Silva, C. (2016). Suicide as derangement of the self-sacrificial aspect of eusociality. *Psychological Review*, 123(3), pp.235–254.
Khan, M. M., Ahmed, A., & Khan, S. R. (2009). Female suicide rates in Ghizer, Pakistan. *Suicide and Life-Threatening Behavior*, 39(2), pp.227–230.
Khan, M. M., & Hyder, A. A. (2006). Suicides in the developing world: Case study from Pakistan. *Suicide and Life-Threatening Behavior*, 36(1), pp.76–81.
Khan, M. M., Naqvi, H., Thaver, D., & Prince, M. (2008). Epidemiology of suicide in Pakistan: Determining rates in six cities. *Archives of Suicide Research*, 12(2), pp.155–160.
Khan, M. M., & Reza, H. (1998). Gender differences in nonfatal suicidal behavior in Pakistan: Significance of sociocultural factors. *Suicide and Life-Threatening Behavior*, 28(1), pp.62–68.

Khan, M. M., & Reza, H. (2000). The pattern of suicide in Pakistan. *Crisis: The Journal of Crisis Intervention and Suicide Prevention*, 21(1), pp.31–35.

Khlat, M., & Courbage, Y. (1995). La mortalité et les causes de décés des Marocains en France 1979 á 1991. *Populations*, 50, pp.447–471.

Lari, A. R., Alaghenhbandan, R., Panjeshahin, M.-R., & Joghataei, M.-T. (2009). Suicidal behavior by burns in the province of Fars, Iran. *Crisis: The Journal of Crisis Intervention and Suicide Prevention*, 30(2), pp.98–101.

Lari, A. R., Joghataei M.-T., Adli, Y. R., Zadeh, Y. A., & Alaghenhbandan, R. (2007). Epidemiology of suicide by burns in the province of Isfahan, Iran. *Journal of Burn Care & Research*, 28(2), pp.307–311.

Mabrouk, A. R., Omar, A. N. M., Massoud, K., Sherif, M. M., & El Sayed, N. (1999). Suicide by burns: A tragic end. *Burns*, 25(4), pp.337–339.

Maghsoudi, H., Garadagi, A., Jafary, G. A., Azarmir, G., Aali, N., Karimian, B., et al. (2004). Women victims of self-inflicted burns in Tabriz, Iran. *Burns*, 30(3), pp.217–220.

Maghsoudi, H., Samnia, R., Garadaghi, A., & Kianvar, H. (2006). Burns in pregnancy. *Burns*, 32(2), pp.246–250.

Marecek, J. (2000). Resisting and remaking gender imperatives: Women's suicide as gendered protest in Sri Lanka. *International Journal of Psychology*, 35(3–4), p.36.

Motlagh, J. (2007, June 22). Self-immolation tragically frequent among Afghan women. *World Politics Review*. Retrieved from www.worldpoliticsreview.com/articles/873/self-immolation-tragically-frequent-among-afghan-women

Naved, R. T., & Akhtar, N. (2008). Spousal violence against women and suicidal ideation in Bangladesh. *Women's Health Issues*, 18(6), pp.442–452.

Nawa, F. (2002, July 26). They prefer death over abuse: Afghan women protesting with self-immolation. *San Francisco Chronicle*. Retrieved from www.sfgate.com/news/article/They-prefer-death-over-abuse-Afghan-women-2818734.php

Nazarzadeh, M., Bidel, Z., Ayubi, E., Asadollahi, K., Carson, K., & Sayehmiri, K. (2013). Determination of the social related factors of suicide in Iran: A systematic review and meta-analysis. *BMC Public Health*, 13(4). doi:10.1186/1471-2458-13-4

Niehaus, I. (2012). Gendered endings: Narratives of male and female suicides in the South African Lowveld. *Culture Medicine and Psychiatry*, 36(2), pp.327–347.

Okasha, A., & Okasha, T. (2009). Suicide and Islam. In D. Wasserman and C. Wasserman (eds.), *Oxford Textbook of Suicidology and Suicide Prevention: A Global Perspective* (pp.49–56). Oxford: Oxford University Press.

Oner, S., Yenilmez, C., Ayranci, U., Gunay, Y., & Ozdamar, K. (2007). Sexual differences in the completed suicides in Turkey. *European Psychiatry*, 22(4), pp.223–228.

Oquendo, M. A., & Baca-Garcia, E. (2014). Suicidal behavior disorder as a diagnostic entity in the DSM-5 classification system: advantages outweigh limitations. *World Psychiatry*, 13(2), pp.128–130.

Othman, N. (2011). Suicide by self-burning in Iraqi Kurdistan: Description and risk factors. *Archives of Suicide Research*, 15(3), pp.238–249.

Panjeshahin, M.-R., Lari, A. R., Talei, A.-R., Shamsnia, J., & Alaghehbandan, R. (2001). Epidemiology and mortality of burns in the South West of Iran. *Burns*, 27(3), pp.219–226.

Pritchard, C., & Amanullah, S. (2007). An analysis of suicide and undetermined deaths in 17 predominantly Islamic countries contrasted with the UK. *Psychological Medicine*, 37(3), pp.421–430.
The Qur'ān (1997). English edition revised and edited by Saheeh International. Jeddah: Abul-Qasim Publishing House.
Rad, F. M., Anvari, M. M., Ansarinejad, F., & Panaghi, L. (2012). Family function and social support in Iranian self-immolated women. *Burns*, 38(4), pp.556–561.
Raj, A., Gomez, F., & Silverman, J. G. (2008). Driven to a fiery death—The tragedy of self-immolation in Afghanistan. *The New England Journal of Medicine*, 358(21), pp.2201–2203.
Rasool, I. A., & Payton, J. L. (2014). Tongues of fire: Women's suicide and self-injury by burns in the Kurdistan Region of Iraq. *The Sociological Review*, 62, pp.237–254.
Rastegar A., Joghataei M. T., Adli, Y. R., Zadeh, Y. A., & Alaghehbandan, R. (2007). Epidemiology of suicide by burns in the province of Isfahan, Iran. *Journal of Burn Care & Research*, 28(2), pp.307–311.
Rezaeian, M. (2008). Islam and suicide: A short personal communication. *Omega: Journal of Death and Dying*, 58(1), pp.77–85.
Rezaeian, M. (2010). Suicide among young Middle Eastern Muslim females. *Crisis: The Journal of Crisis Intervention and Suicide Prevention*, 31(1), pp.36–42.
Rezaeian, M. (2013). Epidemiology of self-immolation. *Burns*, 39(1), pp.184–186.
Rezaeian, M. (2014a). Death by burning in Indian women. *Burns*, 40(8), pp.1816–1817.
Rezaeian, M. (2014b). Social campaigns are needed to stop any forms of self-immolation. *Burns*, 40(2), pp.356–357.
Rezaeian, M. (2015). Self-immolation in Afghan females. *Burns*, 41(3), pp.642–643.
Rezaeian, M. (2017a). The geographical belt of self-immolation. *Burns*, 43(5), pp.245–246.
Rezaeian, M. (2017b). Self-immolation in women: Addressing an urgent human crisis. *International Journal of High Risk Behavior and Addiction*, 6(1), e30976
Rezaeian, M. (in press). Does Durkheim's theory hold any truths for modern day self-immolation? A review on the literature.
Rezaie, L., Hosseini, S. A., Rassafiani, M., Najafi, F., Shakeri, J., & Khankeh, H. R. (2014). Why self-immolation? A qualitative exploration of the motives for attempting suicide by self-immolation. *Burns*, 40(2), pp.319–327.
Rezaie, L., Khazaie, H., Soleimani, A., & Schwebel, D. C. (2011). Is self-immolation a distinct method for suicide? A comparison of Iranian patients attempting suicide by self-immolation and by poisoning. *Burns*, 37(1), pp.159–163.
Rezaie, L., & Schwebel, D. C. (2012). An ecological approach to explain suicide by self-immolation among women in rural Iran. *Neurosciences*, 17(4), pp.309–313.
Saadat, M., Bahaoddini, A., Mohabatkar, H., & Noemani, K. (2004). High incidence of suicide by burning in Masjid-i-Sulaiman (southwest of Iran), a polluted area with natural sour gas leakage. *Burns*, 30(8), pp.829–832.
Saaiq, M., & Ashraf, B. (2016). The menace of self-immolation plaguing low income countries. *Burns*, 42(2), pp.472–473.

Sachedina, A. (2005). End-of-life: the Islamic view. *The Lancet*, 366(99487), pp.774–779.

Shahid, M., & Hyder, A. A. (2008). Deliberate self-harm and suicide: A review from Pakistan. *International Journal of Injury Control and Safety Promotion*, 15(4), pp.233–241.

Shahid, M., Khan, M. M., Khan, M. S., Jamal, Y., Badshah, A., & Rehmani, R. (2009). Deliberate self-harm in the emergency department: Experience from Karachi, Pakistan. *Crisis: The Journal of Crisis Intervention and Suicide Prevention*, 30(2), pp.85–89.

Skaff, J. M. (2013). Gender-based violence in the Middle-East: A review. In C. Garcia-Moreno & A. Riecher-Rössler (eds.), *Violence Against Women and Mental Health: Key Issues in Mental Health* (Vol. 178, pp.12–23). Basel: Karger.

Spehr, S., & Dixon, J. (2013). Protest suicide: A systematic model with heuristic archetypes. *Journal for the Theory of Social Behaviour*, 44(3), pp.368–388.

Syed, E. U., & Khan, M. M. (2008). Patterns of deliberate self-harm in young people in Karachi, Pakistan. *Crisis: The Journal of Crisis Intervention and Suicide Prevention*, 29(3), pp.159–163.

van Bergen, D. D., Eikelenboom, M., Smit, J. H., van de Looij-Jansen, P. M., & Saharso, S. (2010). Suicidal behavior and ethnicity of young females in Rotterdam, The Netherlands: Rates and risk factors. *Ethnicity and Health*, 15(5), pp.515–530.

van Bergen, D. D., Smit, J. H., van Balkom, A. J. L. M., & Saharso, S. (2009). Suicidal behavior of young immigrant women in the Netherlands. Can we use Durkheim's concept of 'fatalistic suicide' to explain their high incidence of attempted suicide? *Ethnic and Racial Studies*, 32(2), pp.302–322.

Van Orden, K. A., Cuckrowitz, K. C., Witte, T. K., & Joiner, T. E. (2012). Thwarted belongingness and perceived burdensomeness: Construct validity and psychometric properties of the Interpersonal Needs Questionnaire. *Psychological Assessment*, 24(1), pp.197–215.

Yasan A., Danis, R., Taman. L., Ozmen, S., & Ozkan, M. (2008). Socio-cultural features and sex profile of the individuals with serious suicide attempts in Southeastern Turkey: A one-year survey. *Suicide and Life-Threatening Behavior*, 38(4), pp.467–480.

Yusuf, H. R., Akhter, H. H., Rahman, M. H., Chowdhury, M. E., & Rochat, R. W. (2000). Injury-related deaths among women aged 10–50 in Bangladesh, 1996–1997. *The Lancet*, 355(9211), pp.1203–1204.

World Health Organization (2014). *Preventing Suicide: A Global Imperative*. Geneva: Author. Retrieved from apps.who.int/iris/bitstream/handle/10665/131056/9789241564779_eng.pdf?sequence=1

Zaidan, S. A. J., Burke, D. T., Dorvlo, A. S. S., Al-Naamani, A., Al-Suleimani, A., Al-Hussaini, A., et al. (2002). Deliberate self-poisoning in Oman. *Tropical Medicine and International Health*, 7(6), pp.549–556.

7 From Psychocentric Explanations to Social Troubles

Challenging Dominant Discourse on Suicide in Ghana

Joseph Osafo

The Mental Health Landscape and Suicidal Behaviour in Ghana

The WHO age-standardized suicide rate per 100,000 for Ghana from 2000 to 2015 has shown a consistent increase for both males (from 15.4 in 2000 to 17.8 in 2014) and females (from 3.6 in 2000 to 3.9 in 2014). The national suicide mortality rate is 6.9 compared to a regional estimate of 8.8% (WHO, 2015). Although these estimates are lower than neighbouring countries such as Togo, Benin, Cote D'Ivoire, Nigeria and Burkina Faso (WHO, 2015), the consistent increase in cases seems to indicate that suicide in Ghana is becoming a public mental health issue (Asante et al., 2017).

Some studies have examined the risks and reasons for suicidal behaviour among various groups of people: students (Asante et al., 2017), and lay persons in a community (Osafo et al., 2015) as well as in a hospital setting (Akotia et al., 2018). Recently, a qualitative psychological autopsy study illuminated how the lived experience of some men intersected with the broader social-cultural context of 'being a man' in Ghana to contribute to suicides (Andoh-Arthur et al., 2017). Other studies have examined general attitudes towards suicidal behaviour from various groups including psychology students (Osafo et al., 2011), health professionals (Osafo et al., 2012; Osafo et al., 2018), law enforcement fraternity such as judges, lawyers and police officers (Osafo et al., 2018), to help better understand the meanings of suicide in Ghana.

Suicidal behaviour is proscribed in Ghana and this is expressed through three of the most powerful social institutions: family, religious community, and the legal (Osafo, 2016). Suicidal behaviour represents a social injury; an act that is perceived to inflict irreparable damage on the social image of the family (Osafo et al., 2011). The fear of such social stigma creates tensions between attempt survivors and their families with dire consequences for the provision of help for victims (Asare-Doku, 2018; Osafo et al., 2015). Commitment to core religious beliefs fosters strong negative views on suicidal behaviour but on the other hand also facilitates a willingness to provide help for suicidal persons and their families (Akotia et al., 2014; Akotia et al., 2018; Osafo et al., 2011b).

Ghana is among several other African countries that have laws against attempted suicide and anyone who abets the commission of the act. According to Ghana's Criminal Code (1960, Act 29, section 57), 'whoever attempts to commit suicide shall be guilty of a misdemeanor.' An attempt survivor may therefore be at risk for criminal apprehension, prosecution and penalization (Adinkrah, 2016). There is some evidence of criminal prosecutions of attempt survivors in Ghana (Adinkrah, 2013). In recent times, however, there have been various calls to decriminalize attempted suicide in the country. Support for decriminalization has come from various groups including judges and lawyers, police, psychologists, and physicians (Osafo et al., 2018; Osafo et al., 2018). Various pressure groups such as the Centre for Suicide and Violence Research (CSVR), Mental Health Advocacy and Mental Health Authority in Ghana and other civil society groups have initiated a petition to seek to expunge this provision in the criminal code.

The government's budgetary allocation for mental health is woefully inadequate. Although there is a mental health policy (which is seeking to address mental health as a public health issue and also protect the rights of sufferers) in place as of 2013, it has yet to be implemented (WHO, 2015). There is a manpower crisis in the health sector. For example, some reports estimate that as of 2011, there were 1,177 (4.88/100,000) trained mental health staff, including only 19 (0.08/100,000) psychologists, and 18 (0.07/100,000) psychiatrists (Roberts, Mogan & Asare, 2014; WHO, 2014). It was estimated that up to 2.4 million people suffered from mental health problems, of which only 67,780 (2.8%) received treatment in 2011. In another report, about 21% of adult Ghanaians surveyed (n=5,391) were reported to have moderate or severe psychological distress accounting for a 7% loss of GDP (Canavan et al., 2013). One of Ghana's WHO Country Cooperation strategic priorities for health is to support the development of policies and plans for implementing interventions to prevent mental illnesses (WHO, 2018) but the continuing delay of implementing the Mental Health Act casts doubt on this strategy.

Reasons for Suicide: Existential Crisis or Mental Illness?

Explanations that locate the causal factors for suicide within the person, such as mental disorders and psychological difficulties (psychocentric perspectives), have come to dominate how the act is understood in Ghana. Accordingly, mental health researchers and workers have applied pressure on governments to increase resource allocation and improve mental health care service delivery in the country. The Chief Psychiatrist, for instance, is frequently heard on various media platforms drawing a strong link between mental illnesses and suicidality, often arguing for a linear link between depression and suicide (Ghanaweb, 2014). During the 2016 World Suicide Prevention Day commemoration, he reiterated this assertion that mental illness accounted for 95% of all suicide cases in the country (Ghanaweb, 2016). Attempts to understand the wider contexts of suicide, however, are also underway. Researchers at the Department of Psychology and the Centre for Suicide and Violence Research (CSVR) have been investigating sociocultural factors in an attempt to understand the reasons for suicidality. Their research has reported that reasons for the act in the Ghanaian context have included (but are not limited to) domestic abuse, faith crisis, loss of job, interpersonal difficulties, loss of face, social taunting, and lack of support (Akotia et al., 2018; Andoh-Arthur et al., 2017; Asare-Doku et al., 2017; Osafo et al., 2015). Gender variations in some of these reasons have been reported: for instance, women engaged in suicide because of patriarchal oppression, and crises in romantic relationships (Sefa-Dede & Canetto, 1992; Akotia et al., 2018), while among men the loss of masculinity, virility and economic control accounted for suicidality (Adinkrah, 2012; Andoh-Arthur et al., 2018). Various meanings of suicide that have thus emerged from such studies in the country include suicide as faith-failure, suicide as a social injury, suicide as a transgression, suicide as an escape from shame, and suicide as a reaction to adverse life circumstances.

The first large cross-sectional study involving more than 500 adults living in the Ghanaian capital, Accra, showed that the biggest indicators of risk for suicidality were poverty, lack of parental warmth, family conflict, and school related discord, much more so than depression (ORID, 2016). In another study involving more than 1900 secondary students, being bullied, physically attacked, involved in a physical fight and food insecurity predicted suicidal ideation (18.2%), plans (22.5%) and attempt (22.2%) along with anxiety (Oppong Asante et al., 2017). In other words, the oft-quoted '90% of people who die by suicide have a mental illness' statistic in suicidology does not resonate with research findings in Ghana. I do not dispute the fact that mental disorders such as anxiety and depression can play a role in the complex pathways of suicidality, but, arguably, the reasons for the act within the socio-cultural context of Ghana reflect more existential issues rather than mental disorders. Qualitative research seems to consistently point to these conclusions (e.g. Hjelmeland & Knizek, 2016), but often such reports are dismissed as unscientific and polemical (Hjelmeland & Knizek, 2017).

Existential Issues as Social Injustice

My point of departure in this piece rests on looking at suicide as an existential issue. I shall define existential issues as circumstances in life – personal, social, economic, political – which challenge the meaning of worthwhile living, creating distress for a person, who as a result might seek death as a better alternative than undignified living. This view resonates with the narratives of suicide from the lived experiences of suicide attempt survivors (Fitzpatrick, 2016; Sanati, 2009). My argument is that there are important social and structural factors involved in suicidality which arise from social, economic, and political contexts. These factors draw context and culture into the understanding of the complexity of suicide and suicidality. Although generally acknowledged, research findings providing strong evidence of the entanglements of culture and suicidality have not received the same recognition as traditional psychological and psychiatric framings of the issue (Hjelmeland & Knizek, 2017). I concur with others that suicidal behaviour cannot be stripped of contexts, and any meaningful and sensitive research and interventions which take this into account will better serve the development of suicidology than it currently appears (Boldt, 1989; Colucci & Lester, 2012).

Psychological models have tended to use concepts and terms such as hopelessness, helplessness or psychache, perceived burdensomeness, or thwarted belongingness in explaining suicide (Joiner, 2005; Joiner et al., 2016; Schlimme, 2018), and psychiatric models focus on mental disorders (Insel & Cuthbert, 2015). Such views explore the interiorities of an individual and implicate psychocentric factors as the primary cause for suicide. In this regard, structural elements such as social, political, and economic factors affecting health and wellbeing are not given sufficient attention. I am not asserting that individual level factors are irrelevant, rather that attention to such micro level elements obscures macro-level factors in Ghana. I would argue that what is killing people in Ghana by suicide are not just mental disorders or psychological problems, but that is the core epistemic claim in mainstream suicidology.

Research in other settings has pointed to the role of larger structural factors. For example, in China, several studies have emphasized the role of socio-political factors in suicide (e.g., Ji et al., 2001; Lee & Kleinman, 2003; Pearson & Liu, 2002; Zou et al., 2003). Wu Fei (2009) argues that the Chinese perspective on suicide is that the act is not just psychocentric but also political, and asserted that 'After a long period of fieldwork on suicide, I have come to understand suicide from the perspective of justice' (Wu, 2009, p. 6). Generally, strong evidence from low and middle-income countries (LMICs) show positive associations between suicide and larger social difficulties such as poverty (i.e. worse economic status, diminished wealth, and unemployment) (Iemmi et al., 2016). In Uganda for instance, social, cultural and political factors such as loss of masculinity for men and a protestation against the oppression of hegemonic masculinity for women are reasons for suicide in Northern Uganda (Kizza et al., 2012). Similarly, Canetto (2015) has argued that suicide is better understood from a human rights perspective rather than from a traditional biomedical one in Islamic settings, where the act reflects more of a desperate rebellion against, or escape from, the suffocating restrictions and abuse women have to endure within their families and societies. In fact, this sociocentric narrative is not only common in the global South but also in the West.

For instance, following the 2007–2008 financial crisis in the UK there was an increase in the number of people who killed themselves, with many of these deaths linked to welfare cuts and austerity measures (Mills, 2018). In the next section I provide examples from Ghana to further illustrate the relationship between social factors, questions of justice and suicide.

Injustice, Suicide and the Law in Ghana

In Africa (and Ghana in particular) it can be seen clearly that existential issues can create extreme difficulties for people (Akyeampong, 2015). The destitution spreading across Africa provides insights into reasons for suicide. Wars and the attendant excesses of genocide, rape, child trafficking, disease, poor mental health services and a host of social ills create daily distress across the continent (Akyeampong, 2015; Jacob et al., 2007). In Ghana reports of homelessness and unemployment have been observed to create psychological stressors and distress (e.g., Canavan et al., 2013; De-Graft Aikins & Ofori-Atta, 2007).

In the following two cases, I shall tease out the social injustices meted out to suicide attempt survivors whose action were driven by an unbearable life of distress. These cases are gleaned from our several community education programs and gatekeeper training on suicide prevention for the past 10 years. These cases reflect two key vulnerable groups: children and ex-convicts.

Case 1

> *During a training workshop for more than 240 judges on a wide range of mental health related issues including suicide and why it should be decriminalized, a magistrate narrated her experience of the social difficulties that push some homeless children on the streets in Ghana to engage in the act. She indicated that two teenagers were arraigned before her court and the prosecutor prayed that the judge should (in accordance with the law that criminalizes attempted suicide) jail these two girls. The judge observed that they looked frail and famished. She enquired from them the reason for their actions and they indicated that they were from the Northern part of the country and were engaged as 'kayaye' (women head porters) but for the past few days they have not made any sales to have decent meals. They have been going hungry for some days and so decided to end it all. The judge told the prosecutor to follow the pathway of referral since there are laws on child protection as well as provision for diverting criminal cases with suspected mental health underpinnings. She asked the prosecutor to refer the young ladies to the social welfare and indicated that she (the magistrate) has a strong conviction that most suicides of children (or young people) in Ghana arise from several forms of social distress.*

The hope of society and humanity rests on children and yet in most children–dominated nations such as in Africa, the reality on the ground is that children are not a core feature in our development agenda (Tefera, 2015). The phenomenon of 'streetism' is a canker in Africa and although several conventions on child rights aimed at protecting and aiding child survival have been ratified in Africa (and Ghana), there continues to be implementation challenges (Kuyini, 2009; UNICEF, 2012). From wars to infectious diseases such as HIV/AIDS, the lives of children in Africa have been reduced to squalor and many have found their way into the streets (Oppong Asante, 2016; UNICEF, 2012). In the literature on street children, two main groups can be identified: those who have a home but are pushed onto the streets as a result of lack of basic needs such as food and those who were born on the street by street mothers (Oppong Asante, 2016). The recent influx of refugees into the country has increased this phenomenon and appears to be adding a third group: refugee-based street children. In 2009, a collaborative project by Department of Social Welfare (DSW) in Ghana, *Ricerca e Cooperazione* (RC), an Italian NGO, Catholic Action for Street Children (CAS) and Street Girls Aid (S.AID) reported that there were 61,492 streets children in Accra and its environs. The majority (about 40%) of these children are from the Northern belt. Streetism is widespread in Ghana and the factors leading to this are well documented (Anarfi, 1997; Mizen & Ofosu-Kusi, 2010; Oduro, 2012; Oppong Asante 2015; Wutoh, 2006). They often lack basic human needs such as access to food, clothing, education and health facilities (Orme Seipel, 2007). Most children in Ghana engage in some economic activities to support their parents and thus are exposed to several stressors. In fact, the Ghana S Survey report (2014) indicated that 22.7% of boys and 20.8% of girls in rural and urban Ghana are involved in economic activities. Further, the percentage of urban children in child labour was 12.4% and that of rural areas was 30.2% (Adonteng-Kissi, 2018), with cultural practices in Ghana impacting on the international and constitutional human rights of children.

The law enforcement agent in the case presented above was very keen on the full application of the anti-suicide law against such vulnerable population. The biggest question is what is the most important thing to do when a person in authority (e.g. police officer) comes across a child or adolescent who is suicidal? The involvement of the police with citizens experiencing mental health problems, and their role in diversion and the provision of community mental health services, have been extensively discussed elsewhere (see Osafo et al., 2017). It is important, however, to indicate that their role in protection and arrests is prioritized over the provision of supportive interventions to vulnerable people. This is a real gap that needs to be addressed through gatekeeper training in the country.

Ghana is recording increasing numbers of suicidal and self-harming behaviours among adolescents in schools in the country. For example, one in five school children (N=1723) in Accra have self-harmed

(Quarshie, 2018). The reasons cited include suppressing personal pain and self-distressing thoughts, to make someone change their mind, to get help from others, to communicate personal pain. This should be a clarion call for strengthening social intervention and safety nets to address the various developmental, mental and social challenges that may conspire to compromise young people's health. In the global mental health discourse, teen mental health is a key priority area for the national developmental agenda. It is my firmest conviction that any society that is keen on criminalizing the behaviours of their youth rather than providing support systems to harness their potential and help them survive the vicissitudes of their developmental trajectory has failed its social obligation.

Case 2

> *A man approaching middle age visited our Centre (CSVR) and narrated his story to us about how he was maltreated by another person who colluded with a judge, and he ended up in prison where he spent four years. He returned from prison without a job and a sick mother to take care of. When the economic burden of having to fend for himself and mother became unbearable, he attempted suicide. He survived this but was being pursued by the police for an arrest. He had still not given up plans for another attempt. In one of the conversations at our Centre he bemoaned thus, 'of what value is a man's life without a job?' The Centre took a social interventionist approach where a needs assessment was conducted, and funds were raised to help him restructure his business. In six months, he has set up the business, and added another one. He sent a message to the Centre during one of our usual check-ups on how our clientele are faring and indicated that, 'Now by the grace of God I have 4,300 GHC (equiv: about 1,000 USD) in my account. The shoe business is also moving on well. If only I can smile today, it is all because of you. I just don't know how to thank you' (CSVR Client001).*

In this case an ex-convict became suicidal following a loss of what provides meaning to life, such as employment or economic support. He already bemoaned the lack of justice for which he was incarcerated, and, in addition, he had lost his job. This circumstance of joblessness could be perceived by him as an existential threat. Paradoxically, his jobless state did not prompt the attention of anyone, but as soon as he attempted suicide the law was unleashed in full force to penalize him. This constitutes an injustice. The daily struggles and difficulties in livelihoods in sub-Saharan Africa is a growing reality as the continent has not been able to lift her populations out of poverty. Close to 50% of Sub-Saharan Africans are reported to be struggling with poverty and more struggle with absolute poverty (Akanle & Adésìnà, 2018). The discourse on development also presents a fundamental dimension of social inequality and struggles for social justice (Akintunde & Omobowale, 2018); it is antithetical for a society to demand moral commitments from its members and without creating the enabling environment to make such commitments possible. Worst of all is to punish those made vulnerable by the same society. Stated plainly, some groups of people become suicidal because of various social distresses and they are punished for experiencing difficulties in living. The widespread poverty and unemployment in sub-Saharan Africa make government interventions to alleviate abject poverty a sine qua non to improving mental health in this context (Akyeampong, Hill & Kleinman, 2015; Omomowo, 2018). Unfortunately, this has not been the focus of many sub-Saharan African governments. Africa bears a significant proportion of the global burden of chronic diseases (Zondi, 2010) and there is a projection that these will increase by 2020. Such chronic diseases have resulted from various challenges such as natural disasters, poor economic performance and military conflicts (Akyeampong, Hill & Kleinman, 2015; Anaemene, 2018). Against this backdrop, social and humanitarian crises could be high in this context and thus makes it myopic and irrational for African societies to punish its citizens who become suicidal following the experience of various distresses.

The discourse on the legal status of suicide has been extensively studied. In a recent review of the laws of 192 countries, 142 have laws and regulations that stipulate punishments, including jail sentences, for assisting or encouraging suicidal behaviour (Mishara & Weisstub, 2016). Ghana is among the many countries in Africa and the world that penalize attempt survivors. The offender could go to jail for about three years or suffer hefty fines (Adinkrah, 2013). The arguments for criminalization of suicide attempts in the country include deterrence, retribution, and safety/health concerns (Hjelmeland et al., 2013; Osafo et al., 2018a; Osafo et al., 2018b). The code remains although sustained advocacy for decriminalization have been mounted against it since 2008 (Osafo et al., 2017). Interest in decriminalization is widening with evidence of support from the judiciary, the police and health professionals (Osafo et al., 2018a; Osafo et al., 2018b; Osafo et al., 2018c). Research evidence does not support the preventative effect of the threat of incarceration and thus it has become one of the prime targets for the International Association for Suicide Prevention (IASP) and the World Health Orgainzation (WHO) to encourage nations to decriminalize (Arensman, 2017; Mishara & Weisstub, 2016). Thus, in the wisdom of such global organizations and I, the rationale for penalization cannot be justified and constitutes one of the gravest social injustices against suicide attempt survivors. When a suicide attempt survivor is criminalized, two forms of messages are sent out: first, we privatize the person's crisis and thereby look for causes within the person's interiority. Second, we absolve the states' liability and obscure other social issues accounting for the victim's distress.

As Reynolds (2016) argues, 'a social justice frame requires us to always examine the social context to understand events' (p. 183).

Beyond Psychocentric Advocacy to Sociocentric Intervention Schemes

Research in Ghana continues to show the extensive role played by social stress, distress and discomfort in suicidality more than medical and personal factors. Precipitants and reasons for suicide have included financial difficulties, lack of support, abandonment, shame, existential struggles and others (Akotia et al., 2018; Osafo et al., 2015). Yet advocacy to improve mental health services in Ghana has biomedicalized the discourse, narrowed the range of options and centred on the competent role of health professionals and government's financing of essential medications for the mentally ill (Osafo et al., 2017). Improving psychiatric services is good, but not sufficient. In fact, there are indications that suicide is higher in countries with better mental health services (Rajkumar et al., 2013). This accounts for the critical need to elevate the discourse on suicide intervention in Ghana beyond improving mental health services. As Hjelmeland and Knizek (2017) assert, 'Psychiatry does have a role to play in suicide prevention, but its importance should be weighed alongside other perspectives and approaches' (p. 489).

The poor economic performance in sub-Saharan countries continues to create poverty at the grassroots level (Dulani et al., 2013). Currently, the international poverty lines are set at $1.90 and $3.10 a day for extreme poverty and poverty respectively at 2011 PPP (World Bank, 2016). In Ghana, the minimum wage for 2018 was pegged at 9.68 Ghana Cedis (a little over 2 USD). In 2008, the Government of Ghana rolled out the Implementation of Livelihood Empowerment against Poverty (LEAP) involving a cash transfer to extremely poor households in rural communities with the overall expectation that it will transform the livelihoods of the extremely poor in rural communities in Ghana (Debrah, 2013). Although LEAP has been found to positively help the rural poor, the capacity to alleviate poverty still remains an expectation (Debrah, 2013). Rapid modernization, urbanization and migration in recent times (Cobbinah & Niminga-Beka, 2017) have have led to changes in the family structure, living arrangements, unemployment, and poverty in Ghana (Baah-Boateng, 2013; Nukunya, 2003). These may constitute significant social stressors contributing to poor lifestyles and ultimately poor health (Agyei-Mensah & de-Graft Aikins, 2010). People's coping resources might be compromised, or they may cope poorly and thus require much more structural support than the provision of medications and psychotherapeutic support systems. If poverty affects people's mental health, then their well-being could be placed at the centre of the political economy, and the injustice of seeing suicide only as an issue of individual mental illness could be ended.

Civil Society Groups, Advocacy Realignment and Policy Formulation

Advocacy needs to be extensive and should call on governments to reduce poverty and create safety nets to protect people who experience distresses which threaten survival. Improvement in mental health provision needs to focus on more than public education on how to refer those in crisis to professionals. In fact, the manpower crisis and meagre resources for mental health services cannot keep pace with the huge demand for caregiving which may follow from such public education. The preceding point thus brings into sharp focus the supportive role civil society and Non-Governmental Organisations (NGOs) can play in bridging the demand and supply gap in the mental healthcare in Ghana. Of note, NGOs in LMICs (including Ghana) have over the years engaged with the mental health sector through advocacy, activism, awareness creation, care provision, or research on different mental health related issues, such as academic-related stress, mental disorders, suicide, autism, epilepsy among others (Das & Chakraborty, 2006; Upadhaya et al., 2014). The successes of the NGOs in the above areas have largely resulted from the fact that they have easy access to local communities, have better understanding of the local contexts, have quick and flexible response mechanism and access to marginalized populations and under-served areas (Upadhaya et al., 2014). From the above, the critical role of NGOs in uncovering local particularities of mental health problems which have sociocentric underpinnings cannot be overemphasized. Particularly, given the agenda for increased deinstitutionalisation of mental health care towards a more community-centred care system, as captured in the Mental Health Gap Action Programme (mhGAP) (WHO, 2008), the needs of marginalized and under-served populations could well be identified and addressed through the activities of such NGOs. The corollary will be a health care system which not only reaches marginalized groups through partnership with non-governmental actors, but also one that valorizes social justice and human right values of the populations it serves.

A social justice and human rights orientated mental health care system would, for instance, prioritize stigma reduction, ensure improved access, affordability, universal coverage, and support for marginalized groups, as well as scaling up government led social interventionist programmes to cover the most vulnerable in society (Sen, 2017). Unfortunately, the largely institutionalized nature of the mental health sector in Ghana, coupled with its inherent resource constraints, manpower deficit, the lack of knowledge of local context, and ineffective collaboration with NGOs, remains a key challenge towards a sociocentric approach to mental health and suicide prevention.

The aforesaid challenges notwithstanding, the activities of more than a dozen NGOs in the mental health sector in Ghana, covering mostly areas where poverty is endemic, continue to give some glimmer of hope.

For example, the operations of Basic needs and Mind Freedom and a few other NGOs, with support from their international partners, have human rights and social justice anchoring, which has seen them commit to meeting the mental health needs, as well as improving general psychosocial conditions, of vulnerable persons in remote areas. Achieving success from such perspectives requires a kind of collaboration where governmental agencies show willingness to leverage on and utilize locally relevant information obtained by NGOs on the situational and experiential needs of local peoples. Further, it requires continuous training and the development of appropriate skills in such community-based NGOs to enable them to deliver efficient health care at the local level. Such an arrangement would be in keeping with the task shifting orientation in mental health care which is noted to be of critical importance in resource-poor settings (Patel, 2012). Shifting tasks in such settings with highly trained non-governmental actors is likely to promote a sociocentric approach to mental health and suicide prevention programmes in resource-poor settings as has recently been advocated in Ghana (Agyapong, Osei, Farren, & Mcauliffe, 2015)

Concluding Remarks

Psychocentric approaches to suicide and suicidality relegate the contribution of rising social stressors and the role they play in poor mental health functioning in contemporary Ghanaian society, and this focus on psychocentric interventions at the expense of structural ones limits the range of prevention responses. As Hjelmeland and Knizek (2017) argue, the continuing dominance of biomedical research in suicidology limits the extent to which 'established truths' in the field can be questioned. In Ghana, such a situation weakens broader advocacy in suicide prevention and narrows the range of participation to only mental health workers (Osafo et al., 2017).

The medicalization of human problems or the human condition leaves no room to interrogate social difficulties and how they contribute to distress and eventually poor mental health in Ghana. Strong indications in the psychological literature in Ghana are pointing towards distress in living and the corollary of mental distress/illness. Thus, treating mental illness and not addressing the social challenges that produce the so-called 'immutable truth' implicating mental illnesses as major risks for suicidality in Ghana is an exercise in futility. For example, it is unfathomable to 'treat suicide with a pill' when the suicidal person says, 'I have no job and so I feel useless'. The vicious cycle of poverty and mental distress in Africa will persist until African governments and mental health researchers shift from the psychocentric approach to the vigorous pursuit of improving the poor living conditions which affect health in general and mental health in particular.

Structural transformations that will ameliorate human problems should receive serious considerations as part of the package in improving mental health of Ghanaians. Pursuing a psychocentric agenda by advocating for better mental health care services, training more health workers, improving suicide risk assessment competences are all important goals but are skewed and do not facilitate holistic and fruitful discussions on suicide prevention. As Vikki Reynolds argues;

> Suicide is not something that happens to one person, and it is not something that one person does. Nobody simply kills themselves. Events occur in context, and . . . we have to structure into our analysis of a person's death the context of social injustice in which they lived.
>
> (2016; p. 170)

There is no doubt that Africa is a continent whose mental illness load keeps increasing as a result of various social troubles. However, the adoption of psychocentric approaches without a corresponding commitment to improving people's living conditions will not yield good results. It may appear logical and feasible but it lacks the sense of a sustainable developmental agenda.

The psychocentric views and approaches can co-exist with the sociocentric. I am not asserting an exclusionist agenda. I am arguing for a broader perspective that creates synergy more than a silo. This perspective resonates with the perspective of Giddens (1965) on suicide expressed half a century ago:

> To admit that psychology can properly contribute to the analysis of suicide does not mean that suicide, in certain aspects – particularly as a demographic phenomenon – cannot be studied sociologically; conversely, to accept that social factors play a role in the aetiology of suicide does not entail the exclusion of other factors as having causative forces.
>
> (p. 10)

In conclusion, suicidality in Ghana is not necessarily solely the result of mental illness. Social, economic, and political factors may lead to distress and eventually suicide. Suicidology is at its embryonic stage in Ghana, and we shall effectively serve the field and people better if we broaden the discourse on mental health improvement strategies to include social and structural interventions in the country.

References

Adinkrah, M. (2012). Better dead than dishonored: Masculinity and male suicidal behavior in contemporary Ghana. *Social Science & Medicine*, 74(4), 474–481.

Adinkrah, M. (2013). Criminal prosecution of suicide attempt survivors in Ghana. *International Journal of Offender Therapy and Comparative Criminology*, *57*(12), 1477–1497.

Adinkrah, M. (2016). Anti-suicide laws in nine African countries: Criminalization, prosecution and penalization. *African Journal of Criminology & Justice Studies*, *9*(1), 279–292.

Adonteng-Kissi, O. (2018). Parental perceptions of child labour and human rights: A comparative study of rural and urban Ghana. *Child Abuse & Neglect*, *84*, 34–44.

Agyapong, V. O., Osei, A., Farren, C. K., & Mcauliffe, E. (2015). Task shifting of mental care services in Ghana: Ease of referral, perception and concerns of stakeholders about quality of care. *International Journal for Quality in Health Care*, *27*(5), 377–383.

Agyei-Mensah, S., & de-Graft Aikins, A. (2010). Epidemiological transition and the double burden of disease in Accra, Ghana. *Journal of Urban Health: Bulletin of the New York Academy of Medicine*, *87*(5), 879–897.

Akanle, O., & Adésìnà, J. O. (2018). Introduction: The Development of Africa: Issues, Diagnoses and Prognoses. In *The Development of Africa* (pp. 1–8). Cham: Springer.

Akintunde, A. A., & Omobowale, A. O. (2018). Conceptualizing and Framing Realities of Africa's Development. In *The Development of Africa* (pp. 9–28). Cham: Springer.

Akotia, C. S., Knizek, B. L., Kinyanda, E., & Hjelmeland, H. (2014). "I have sinned": Understanding the role of religion in the experiences of suicide attempters in Ghana. *Mental Health, Religion & Culture*, *17*(5), 437–448.

Akotia, C., Hjelmeland, H., Knizek, B. L., Kinyanda, E., & Osafo, J. (2018). Reasons for attempting suicide: An exploratory study in Ghana. *Transcultural Psychiatry*, *56*(1), 233–249.

Akyeampong, E. (2015). A Historical Overview of Psychiatry in Africa. In *The Culture of Mental Illness and Psychiatric Practice in Africa* (pp. 24–49). Bloomington: Indiana University Press.

Akyeampong, E., Hill, A. G., & Kleinman, A. M. (Eds.). (2015). *The Culture of Mental Illness and Psychiatric Practice in Africa*. Bloomington: Indiana University Press.

Anaemene, B. (2018). Health and Diseases in Africa. In *The Development of Africa* (pp. 207–226). Cham: Springer.

Anarfi, J. K. (1997). Vulnerability to sexually transmitted disease: Street children in Accra. *Health Transition Review, 7*(supplement), 281–306.

Andoh-Arthur, J., Knizek, B. L., Osafo, J., & Hjelmeland, H. (2018). Suicide among men in Ghana: The burden of masculinity. *Death Studies*, *42*(10), 658–666.

Arensman, E. (2017). Suicide prevention in an international context. *Crisis*, *38*(1), 1–6.

Asante, K. O., Kugbey, N., Osafo, J., Quarshie, E. N. B., & Sarfo, J. O. (2017). The prevalence and correlates of suicidal behaviours (ideation, plan and attempt) among adolescents in senior high schools in Ghana. *SSM-Population Health*, *3*, 427–434.

Baah-Boateng, W. (2013). Determinants of unemployment in Ghana. *African Development Review*, *25*(4), 385–399.

Canavan, M. E., Sipsma, H. L., Adhvaryu, A., Ofori-Atta, A., Jack, H., Udry, C., . . . & Bradley, E. H. (2013). Psychological distress in Ghana: Associations with employment and lost productivity. *International Journal of Mental Health Systems*, 7(1), 9. doi:10.1186/1752-4458-7-9

Canetto, S. S. (2015). Suicidal behaviors among Muslim women. Patterns, pathways, meanings, and prevention. *Crisis*, *36*(6), 447–458.

Cobbinah, P. B., & Niminga-Beka, R. (2017). Urbanisation in Ghana: Residential land use under siege in Kumasi central. *Cities*, *60*, 388–401.

Das, A. K., & Chakraborty, S. (2006). Role of NGOs and voluntary Societies in Mental Healthcare in West Bengal: A critical appraisal. In *Emerging Health Challenges and the Response of Indian Healthcare System*. Centre de Science Humaines and Delhi School of Economics. Retrieved June 21, 2011, from https://impactstory.org/AnupKumarDas/product/3iezvuc7ngdgqntw3oztdqs8

Debrah, E. (2013). Alleviating poverty in Ghana: the case of livelihood empowerment against poverty (LEAP). *Africa Today*, *59*(4), 41–67.

De-Graft Aikins, A., & Ofori-Atta, A. L. (2007). Homelessness and mental health in Ghana: Everyday experiences of Accra's migrant squatters. *Journal of Health Psychology*, *12*(5), 761–778.

Fitzpatrick, S. J. (2016). Stories of suicide and social justice. *Philosophy, Psychiatry, & Psychology*, *23*(3), 285–287.

Ghanaweb. (2014, August 27). Suicide is a disease not a crime. Retrieved from www.ghanaweb.com/GhanaHomePage/NewsArchive/Suicide-is-a-disease-not-a-crime-Dr-Akwasi-Osei-323014

Ghanaweb. (2016, September 13). Decriminalize suicide—chief psychiatrist. Retrieved from www.ghanaweb.com/GhanaHomePage/health/Decriminalise-suicide-Chief-Psychiatrist-469408

Giddens, A. (1965). The suicide problem in French sociology. *The British Journal of Sociology*, *16*(1), 3–18.

Insel, T. R., & Cuthbert, B. N. (2015). Brain disorders? Precisely. *Science*, *348*(6234), 499–500.

Hjelmeland, H., & Knizek, B. L. (2016). Qualitative evidence in suicide: Findings from qualitative psychological autopsy studies. In K. Olson, R. A. Young, & I. Z. Schultz (Eds.), *Handbook of Qualitative Health Research for Evidence-based Practice* (pp. 355–371). New York: Springer Science and Business Media.

Hjelmeland, H., & Knizek, B. L. (2017). Suicide and mental disorders: a discourse of politics, power, and vested interests. *Death Studies*, *41*(8), 481–492.

Jacob, K. S., Sharan, P., Mirza, I., Garrido-Cumbrera, M., Seedat, S., Mari, J. J., . . . & Saxena, S. (2007). Mental health systems in countries: where are we now? *The Lancet*, *370*(9592), 1061–1077.

Ji, J., Kleinman, A., & Becker, A. E. (2001). Suicide in contemporary China: a review of China's distinctive suicide demographics in their sociocultural context. *Harvard Review of Psychiatry*, *9*(1), 1–12.

Joiner, T. (2005). *Why People Die by Suicide*. Cambridge, MA: Harvard University Press.

Joiner, T. E., Hom, M. A., Hagan, C. R., & Silva, C. (2016). Suicide as a derangement of the self-sacrificial aspect of eusociality. *Psychological Review*, *123*(3), 235–254.

Kizza, D., Knizek, B. L., Kinyanda, E., & Hjelmeland, H. (2012). Men in despair: A qualitative psychological autopsy study of suicide in Northern Uganda. *Transcultural Psychiatry*, *49*(5), 696–717.

Kuyini, A. B., & Mahama, F. K. (2009). Implementing child rights and protection law in Ghana: Case study. Retrieved April 29 (2009): http://challengingheights.org/wp-content/uploads

Lee, S., & Kleinman, A. (2003). Suicide as Resistance in Chinese Society. In E. Perry (ed.), *Chinese Society* (pp. 294–317. London: Routledge.

Mills, C. (2018). "Dead people don't claim": A psycho-political autopsy of UK austerity suicides. *Critical Social Policy*, *38*(2), 302–322.

Mishara, B. L., & Weisstub, D. N. (2016). The legal status of suicide: A global review. *International journal of law and psychiatry*, *44*, 54–74.

Mizen, P., & Ofosu-Kusi, Y. (2010). Asking, giving, receiving:friendship as survival strategy among Accra's street children. *Childhood*, *17*(4), 441–454.

Oduro, G. Y. (2012). 'Children of the street': Sexual citizenship and the unprotected lives of Ghanaian street youth. *Comparative Education*, *48*(1), 41–56

Omomowo, K. E. (2018). Poverty in Africa. In *The Development of Africa* (pp. 69–94). Cham: Springer.

Oppong Asante, K. (2016). Street children and adolescents in Ghana: A qualitative study of trajectory and behavioural experiences of homelessness. *Global Social Welfare*, *3*(1), 33–43.

Osafo, J., Akotia, C. S., Andoh-Arthur, J., & Quarshie, E. N. B. (2015). Attempted suicide in Ghana: Motivation, stigma, and coping. *Death Studies*, *39*(5), 274–280.

Osafo, J., Akotia, C. S., Andoh-Arthur, J., Boakye, K. E., & NB Quarshie, E. (2018). "We now have a patient and not a criminal": An exploratory study of judges and lawyers' views on suicide attempters and the law in Ghana. *International Journal of Offender Therapy and Comparative Criminology*, *62*(6), 1488–1508.

Patel, V. (2012). Mental Health for All, by All: Ted Global. Accessed 23.09.2018 from www.youtube.com/watch?v=gS-p4Piggy8

Pearson, V., & Liu, M. (2002). Ling's death: An ethnography of a Chinese woman's suicide. *Suicide and Life-Threatening Behavior*, *32*(4), 347–358.

Reynolds, V. (2016). Hate kills: A social justice response to suicide. In J White, I Marsh, M.J. Kral and J. Morris (eds.) *Critical suicidology: Transforming Suicide Research and Prevention for the 21st Century*. Vancouver: UBC Press, 169–187.

Sanati, A. (2009). Does suicide always indicate a mental illness? *London Journal of Primary Care*, *2*(2), 93–94.

Schlimme, J. E. (2018). A Phenomenological Approach to Suicidal Mental Life. In Pompili, M. (ed.), *Phenomenology of Suicide* (pp. 31–37). Cham: Springer Nature.

Tefera, B. (2015). The situation of street children in selected cities of South Sudan: Magnitude, causes, and effects. *Eastern Africa Social Science Research Review*, *31*(1), 63–87.

United Nations Children's Fund (UNICEF). (2012). *The State of the World's Children 2012: Children in an Urban World*. New York: Author.

Upadhaya, N., Luitel, N. P., Koirala, S., Adhikari, R. P. et al. (2014). The role of mental health and psychosocial support in governmental organizations: reflections from post conflict Nepal. *Interventions*, *12*(1), 113–128.

World Health Organization. (2015). Global Health Observatory data repository. Geneva: World Health Organization.

World Health Organization. (2008). MhGAP: Mental Health Gap Action Programme: Scaling up care for Mental, Neurological, and Substance Use Disorder. Geneva: Word Health Organization.

World Health Organization. (2018). *WHO country cooperation strategy at a glance: Ghana* (No. WHO/CCU/18.02/Ghana). Geneva: World Health Organization.

Wu, F. (2009). *Suicide and Justice: A Chinese perspective*. New York: Routledge.

Wutoh, A. K., Kumoji, E. K., Xue, Z., Campusano, G., Wutoh, R. D., & Ofosu, J. R. (2006). HIV knowledge and sexual risks behaviours of street children in Takoradi, Ghana. *AIDS and Behaviour*, *10*(2), 209–215.

Zou, S. H., Zhang, Y. L., & Dang, H. H. (2003). Association between domestic violence and suicide in patients with depression. *Chinese Journal of Psychiatry*, *36*(4), 238–241.

Part III

8 I Am a Suicide Waiting to Happen
Reframing Self-Completed Murder and Death

Bee Scherer

Introduction: The Social Justice Turn

As an intersectional, queer-(trans)feminist thinker, I maintain that the chaotic complexity of all intersectional identity facets—including sex, gender identity, sexuality, dis/variability, neurodiversity, race, ethnicity, cultural traditions & religious beliefs; age group, class, socio-economic status, legal status etc.—constitute the shifting and fluid mosaic of our identity negotiations within societal contexts in the tension of 'equal—unequal', 'just—unjust' social participation and opportunities. When we look at the systemic failings of our societies to provide a nurturing and inspiring context for the thriving of our embodied identity performances, the unique intersectional cocktail behind each individual embodied experience of oppression, stigma, marginalization, exclusion and violence becomes explosive; this volatile messiness becomes urgently important both for our advocacy and solidarity work, and in the radical challenges we make to the systemic societal scripts which produce sustained traumata that lead to self-completed deaths. The nascent Critical Suicidology movement could be described as the long overdue and crucially relevant Social Justice turn in the thinking around what—for the time being, I keep calling "suicide"—although I believe the term to be misleading and ultimately a misnomer.

Remota itaque iustitia quid sunt regna nisi magna latrocinia? (Indeed, without justice what else are polities but thug-realms?) A Post-Nicene church father, Augustine of Hippo, poses this rhetorical question poignantly in his Christian-utopian writing *City of God* (*De Civitate Dei* IV. 4) in around 400 CE. *Iustitia* (justice) and its Greek equivalent δικαιοσύνη (*dikaiosýnē*) have been a central topic in Classical Philosophy ever since Plato explored this concept in his *Republic* (*Πολιτεία politeía*) roughly 800 years before Augustine. By calling the lack of justice 'gang rule' ('robbery, band of robbers', *latrocinium*), does Augustine echo the opening argument made by the interlocuter Thrasymachos in Plato's *Republic*? Thrasymachus maintains that justice is the rule of the more powerful: justice is 'that what is beneficial for the stronger' (τὸ τοῦ κρείττονος συμφέρον, Pl. *R*. 1.338c). As shown in Plato's later writing, his monumental dialogue *Laws* (Νόμοι *Nómoi*, Pl. *Lg*. 714), Thrasymachus' legal-political view appears to support the Athenian oligarchic rule of his time.

Classical Greek Political Philosophy maintains striking relevance for contemporary politics in the Global North. Thrasymachus' position eerily substantiates current political maneuverings —such as Brexit and the election of Donald Trump. Global Northern contemporary politics exemplify how in neoliberal, late-capitalist plutocracies and media-cracies, the self-interest of the powerful—the privileged, rich, and the populist manipulators—is undermining political and social justice (e.g. in terms of wealth distribution) under the pretense of democracy. Whether the rise of populism in the Global North is linked to *economic insecurity* or *cultural backlash* (Inglehart and Norris 2016), the growing inequality appears to advance plutocratic political power (Epp 2018). Neo-Darwinist social coldness disguises itself in maxims of self-realization and individual responsibility and opportunity in the face of severely unequal conditions. Social injustice is masked by capitalist mytheme such as the *The American Dream* that 'life should be better and richer and fuller for every man, with opportunity for each according to his ability or achievement' (Adams 1931: 404), and by cognitive elite narratives such as *The Bell Curve* (Herrnstein and Murray 1994) that downplay the role of socio-economic status and its intersectionalities (such as race, sex/ gender, sexualities etc.) for Social Injustice. Hence, for our contexts, we can state Augustine's dictum more precisely: a state without *social* justice is simply gangland.

But how does Social Justice relate to such a seemingly private, individual phenomenon as a 'suicide'? Why does such a phenomenon that is seemingly so evidently embedded in psychological and/or psychiatric domains need to be looked at from a social-critical, *Social Justice* perspective? The emerging field of Critical Suicidology (see White, Marsh, Kral and Morris (eds.) 2016), including the contributions by Vikki Reynolds (2016), Jennifer White (2015), Tom Widger (2015) and others (see Marsh 2015) is providing a much-needed counterweight to prevailing policy and prevention discourses of compartmentalization and individual pathologization of self-completed deaths. Taking my cue from there, I want to argue that "suicide" is a misnomer that aids a particular and harmful societal discourse of exclusion, abjection and Othering; privatizing, individualizing, and pathologizing death ideations, wishes, and resolves, and self-completed deaths function as defense mechanisms of structural and systemic inequalities and violence. Such inequalities and violence lie at the core of neo-liberal late-capitalist (hetero-/cis-) patriarchy—the oppressive societal order manifesting, indeed, the thug-rule about which Augustine warned as the absence of justice in the quoted passage from his *City of God* (IV. 4) . Compartmentalizing and pathologizing the manifesting effects and symptoms of systemic inequalities including self-completed deaths constitute self-serving mechanisms of protecting the unjust status quo.

In this context it is useful to adduce a key philosophical concept of the cognitive linguist George Lakoff connected with the construction of centers which also (must) create margins: the idea of prototypes (Lakoff 1987). The Lakoffian prototype is the ideal yet—in terms of existence in the real world—empty center of a cognitive category, against which the *realia* (phenomena) are observed, measured, and judged. Lakoffian prototype centers exert a conceptual tyranny shaping cognition. Translating this observation into Social Theory in terms of belonging and identity, Lakoffian prototype centers exert the systemic tyranny (see Scherer 2016: 261) that create margins of delineated belongings that create the Other. This systemic oppression constitutes nothing more than the rule of those intersectionally strongest in the context of the underlying societal normativities and scripts focusing on male, gender binary, cis, hetero(normative), white, unimpaired, neuro-'typical', reproductive/pre-menopausal, affluent, upper-(middle-)class, body-normative, mainstream (ir)religious, legal (etc.) citizens. The constructed ideal and its ultimately uninhabitable center of scripted societal normativities and their underpinning discourses—such as the negating of social responsibility and equality through syllogistic rhetorics of 'equity' or 'equal opportunities', 'self-made success, wealth, and power'—create ever fluctuating and renegotiated margins of abjection as being individually born, inscribed, unjust burdens. Where unjust society creates a lived embodiment of marginality, normative-discursive abjection and failure, living itself becomes the burdensome negotiation of a hostile environment generated by an unsuitable template; identity performance and life itself become a struggle for belonging—to partake in an unachievable center, provoking a vicious circle of alienating and desynchronizing experiences of rejection. I argue that this struggle is not only *traumatic* for the excluded Other. This struggle kills. The societal norm-scripts kill. In a cynical reversal of accountability the victims are blamed by means of the conceptualization of their deaths according to the capitalist alienation tactics: the compartmentalizing and individualizing of complex and interconnected nexus of embodied experiences: the labels 'self-murder' and 'suicide' absolve the thug-land apologists and reaffirm the unsuitable normative templates that create comfortable advantage for the κρείττονες (*kreíttones*)—the more powerful and privileged who, thus, can easily abrogate any social responsibility. Therefore, the label 'suicide' is a terrible and often calculated misnomer and an instrument of victim-blaming: the ultimate devaluation of those who succumb to social injustice.

What Suicidology needs is a Social Justice turn. The mournful outrage of survivors and of victims needs to be re-focalized upon the systemic violence and injustices that produce the killing wounds.

The Double Chrysippus

I feel myself reassured about the Social Justice turn in suicidology by echoes and lessons from the past. The Stoic philosopher Chrysippus of

Soloi (Χρύσιππος, fl. mid 3rd c. BCE)—who is celebrated as this ancient philosophic school's second founder—appears to foreshadow a Social Justice perspective on 'suicide.' The self-completed death of the founder of the Stoa, Zeno (Ζήνων) of Kition (died around 262 BCE), already testifies to the Stoic view that the self-chosen departure from life is by itself neutral and can be the ethical and honorable choice for the wise—a view in line with earlier Greek culture and philosophy. Chrysippus (*SVF* III fr. 768 von Arnim, pp. 191–2) compares self-completed departure from life with the breaking up of a party. He likens five different scenarios that necessitate the ending of a feast to the rationales for (the necessity of) self-chosen death. Those reasons (τρόποι *trópoi*) can broadly be aligned with Durkheim's 'altruistic' and 'fatalistic' modes and are (p. 192): 'due to great necessity' (διὰ χρείαν μεγάλην *dia chreían megálēn*) for the greater good; because of coercion—'because of the tyrants who gatecrash (sc. the party of our life) and force us either to unethical behavior or to reveal secrets'; because of prolonged illness (διὰ μακρὰν νόσον *dia makrán nóson*); because of poverty (διὰ πενίαν *dia penían*); because of the loss of mental faculties (διὰ λῆρον *dia lēron* – 'delirium'). Hence, Chrysippus explicitly includes living in socio-economic injustice (πενία *penía* 'poverty') among his five reasons of justified self-completed death.[1]

Of course, there is the other Chrysippus who provides a haunting echo for me personally and for Social Justice advocacy: according to early Greek myth (see Gantz 1993 II, pp. 488–92), the young son of Pelops, the Tantalide king of Pisa (Peloponnese, Greece), was abducted and raped by king Laios of Thebes; in one of the two dominant versions of the myth, possibly derived from Euripides' play *Chrysippos* (5th c. BCE, lost apart from small fragments), the raped boy kills himself. The killing wounds of child sex abuse— ubiquitous through times and places—are prime examples for the genealogy of death resolves and self-completed deaths; carrying such wounds condemns the victims often to an enduring struggle to survive a soul-murder that in many cases is nothing else but a slow, delayed murder barely survived for a time but often eventually completed by the victims themselves.

While Chrysippus, the philosopher, teaches us that Social Justice perspectives on self-completed death have been recognized since antiquity, Chrysippus, the mythic boy victim of rape, compels us to look beyond individual circumstances and to consider that Social Justice advocacy needs to challenge, disrupt and dismantle the variable societal power structures that enable the individual killing wounds—in this case through child sex abuse.

The Case of Trans*

Widening the important impulse derived from the Double Chrysippus—the focus on both the system *and* the individual trauma—I emphatically support the turn from individually framing and pathologizing occurrences of self-completed deaths towards a decisive critique and change of the systemic framework that enables, encourages and facilitates traumatic social injustices and unchecked power imbalances. The high prevalence of self-completed death ideation, attempts, and completions in marginalized and abject populations attests to both the systemic and the individual experiences of social injustice at the heart of self-completed deaths.

For example, a meta-analysis of trans* mental health and social well-being surveys reveals that between two thirds and three quarters of trans* people experience harassment—with particular subgroups such as trans women of color and sex workers and particular intersectionalities according to age, race, occupation, employment status and class featuring as the most vulnerable (Scherer 2018). In the navigation of their daily lives the overwhelming majority of trans* people face unjust burdens and individual, structural and systemic discrimination. This sufficiently explains the high prevalence of depression, self-harm, drug usage and self-completed death ideation, attempts and completion among the trans* populace. However, in cruel irony, discriminatory discourses and practices—be they religiously and/or culturally underpinned—regularly point to high 'suicidality' or 'suicidal ideation' in abject populations such as LGBTIQ+ people as an inferred proof of the moral inferiority of this group, concluding that LGBTIQ+ identity performances demonstrate an inherent mental disorder. Yet, a meta-analysis of research on the link between perceived marginalization and worse mental health (Pascoe and Smart Richman 2009) clearly demonstrates a consensus in in recent research: it is not the marginalized abject that is "mentally 'disordered' but that abjection, rejection, stigma and systemic societal aggression that creates the mental distress. The systemic violence of marginalization causes the mental distress that manifests, for example, in alarmingly high self-completed death numbers for trans* people in general and for LGBTIQ+ youth (Scherer 2018). Taking the heightened prevalence of drug usage and risk-taking behavior within segments of the LGBTIQ+ community into consideration, risk-seeking and unhealthy behavioral patterns appear, again, not as proof of moral degeneration but as reactions to the undue systemic mental pressures on this group; such behaviors appear as less constructive attempts to develop resilience or as expressing unhealthy coping mechanisms, often akin to semi-conscious, prolonged phased self-completed deaths.

Trauma beyond Healing: Phonoïc Wounds

The Social Justice turn in Suicidology urges us to look at the systemic causes for both gradual and sudden self-completed death among people living with social injustices; doing so, we also need to examine the concrete irresolvable traumatic experiences, which express, perform, and focalize such systemic causes and traumata. These traumata occur and get inscribed in the embodied experiences of intersectionally marginalized, disenfranchised and oppressed people whose social trauma often proves deadly. Just as 'suicide' appears to me to be a misnomer so does 'trauma' when it leads to slow death: in these cases, 'trauma', Greek for 'wound' (τραῦμα), becomes homicide or murder, Greek 'phonos' (φόνος). Experiences are often more than traumatic, they are *phonoïc.*

I maintain that we should consider abandoning the term 'suicide' altogether. The less emotive term 'self-completed death' appears to be more appropriate in general. The term 'self-completed death' is even appropriate at those rare occasions of a truly Durkheimian 'altruistic' *Freitod* (voluntary death)—a self-sacrifice—that is consciously enacted for a higher ethical good.[2]

Using the term 'self-completed death' affords more space and opportunity for non-judgmental listening and counsel. From a Social Justice perspective, most 'suicides' i.e. self-completed deaths cannot be called 'self-murder' i.e. 'suicides' properly: the illusion of the extent of individual agency that this loaded term carries only serves to absolve the system that creates the social injustice. Social injustice-induced and/or -underpinned self-completed deaths are not really suicides; those self-completed deaths are, in fact, delayed, self-completed murders. Of course, in legal terms, different jurisdictions and criminal codes operate various legal definitions for homicides such, in English law, 'murder', 'voluntary manslaughter' and 'involuntary manslaughter.'

Using the strong term '(delayed) murder' for self-completed deaths is not meant to suggest a simplistic *passe-partout* concept or ready-made legal evaluation. 'Murder' serves to point to the underlying societal agency and *mens rea*—or the *mentes reae* creating and sustaining assentingly and willingly the systems that kill—often with delay and over a prolonged period of time: the mechanics of social deprivation, marginalization, power abuse and institutional/organizational protectionism (as in the case of clerical sexual abuse) which induce and/or underpin self-completed deaths have direct, arguably intentional, systemic support within communities and societies. Individual power brokers might claim that they do not intend the effects these systems have but their support of the very systems that clearly kill makes them co-accountable for homicide.

For example, take the case of veterans, sent off as pawns of late-capitalist or nationalist interests, returning from the trauma of the killing fields; many, having served their function to a cynical society which willingly made them killers, slowly spiral into self-destruction, unable to make sense of their alleged heroism in the face of the reality of horror. Or take the transwoman of color who has been denied the resources and strategies of resilience and succumbs to the hopelessness and inevitability of stigma, abuse, violence and poverty. Or take the mentally diverse or 'variable' person who signs themselves out of a life without respect, love and basic inclusive access to opportunities. In all those cases, why are we calling 'suicide' what should be called 'murder' or, at least, 'homicide'? Where systemic injustice has translated into sustained trauma it should be called out and appropriately named: delayed, self-completed murder. Systemic, intersectional social injustices create sustained wounding—traumatic experiences which often become phonoïc: killing wounds.

Testimonial

As scholars and activists, we need to bear witness to the killing wounds around us. I bear witness to my own phonöic experiences which shaped my slow, continuing murder and leave me continuously surprised that I am, for now, still breathing, still alive.

I am a suicide waiting to happen.

I was murdered when I was born and put into a binary gender box.

I was murdered every day in junior high school when the heavy lids of the metal rubbish containers closed over me, burying me into a reeking abyss of darkness which swallowed me as dehumanized refuse.

I was murdered by gossip, exclusion, and ostracisms of senior high school and at university; and by the name-callings and beatings; only my body survived, by an inch, after one particular instance of bashing—for now.

I was thoroughly and routinely murdered again and again as young person when Christ looked phlegmatically on from his wooden cross while I was raped.

I was murdered many times. I do not ask for sympathy; I ask for respect and action.

So far, I survived my murder by becoming a—another—smartass scholar; but also, more than that: an activist. Against an irreparable loss of meaning I can only set as purpose the fight against the systems that allowed my murders.

I know the shadows.
I know they will come.
I know eventually I will embrace them, as lovers.
Until then I will fight.

Conclusion: From Victim-Blaming to Death Wish Counseling

Turning Suicidology into Social Justice activism needs to give voice to all those, all of us, who were killed, who were murdered. I ask for two things:

First, let us celebrate survivors and victims of traumatic and phonoïc injustice. For instance, those whose souls were murdered by child abuse are rightly called *survivors* of abuse and trauma; *temporary survivors* in many cases. We need to acknowledge that not all survive; not all can find resilience in network, humor and meaning- and purpose-making; not everyone is able to reconstruct meaning out of the ruins of an utterly destroyed and meaningless life after the murder of the soul—be that a murder in one dramatic event which expresses systemic injustices and power imbalances, or a murder by constant phonoïc micro-aggressions and micro-killings. I want to celebrate all of them and us; and remember in fondness those we have lost to delayed self-completed murder. As is written on many Jewish gravestones:

זָכוֹר לֹא תִּשְׁכָּח *(zākhor . . . lo tiškaḇ—Remember . . . don't forget* (cf. Dəvarim/Deuteronomy 26, 17.19)[3]

Secondly, let us stop blaming the victim, stop reducing, rationalizing and minimizing the real, systemic violence behind those murders and create meaning, or at least purpose, for our own wounded selves through that kind of activism and advocacy that explodes the centers which create margins and suffering; let us dream and create ways of being and becoming which celebrate each of our sameness and uniqueness without Othering and stigma, with true empathy and respect.

A decisive step to end the victim-blaming compartmentalization as individual acts of self-completed deaths is to carefully erase the judgmental language and patronizing pathologization of people with self-completed death ideation, wish and/or resolve. 'Suicide prevention', 'suicide helpline' etc. carry as terms and concepts the individualized burden and stigma of those living with phonöic experiences: the term 'suicide' wrongly overemphasizes self-agency and individual burden over the systemic phonoïc wounding and victimization. 'Prevention' and 'helpline' as terms are loaded with both ethical and medical-psychiatric judgements cast back at the individual with death ideation, wish and/or resolve. The terms speak of an agenda that fails to recognize that in many cases the homicide, the murder, has already happened. So, instead, I propose to rethink 'suicide prevention' in terms of counselling: non-judgemental and result-open explorations of the wounds that may or may not be phonoïc; the resolve to end the wounding or killing pains can be more empathically explored without the medico-psychiatric public health agenda implied in 'prevention' that reduces service users to socio-psychic problems. We might want to call such services 'end-of-the-road counselling' or 'death (resolve) counselling'. By doing so, we can take seriously both the autonomy and agency of those living with death wishes and/or death resolves due to delayed murders or ethical deliberations; and the pain of those surviving loved ones of self-completed deaths who understandably might feel upset by any reframing from 'prevention' toward result-open counselling.

My rationale for suggesting rethinking suicide prevention as 'death resolve counselling' focusses very much on those living with phonöic wounds and takes its cue from the experience of counselling people with unwanted pregnancies. Death wish counselling places emphasis on ethical value-neutrality and the bodily autonomy of the subject. Of course, the problem with agency is that any true agency (if it can exist at all) needs to be reflective and empowered. Decisions and resolves that feel autonomous can be insufficiently explored and can benefit from non-judgemental exploration. Unemancipated forms of self-convinced agentive action resulting in various degrees of suffering and harm for oneself and others can reflect the succumbing to any given, overwhelming societal, cultural (or sometimes religious and ideological) script rather than constituting the result of agentive value negotiations. E.g., in LGB (Lesbian, Gay, Bisexual)-repressive societies, non-heterosexuals might 'decide' to marry an opposite-sex partner in order the fulfil the reproductive, monogamous nucleolar hetero-norm, despite the high likelihood of sustained mental harm and suffering for themselves and their direct environment. In how many cases would such an action be the result of emancipated and agentive value negotiation leading to a conscious sacrifice of one's own sexual/intimate happiness in support of repressive societal scripts? Rather, in most cases, such decisions would be pseudo-agentive submission to the overpowering burden on normative scripts.

I envision death resolve counselling to be firmly grounded in an ethos that prioritizes the thorough reflection on the agentive structures and possibilities at disposition. Death resolve counselling would need to decisively differentiate between pseudo-agentive death wishes and autonomous resolves. Despite the pain that an—in principle—result-open counselling for those living with death ideations might cause those bereaved by self-completed deaths I feel that a safe, less agenda-driven space to discuss death ideation and resolves might paradoxically be 'more preventative' (further delaying) by virtue of its destigmatizing and strongly empowering nature; in the end, pragmatically, it might even lead to less self-completed deaths.

We need to face the uncomfortable possibility that self-completed deaths can be free, emancipated, autonomous, and ethically acceptable decisions. Without falling into the extremes of fetishizing or heroizing voluntary death (*Freitod*), it appears to be ethically imperative (and expedient!) to drag death ideation, wishes, and resolves out of the pathology and the silence, and into an open honest discussion that might give people who are living with delayed murder—like myself—an opportunity to be taken seriously and to breath and, possibly, to fight another day. In terms of transforming phonoïc suffering for Social Justice I advocate defying the phonoïc wounds for as long as possible and making them visible; as a feminist practice, my killing wounds show the private as the public and as the politically potent and revolutionary.

The heteronomous delayed death can become autonomous *résistance* to the systems that kill and the opportunistic killers it enables and creates. By fighting to further delay the homicide already committed we can powerfully speak to the utopia of *civitas iusta* (the just society) and create a less unjust society.

Notes

1 Interestingly, the socio-economic privileged (eclectic) Stoic writer Seneca the Younger (died 65 CE) appears to reject Chrysippus' tropos of poverty. In Seneca's short, mature work —a reflection on theodicy entitled *De Providentia* ('On Providence'), God admonishes humankind to disregard poverty (*contemnite paupertatem*), suffering (*dolor*), death (*mors*) and fate (*fortuna*, Sen. *de prov.* 6, 6) while pointing to the open exit door to flee if one doesn't want to fight: *patet exitus—si pugnare non vultis, licet fugere* (Sen. *de prov.* 6, 7 cf. *ep. mor.* 70, 14 and 24). *Patet exitus* is echoed by Epictetus (died 134 CE) Arr. *Epict.* 1, 24, 20: μέμνησο ὅτι ἡ θύρα ἤνοικται *mémnēso hoti hē thýra ḗnoiktai* – remember that the door is open).

2 E.g. in the Stoic sense as discussed earlier; or in case of the cases of acceptable self-chosen deaths in Buddhist traditions, in particular those traditions that base themselves on the *Lotus Sūtra* (*Saddharmapuṇḍarīka Sūtra*, Chapter 23 [= 22 Sanskrit]; Benn 2009). Secular and Social Darwinist heroization of self-completed Death is reflected in the German term *Freitod* ('voluntary death, literally: 'free[-will]-death') which first came into use in the 1900s and popularized in the first half of the 20th century. *Freitod* was viewed as an alternative to the stigmatizing term *Selbstmord* (self-murder), thought to reflect Christian taboos and moral judgment (see Goeschel 2009: 20–21).

3 The Judaeo-European call for memory as resistance-in-action is in contrast to the Greco-European tradition of philosophy of history expressed in Thucydides' chapter on method in his *Archaeology* at the beginning of his work on the *Peloponnesian War* (i.22, 4). Here, pessimism about the nature of humankind (κατὰ τὸ ἀνθρώπινον, *kata ton anthrōpinon*) mixes with fatalism. Thucydides' τὸ σαφὲς σκοπεῖν (*to saphes skopein*), to examine in all clarity the past, does not entail any necessary or even possible recourse to changing the present and future: rather the future will to a great degree repeat the past: τῶν μελλόντων ποτὲ αὖθις . . . τοιούτων καὶ παραπλησίων ἔσεσθαι (*tōn mellontōn pote authis . . . toioutōn kai paraplēsiōn esesthai*).

References

Adams, J.T. 1931. *The Epic of America*. New York: Blue Ribbons Books.

Benn, J.A. 2009. The Lotus Sūtra and Self-Immolation. *In*: S.F. Teiser and J.I. Stone, eds. *Readings of the Lotus Sūtra*. New York: Columbia University Press, 107–131.

Epp, D. 2018. Policy Agendas and Economic Inequality in American Politics. *Political Studies* 66 (4), 922–939.

Gantz, T. 1993. *Early Greek Myth: A Guide to the Literary and Artistic Sources*. 2 vols. Baltimore and London: The John Hopkins University Press.

Goeschel, C. 2009. *Suicide in Nazi Germany*. Oxford: Oxford University Press.

Herrnstein, R.J. and Murray, C.A. 1994. *The Bell Curve: Intelligence and Class Structure in American Life*. New York: Free Press.

Inglehart, R F. and Norris, P. 2016. Trump, Brexit, and the Rise of Populism: Economic Have-Nots and Cultural Backlash. *HKS Working Paper No. RWP16-026*. Available at SSRN: https://ssrn.com/abstract=2818659 or http://dx.doi.org/10.2139/ssrn.2818659 (accessed 8 December 2018).

Lakoff, G. 1987. *Women, Fire, and. Dangerous Things: What Categories Reveal about the Mind*. Chicago and London: The University of Chicago Press.

Marsh, I. 2015. 'Critical Suicidology': Toward an Inclusive, Inventive and Collaborative (Post) Suicidology. *Social Epistemology Review and Reply Collective*, 4 (5), 6–9.

Pascoe E. A. and Smart Richman, L. 2009. Perceived discrimination and health: A meta-analytic review. *Psychological Bulletin*, 135, 531–554.

Reynolds, V. 2016. Hate Kills: A Social Justice Response to Suicide. *In*: White, Marsh, Kral and Morris, eds., 168–187.

Scherer, B. 2016. Variable Bodies, Buddhism and (No-)Selfhood: Towards Dehegemonised Embodiment. *In*: C. Mounsey and S. Booth, eds. *The Variable Body in History*. Oxford: Peter Lang, 247–263.

Scherer, B. 2018. Beyond Heteropatriarchal Oppression: Inhabiting Aphallic Anthroposcapes. *In*: B. Scherer, ed. with P. de Vries. *Queering Paradigms VII: Contested Bodies and Spaces*. Oxford: Peter Lang, 65–80.

White, J. 2015. Shaking Up Suicidology. *Social Epistemology Review and Reply Collective* 4 (5), 1–4.

White, J., Marsh, I., Kral, M. and Morris, J., eds., 2016. *Critical Suicidology: Transforming Suicide Research and Prevention*. Vancouver: UBC Press.

Widger, T. 2015. 'Suicidology as a Social Practice': A Reply. *Social Epistemology Review and Reply Collective* 4 (3), 1–4.

self murder

Daniel G. Scott

I was murdered many times. I do not ask for sympathy; I ask for respect and action.

Bee Scherer

i am, that one said,
a suicide waiting to happen.
i have been murdered
many times already,
wounded with many blows:
torn, assaulted, raped
and claim the right to make,
that one said,
the murder complete
with my own hands
in my own time.

there are those
who desire
to stop me, take from me
my own hands.
add wounds
to wounds
murder my self
again and again
to keep me from dying.

i only know
that one said,
i do not want more
taken from me,
or added on –

not pity, not shame.
nor control of my death.

i have been murdered
enough already
and will complete
the murder of my self
when i choose.

9 It Takes a Village

The Nonprofessional Mental Health Worker Movement

Rebecca S. Morse, Michael J. Kral, Maura McFadden, Janet McCord and Lory Barsdate Easton

Introduction

> "The lay volunteer was probably the most important single discovery in the fifty-year history of suicide prevention."
>
> (Dublin, 1969 – The first meeting of the American Association of Suicidology)

A social justice perspective on suicide risk and prevention identifies the disparities in access to mental health services and the need for compassionate, culturally attuned, and community-informed approaches to mental health care. It is particularly important to consider the connection between mental health services and suicide risk, assessment, and treatment through a social justice lens. Increasingly, we are seeing suicide framed as a public health issue, yet efforts in suicide prevention have not followed a public health model, that is, they have emphasized individual pathology and treatment rather than the overall health of the public. A broader public health approach, informed by a perspective grounded in social justice, is required – truly, it will take a village.

Recruiting and training "ordinary" or lay people to help individuals with mental health issues is a relatively new response counterbalancing the biomedical approach to mental health care. This chapter offers a review of what is considered the paraprofessional mental health movement – a social justice movement of good people wanting to alleviate the pain of others, utilizing technology as well as community relationships to address pain, agitation and suicidal crises.

History of Paraprofessional Movement

Paraprofessional Definition

Historically, "mental health care professionals" included those who are educated academically, or through vocational training, and have obtained certification, scholastic credentials and/or licensure to substantiate their training, and competency to serve those in need of mental health services. This can include, but is not limited to, those from the fields of education, social work, nursing, counseling, psychiatry, and psychology. "*Paraprofessionals*" is a term that is more ambiguous, and in the literature both more inclusive, and vague, in terms of the scope of who *is* a paraprofessional. Paraprofessionals can include any lay person who works with those in need, and does not necessitate corresponding credentials, licensure, or degree(s). Additionally, at the broader end of the spectrum, it includes everyone from trained and paid staff to those who work strictly on a volunteer basis, and may or may not include formalized training. For the purposes of this chapter, we are going to focus on the volunteer perspective, and argue that the most successful in helping those in crisis are those who are both formally and informally trained. Informal training might include as-you-go mentorship, where helping skills are modeled and scaffolded (encouraged or "built up" via feedback and opportunities to self-correct). Formalized training is more scripted, and may involve classes, supervised interactions with clients, and/or manualized procedural protocols.

Inside Out: From Institutions to Communities

The Mental Health Study Act of 1955 (Public Law 84–182) (Stockdill, 2005), and the subsequent recommendations and efforts of the National Institute of Mental Health to offer the least restrictive environment possible, led to the deinstitutionalizing of the mentally ill and the subsequent closure of the vast majority of psychiatric hospitals. More broadly, the 1950s saw the advent of mental health care reform around the world, as psychiatric hospitals, which had increasingly been administered like prisons, became overcrowded, and the development of anti-psychotics accelerated. Structurally, community mental health services eliminated the oppressive and often abusive environment of the psychiatric hospital. With the move away from one-size-fits-all institutionalization for those with mental health treatment needs, those who could manage to live at home could do so, while those needing additional supportive care could be in group homes. Overall, the goal was to enhance human dignity both through integration of mental health patients within communities and by encouraging communities to take collective responsibility for the needs of some members of their community. But at the crux of the problem, not enough credentialed mental health caregivers were available for the number of deinstitutionalized individuals now living within communities.

Outside In: Biomedical Influence on Mental Health Care

One of the prevailing limitations to mental health care is grounded in the context of its development, the overarching influence of the biomedical model. Despite being deeply rooted in philosophy – which by its very nature is holistic – much of our current approach to understanding and treating, mental health disorders is an attempt to emulate the biomedical approach to healthcare. It is overly simplistic to vilify the biomedical approach as reductionistic (cure the disease, versus treating the person); nonetheless, in medicine we look to indices of efficacy and curative interventions. Similarly, in mental health care, we often focus on symptom management, instead of understanding the greater picture of the individual – functioning as an active agent, and interacting both within and on a larger framework of family, community, society, and time.

An Interactionist Approach

Bronfenbrenner (2005) proposed a Bio-Ecological Systems theory of human development, in which a person is considered within the context of their environment and experiences. His model was interactional in nature – considering the environment as working on the individual, the individual working on the environment – and he further stratified the environment and their respective interactions into five levels. At the outermost level is the chronosystem, which encompasses unique events which can shape both societal and individual development (e.g. growing up before, during, or after 9/11; development of life-saving vaccines), and individual transitions (e.g. graduating high school, birth of a child, being widowed). At the macro level is the overarching society and culture in which the person develops (e.g. public health care policies, the individual's socioeconomic status). At the exosystem level are the indirect environmental elements (e.g. the effect on the child of workplace policies for their parent). At the mesosystem level are the interactions between environmental elements which directly affect the individual (e.g. parent-teacher conferences, connections with the immediate or local neighborhood and community). At the core is the micro-system: the individual, and their immediate surroundings and relationships (home, family, etc.). Further, transactional approaches which expanded Bronfenbrenner's work have demonstrated that early interventions are best in terms of both intrinsic psychological (nature) and environmental (nurture) factors (Sameroff & MacKenzie 2003).

Public health policies and approaches are often implicated at the chrono and macro system level, that is, they are influential on the individual, but limited in immediacy and flexibility to act or react to an individual's needs or crises. Issues of social justice are often most apparent at the macro and exosystem levels; it is here that barriers to mental health care (availability, access, avoidance of support, etc.) limit the ability of well-intended public policies and governmental resources to help those most in need of those policies and resources. Discrepancy of supply to demand, access to care, and reduction of stigma can be ameliorated at the meso/microsystem level by using within-community, peer-to-peer mental health care support and crisis services.

Social Justice Implications

Although mental health care was increasingly deinstitutionalized, and outpatient access to mental healthcare was beginning to expand, not all had equal access to receive or provide mental health care (McGuire & Miranda, 2008). Those of minority populations and individuals of low socioeconomic status were locked out of opportunities to obtain the education, and thus the credentials, to respond to the needs of their communities as fully trained and credentialed professionals. Additionally, there was a general dearth of credentialed professionals available to work in community mental health (Delworth 1974; Gartner & Reissman 1974). Simultaneously, psychiatrists were decreasingly interested in working in the area of community mental health (Ribner 1980). As a result, consumers had limited access to both traditional and research-informed services. Paraprofessionals, who were able to receive some training and provide mental healthcare to the community, were able to be a "bridge to the poor" (Delworth 1974; Gartner & Reissman 1974) and crisis hotlines were seen as necessary to augment community mental health and as a stop-gap to assist those in need who had limited access to traditional care (Rosenbaum & Calhoun 1977).

We would suggest that the paraprofessional movement developed as a response to these inherent disparities in resources and thus is a function of the social justice movement. This prevailing movement offers amelioration of distress to those in crisis, provides a listener who can help, and affirms that everyone has a right to be heard regardless of their race, orientation, sex, gender, religious affiliation, age, size, or abilities. The increased reliance on trained paraprofessionals, driven initially by the paucity of credentialed clinicians, gained momentum as a social movement.

In addition to addressing the lack of resources, the use of paraprofessionals as part of the social justice movement brought needed mental health services to people in crisis who might not otherwise seek professional help and addressed inequities in mental health care, particularly for minorities. Collective memories are long, and mistrust between those who have been socially marginalized and the medical community is deeply rooted in the historical context of discriminatory treatment and even abuse and malpractice (e.g. intergenerational trauma). As noted in the introduction to this volume, a social justice approach addresses the needs of those with limited access to care or who are reluctant to seek out professional care. In this sense, the paraprofessional movement fits with a public health perspective.

Many paraprofessionals share social identity with their target population, forming a bridge between professional agencies and communities, therefore helping to reduce or minimize distrust (Kalafat & Boroto 1977).

Often, crisis centers utilize ethnic minority paraprofessionals to work within their own ethnic minority populations (Andrews et al. 2004; Giblin 1989) allowing for a within-group approach to mental health care that can reduce both stigma and stereotype threat. In some rural areas, such as Montana in the United States, veterans trained as community emergency medical technicians are available to help their fellow veterans in crisis, at the same time decreasing the social isolation frequently experienced by rural veterans. Similarly, certified peer specialists are an example of trained paraprofessionals who provide valuable supportive care for individuals coping, or seeking to cope, with mental illness with face-to-face support services and crisis phone and/or text lines. Trained paraprofessionals provide support services for individuals who might not otherwise have access due to ethnic, social and socio-economic boundaries. Such care enhances both public health and individual human dignity.

Social Justice and Difference Anxiety

Another element that may contribute to the success of non-professional mental health volunteers is that the volunteers are more likely to share the social and cultural background of the people whom they serve. These similarities can reduce "difference anxiety," that is, stress reactions that often arise before and during cross-group encounters. Difference anxiety is specific to intergroup interactions and arises in many interracial encounters and in contacts with other social groups viewed as being different in some significant way, including encounters with persons with mental illness (Stephan 2014; Greenland, Xenias & Maio 2012). Difference anxiety drains cognitive resources and engages vigilance, guardedness, and other psychological mechanisms that can interfere with developing interpersonal relationships (Godsil & Richardson 2017; West, Pearson & Stern 2014; Bergsieker, Shelton & Richeson 2010; Amodio 2009; Vorauer 2006; Stephan & Stephan 1985). Difference anxiety further may activate implicit bias, unconscious prejudice, and subconscious stereotypes (Amodio & Hamilton 2012). In the context of mental health service delivery, difference anxiety can induce impression management efforts and conscious and unconscious stress/coping strategies that in turn can interfere with building rapport, gathering critical clinical information, and helping the client to self-focus (Okun, Chang, Kanhai, Dunn & Easle, 2017; Trawalter Richeson & Shelton 2009). More broadly difference anxiety plays a role in healthcare provider/patient dynamics which are associated with worse health outcomes (Godsil & Richardson 2017). The quality of the alliance between care provider and client is critically important to mental health outcomes (Constantino, Morrison, Coyne & Howard 2017; Wampold, Baldwin, Holtforth & Imel, 2017; Zimmerman & Bambling 2012). When peers and other non-professionals provide mental health support to members of their own communities and social groups, one potential impediment to a therapeutic alliance is diminished.

Characteristics of Crisis Centers and Paraprofessionals

Crisis Centers

Crisis centers have been a significant factor in suicide prevention. In 1953 Chad Varah, an Anglican clergyman in London, founded a crisis telephone service called Samaritans staffed by volunteers for the suicidal and distressed. There are now Samaritans' branches in almost eighty countries (Varah 1985) and Varah's notion of "befriending" has been extended internationally. On local levels Samaritans organizations work to improve the safety of their communities, focusing on crisis and suicide prevention. For example, the Samaritans of New York is, according to their website, the "only community-based organization in the NYC-Metropolitan area solely devoted to preventing suicide and helping people in crisis" (see http://samaritansnyc.org/about-samaritans/). As a matter of policy, their services are provided to anyone who needs them, without regard to socio-economic status, religion, sexual or gender identity, age or culture.

Volunteer Groups

A practical example demonstrating how quickly nonprofessional, volunteer-led programs can proliferate following an initial founding is the case study of The Compassionate Friends. The organization was founded in Coventry, England in 1969 by Reverend Simon Stephens. A chaplain at Warwickshire Hospital in England, Rev. Stephens was counseling two grieving families who had both lost children. He discovered that the families were able to give each other a support, as mutual survivors of child loss, that he was not able to give as a chaplain, and together Stephens and the families founded the first chapter of The Compassionate Friends. The first chapter in the United States was established in 1972, and formally incorporated in 1978. From this meeting of a chaplain and two families, The Compassionate Friends has expanded to include 600 local chapters, spanning 50 states, Washington, DC, and Guam (The Compassionate Friends 2018).

Suicide Prevention Centers

In 1958 Edwin S. Shneidman and Norman Farberow, along with Robert E. Litman and Sam (Mickey) Heilig, started the Los Angeles Suicide Prevention Center (LASPC) with a grant from the National Institute of Mental Health (Morris 2011). The program, now known as Didi Hirsch Mental Health Services, was the first scientifically and clinically based program to study and prevent suicide in the United States and became a model for crisis centers across the United States. After the founding of the LASPC, paraprofessional contributions continued to expand greatly in the 1960s (Christensen, Miller, & Monoz 1978). In 1963, the center trained nonprofessionals to answer crisis calls and expanded the crisis line to 24-hours a day. They dealt with individuals who were in an acute state of distress and needed active intervention. The volunteers, who mainly consisted of housewives, were trained as counselors and used their home telephones to receive calls. In 1981, the center began to organize support groups for those bereaved by suicide, facilitated by trained volunteers. Heilig et al. (1968) summarized their views on the changing role of the nonprofessional volunteer stating:

> A significant aspect of this development has been the involvement of the community and its members in the concern for its own mental health. The citizen as well as the mental health professional can exert a personal, positive force toward the mental health of his community . . . More specifically, roles are now being developed in which the citizen can play an active role, including direct therapeutic interaction with emotionally disturbed individuals. This conception of the citizen's role is markedly different from the approach in past years when the volunteer's activities had been considered ancillary and indirect . . .
>
> (p. 287)

Programs such as the Samaritans, LASPC, and The Compassionate Friends developed at a time when there was an increasing need for mental health workers (Pattison & Elpers 1972), as previously mentioned, correlating with the increase in deinstitutionalization of psychiatric patients.

The LASPC was a model for crisis centers that are now in almost every city in the U.S. and Canada. Centers continue to be facilitated by trained, nonprofessional volunteers whose counseling skills are primarily developed through experience (Abbey, Madsen, & Polland 1989; Levitt et al. 2011; Sakowitz & Hirschman 1975). Hotlines, survivor support groups, and more recently, crisis text lines, have emerged in many communities throughout the United States (Gregory 2015). Texting 741741 from anywhere in the U.S. will connect with a responder with the local text line center closest geographically to the texter. The speed of response is linked to the amount of volunteer support on a local level. Textlines are staffed almost exclusively by trained volunteers (Crisis Text Line 2018).

In a study of interpersonal characteristics of hotline paraprofessional counselors, Rek and Dinger (2016) found that the counselors fell into three groups: submissive-altruistic (liked, others first), helpful-influential (impact driven), and friendly-harmonious (connection/supported). Most paraprofessionals report that the experience has had an extensive positive influence on their lives and has been a growth experience. In addition to serving others and hoping to make a difference, paraprofessionals often are secondarily motivated by a desire to experience self-development through intellectual and social engagement. Much earlier, Heilig et al. (1968) found that volunteers sometimes felt as though they were benefitting from self-development and a sense of purpose, but that sometimes they could feel antsy and discouraged when there was not that much work for them to do. Positive gains in self-development and enjoying a sense of purpose are important, yet they often rate their sense of prestige and opportunities for advancement below that of social workers, psychologists, and teachers (Birenbaum & Ahmed 1978). Paraprofessionals have been accepted by both professionals and clients in mental health services (Alley & Blanton 1976). Paraprofessionals are able to work together with professionals (Hall & Epp 2001) and engage in many of the same activities that professional mental health workers perform (Bartels & Tyler 1975).

Paraprofessionals have worked in many different settings such as school mental health programs (Terrell 1972), outpatient child guidance clinic(s) (Durlak 1979a), in special education (Jones & Bender 1993), in schools (Tierney et al. 1990), as peer educators on university campuses (Catanzarite & Robinson 2013), and as university resident assistants (Taub et al. 2013). They have worked with various populations including northern Canadian Indigenous communities (Minore & Boone 2002), Native American communities (Cwik et al. 2014; Goldston et al. 2010; Gone & Alacantra 2007), the military (Nolan & Cooke 1970), children in general (McWilliams 1972), rural communities (Shybut 1982), as older adult paraprofessionals working with older adults (Gatz, Hileman, & Amaral 1984), as certified peer specialists, and as homosexually-oriented individuals counseling those of similar orientation (Enright & Parsons 1976).

Paraprofessionals have helped individuals facing various difficulties including individuals with learning disabilities (Lindsey 1983), people with eating disorders (Lenihan & Kirk 1990), disturbed children (Vander Kolk 1973), juvenile delinquents (Gordon & Arbuthnot 1988), as drug counselors for individuals facing addiction (Aiken et al. 1984), and elderly individuals with depression (Guerrero-Berroa & Phillips 2001). They have served as an online support group (Gilat & Shahar 2009), in rehabilitation (Hetherington 1995; Smith 1973; Wallace 1970), in treating alcohol abuse (Cooke, Wehmer, & Gruber 1975), as family counselors with chronically ill children (Pless & Satterwhite 1972), as counselors in family therapy in general (Umbarger 1972), as community instructors (Signell 1975), doing program evaluation (Sorensen & Galano 1976), as consultants (Cowen, Trost, & Izzo 1973) and in education, health, social services, family planning, urban planning, police work, and corrections (Gartner & Riessman 1974). As a result of working with diverse groups of individuals in crisis, paraprofessionals experience increased empathic abilities and heightened sensitivity towards other's problems (Heilig et al. 1968).

Beyond Crisis Centers: Gatekeeper Approaches

The term "gatekeeper" first appeared in published research in 1971 in an article by Dr. John Snyder and was defined as "any person to whom troubled people are turning to for help" (Snyder 1971, p.39). In general, gatekeepers are defined as individuals who have face-to-face contact with many members of their communities as part of their daily lives, and they are considered to be gatekeepers if they have appropriate training to identify individuals who are at risk for suicide and to take action to help the individuals get the assistance they need (Burnette, Ramchand, & Ayer 2015). The United States military initiated a variety of gatekeeper strategies to reduce suicide among active duty military, but other gatekeeper strategies are used in schools, universities, medical facilities and communities. Those in gatekeeping roles are able to refer individuals at risk for suicide to specialized providers. In addition to benefit from increased accessibility to a population in need, these providers benefit from having a connection to the individual's community who can contribute to that individual's ability to find community resources (Office of the Surgeon General 2012).

Gatekeeper training programs target increasing awareness and knowledge of those in gatekeeping roles, as well as increasing help-seeking behaviors in populations at high risk for suicidal ideation and attempts (Lipson 2013). In general, gatekeeper trainings include instruction about suicide, with emphasis on risk factors and warning signs, an examination of beliefs and attitudes about suicide and suicidal people, and whether or not participants in training consider suicide to be preventable (Robinson et al. 2018). By discussing suicidality and mental illness, gatekeeper trainings strive to reduce stigma and the reluctance some feel about intervening in a crisis. Organizations offering gatekeeper trainings in the community assume that, in one way or another, everyone is a gatekeeper and we can all stay aware of those around us, and keep our eyes and hearts open to help our neighbors.

The United Nations (1996), as well as The United States Office of the Surgeon General and the National Action Alliance for Suicide Prevention (2012), endorse gatekeeping as effective in preventing suicide and provide lists of recommended gatekeeper training programs. One of the most popular gatekeeper training programs is "Question, Persuade, Refer," or QPR for short. This training was originally created over three years collaboratively between Spokane Mental Health and Paul Quinnett, with input by a variety of organizations. In 1999, the QPR Institute was established as an independent organization, and the Institute has been conducting trainings of Master Trainers who in turn train local QPR community trainers. QPR trainings have demonstrated effectiveness in improving trainees' knowledge, perceived capacity and self-efficacy in suicide prevention efforts, and suicide prevention behaviors (Hangartner 2018).

Certified QPR trainers are asked to conduct QPR trainings in their communities to groups no larger than 40. The QPR Institute recommends that a QPR community training should last no more than 90 minutes, and is best facilitated by two trained individuals. The goal of the training is so ordinary citizens can recognize the warning signs of suicide, know how to offer hope to a person in crisis, and know how to get help and possibly save someone's life. Trainers are required to have QPR Institute booklets and wallet cards with emergency information to hand out to those community members they have trained. The overall goal is to help individuals in a community understand what suicide is – and is not – and to learn how to ask someone if they are considering ending their lives. As such, it is a social justice approach to suicide prevention in that the goal is to increase the number of people who have an enhanced awareness about suicide, and a skill set that includes how to ask someone about suicide.

QPR is one of many gatekeeper training approaches used around the world, including Applied Suicide Intervention Skills Training (ASIST) by LivingWorks; Ask, Care, Escort (ACE) used in the United States Army, and dozens of locally developed gatekeeper trainings for specific communities. These programs help a local community take collective responsibility for suicide prevention and enhanced relationships across a community, reducing isolation.

Outcomes related to gatekeeper training vary based on the gatekeeper training itself as well as the individual characteristics of participants being trained. For example, in a study of school-based gatekeeper trainings funded by Garret Lee Smith Memorial grants, Condron et al. (2015) found that the amount of time an individual spends with youth as well as the professional role that individual fulfills is related to the number of at-risk youth they are able to identify. Individuals who participated in longer gatekeeper trainings identified, on average, more at-risk youths than those who participated in shorter gatekeeper trainings. The difference found was small, though significant, and when applied to a large number of schools and trainees, could reach a large number of at-risk students. Trainees who undergo a more in-depth gatekeeper training are able to identify and refer youth to appropriate services at a higher rate than individuals who undergo briefer trainings (Condron et al. 2018).

In a review of the literature regarding gatekeeper training for those serving adolescent and young adult populations, Lipson (2013) found that research is often focused on outcomes such as beliefs, knowledge, and self-efficacy of trainees, and there is a paucity of research regarding behavioral changes in trainees and population-level changes in outcomes. In addition, the results of this review indicate that positive changes found often diminish over time. These improvements and deficits in outcomes have also been found in research on gatekeeper trainings which occur specifically in school settings (Mo, Ko, & Kin, 2018). In a broader review of the literature on gatekeeper trainings, Burnette, Ramchand, & Ayer (2015) suggest that there is some research evidence that gatekeepers have increased knowledge about suicide and more adaptive beliefs about prevention and decreased reluctance so intervene. They caution, however, that research has not assessed how the knowledge, beliefs, and skills learned in gatekeeper training are best translated into significant behavioral changes. Although there is a limited number of randomized controlled trials comparing suicide prevention programs, there is enough evidence to indicate that gatekeeper training, in combination with recurrent mental health and suicide screening, is an effective suicide prevention intervention strategy (Robinson et al. 2013).

Effectiveness of Paraprofessionals

A survey of topic areas in the Community Mental Health Journal between 1965 and 1977 showed that articles on paraprofessionals ranked 6 out of 38 topics (Lounsbury et al. 1979). In the years following the opening of the Los Angeles Suicide Prevention Center, Heilig et al. (1968) conducted a study of the use of volunteers in the evaluation and handing of suicidal crisis at the LASPC. Volunteers were found to be proficient in obtaining information from callers and mobilizing their resources. More than their professional colleagues, volunteers were able to offer direct and friendly relationships to callers in crisis. One limiting factor of the usefulness of volunteers at the LASPC was that although bringing in trained volunteers increased the amount of work able to be accomplished, this increase in the number of individuals answering calls and responding to callers can interfere with the ability to keep track of cases and communicate their content clearly. The study concluded that the most important factors in increasing efficacy of the use of volunteers was a focus on enthusiasm, interest, coordination, and direction of the staff.

Durlak (1979b) reviewed 42 studies comparing the effectiveness or professional and paraprofessional helpers and found that clinical outcomes of the paraprofessionals were equal to, or significantly better than, those from professionals. Some studies suggest that volunteers who are not trained or who are lesser trained are not as effective (Armstrong 2010). Gilat, Tobin, & Sharhar (2012) found that one benefit of training for paraprofessionals is that they were more likely to use emotion-focused strategies and more therapeutic-like cognitive-focused strategies than individuals in the community who are not trained. Armstrong (2003) found, however, that training for paraprofessionals had minimal effect on process issues.

In general, professional training is not a prerequisite for effective helping (Berman & Norton 1985; Bright, Baker, & Neimeyer 1999; Creaser & Carsello 1979; Summers, Faucher, & Chapman 1973; Getz, Fujita, & Allen 1975; Garber-Epstein et al. 2013; Hoffman & Warner 1976; King et al. 2003; Morgan & King 1975; Pope et al. 1976; Rickel, 1982; Siegel 1973; Stein & Lambert 1984; Steisel 1972; Simonson & Bahr 1974). Male college students in time-limited psychotherapy improved as much when they were seen by college professors as students being seen by highly experienced psychotherapists (Strupp & Hadley 1979).

There has been research on the effectiveness of crisis centers, and the evidence is mixed. Some are believed to help, but there appears to be a limited effect on youth suicide prevention (Lester 1997; Frankish 1994; Dew et al. 1987), to the extent to which suicide prevention can be measured. One study found that almost all high school students knew about the crisis hotline in their community, but only 5.6% had used one. Most callers who identified as suicidal expressed problems with family, self-esteem, and drugs and alcohol (Gould & Kramer 2001). Some studies, however, have detected a reduced suicide rate among young white females, who make up most of the callers to these centers (Miller et al. 1984).

There is some evidence that crisis call centers are effective in Canada (Leenaars & Lester 1995, 2004) and in Japan (Lester, Saito, & Abe 1996, 1997; Stein & Lambert 1984). Besides looking at the suicide rates, these centers are found to help people with decreased depressive mood and hopelessness; they have decreased suicidality, and are able to make a safety contract (Gould, Kalafat, & Munfakh 2007; Mishara & Daigle 1997). Most centers provide Rogerian nondirective counseling (Mishara & Daigle 1997) although some do provide more direct counseling (Daigle & Mishara 1995). Different centers tend to provide different types of counseling (Powell 1976).

There has also been some research on the effectiveness of suicide loss survivor support groups. These groups differ in their leadership, with group facilitators sometimes being mental health professionals, sometimes trained facilitators who are survivors of suicide loss, and sometimes by untrained suicide loss survivors. Farberow (1992) evaluated the survivor support group at the Los Angeles Suicide Prevention Center, which was co-facilitated by a mental health professional and a trained suicide loss survivor. Compared to a control group, they reported an increase in positive outcome and the vast majority of members felt that participating in the group had helped them. Reviewing these positive results, however, McIntosh (2017) found that most of the studies evaluating suicide loss survivor support groups find positive effects, but the research methodologies are usually weak. Current research on the area of crisis centers, hotlines, and support groups is limited.

The training of paraprofessional counselors focuses on relationship building skills (Danish & D'Augelli 1976). This leads to better rapport, greater trust, and attachment which in turn leads to more social support and more healing. Post training, paraprofessionals demonstrate increased substantive knowledge, interviewing skills, correctness of clinical judgments and referral suggestions, and overall crisis intervention competence (Schinke et al. 1979). These trained paraprofessionals were found to be more "helpful" than their untrained nonprofessional counterparts (D'Augelli & Levy 1978). Although research supports some positive outcomes, crisis centers and paraprofessionals exhibit some weaknesses. Without training, or when training is inadequate, or not coupled with trained supervision, failures happen. Many centers have a high rate of turnover and burnout (Littlefield & Koff 1986) and older research suggested they do not successfully reach suicidal elderly (Adamek & Kaplan 1996).

Mixed Messages

Thus far, we have reviewed numerous studies spanning several decades, which offer conflicting evidence in terms of the training requirements, and effectiveness, of paraprofessionals. Armstrong (2010, 2003) has identified the key issue of inconsistency in program evaluation. In support of, and in addition to, Armstrong's work, we would assert that there are two primary reasons for this inconsistency: 1) Issues inherent to program evaluations: Individual research studies only capture a "snapshot" of any given program, that is, of one group of volunteers, and one group of clients, at one point in time. Similar to a candid photograph, chance has a role, because any one "capture" might be worthy of pride, but it might be equally worthy of disappointment. Even studies which attempt to expand beyond a one-time event and track later developments are rife with attrition (people who are unreachable or unable/unwilling to participate) and are limited in scope due to constraints such as confidentiality, lack of funding, or even lack of interested researchers; 2) Issues inherent to replicability: The field of social sciences is currently struggling with what some have termed the "Replication Crisis," an inability to appropriately reproduce outcomes to commonly accepted psychosocial phenomena, purportedly due to issues such as inadequate or misleading disclosure and non-transparency of methodology, chance events, or researcher bias in reporting data which are considered "outliers" or missing (random or not) (Pashler & Harris 2012; Open Science Collaboration 2015). In the context of paraprofessional training and service delivery, replicability is inherently challenging, which further compounds the challenges in demonstrating empirically the effectiveness of both training programs and the paraprofessional interventions themselves. Accordingly, we would offer that there would be greater utility to consider such programs and interventions in terms of relative *success*, as opposed to *effectiveness*. Measures of effectiveness may lack the sensitivity or be inappropriate to fully evaluate the nuance of the indices of a successful crisis intervention at the individual (micro) and community (meso) levels.

Current and Future Developments

Mental Health First Aid

Mental Health First Aid is a standardized public education program designed to increase public mental health literacy and to address the reality that family members, friends, neighbors, co-workers, and other members of the public often can be the first to respond to someone developing a mental health crisis (Kitchener & Jorm 2008; Kitchener & Jorm 2002; Jorm 2000). Developed in Australia in 2001, the program has been adopted in more than 20 countries (Hadlaczky, Hokby, Mkrtchian, Carli & Wasserman 2014). In the US Mental Healthcare First Aid was introduced by the National Council for Behavioral Health, and information on the US program is available through www.mentalhealthfirstaid.org. The program has been offered in all 50 states and is available to the public through local government programs in many cities and counties, and in the 10 years since its introduction in the US more than 1 million individuals in the US have received the training (www.mentalhealthfirstaid.org).

Based on the first aid paradigm for physical injury, Mental Health First Aid teaches members of the public how to recognize signs of a mental health problem and provides a 5-step action plan that anyone can use to assist someone in psychological distress: Assess for risk of suicide or harm, listen nonjudgmentally, give reassurance and information, encourage appropriate professional help, and encourage self-help and other supportive strategies (Lucksted, Mendenhall, Frauenholtz & Aakre 2015; Kitchener & Jorm 2008). In addition to the action plan, Mental Health First Aid training includes an introduction to the symptoms and risk factors for a number of mental health problems and provides information on local and national mental health resources (El-Amin, Anderson, Leider, Satorius & Knudson 2018; Kitchener & Jorm 2002). Youth Mental Health First Aid, a modified training program focusing on emotional problems and psychological disorders among young people, provides trainees with similar tools and education (Aakre, Lucksted, & Browning-McNee 2016).

Mental Health First Aid has been found to increase trainees' knowledge regarding mental health, decrease their negative attitudes about mental illness, increase their appreciation of the distress experiences in mental illness and their empathy for persons with mental health issues, and increase their confidence in trying to provide help (El-Amin et al. 2018; Aakre et al. 2016; Lucksted et al. 2015; Hadlaczky et al. 2014; Morawska et al. 2013). As a tool to increase the mental health literacy of the public, Mental Health First Aid can help to counteract the stigma of mental health problems, which is a significant public-health related obstacle in suicide prevention (Hadlaczky et al. 2014). Equating "first aid" for mental health problems with the first aid for physical injuries makes them both routine responses to someone in need that can be administered by a conscientious passerby (El-Amin et al. 2018). Mental Health First Aid empowers trainees to ask questions about suicide and self-harm risks and "#bethedifference" where they previously may have been hesitant to try to help (Lucksted et al. 2015). And by engaging members of their own community Mental Health First Aid reduces the social distance between the person suffering a mental health crisis and someone who can help (Morawska et al. 2013).

Paraprofessionals and Technology

Recently there has been an increase in research on the relationship between the internet and suicide. Some research seems to suggest that the internet is linked to an increase in suicidal behavior, but at the same time there is an increase in potentially effective prevention and postvention strategies, such as online chats and support groups (Krysinska et al. 2017; Robert et al. 2015).

Preliminary research shows that online interventions, such as social media, can increase positive outcomes (Mokkenstorm et al. 2017), be cost-effective (van Spijker et al. 2012), and be viewed as safe and acceptable by participants (Robinson et al. 2015). Additionally, online interventions can also support in-person or over-the-phone interventions by being used as a point of first contact with crisis centers and hotlines (Predmore et al. 2017). Technology-based interventions using trained paraprofessionals as "coaches" can provide mental health support on an ongoing basis and with lowered barriers to access. For example, MindRight, a technology nonprofit, provides proactive mental health coaching to youth on a text messaging platform using trained volunteer coaches supervised by mental health professionals (https://getmindright.org/).

The rise in cell phone use, particularly the possibility of communicating to others through text, has allowed for the development of text-based interventions. Nancy Lublin, founder and CEO of DoSomething.org and the creator of the National Text Crisis Line shares in a TEDTalk why she founded the text line. DoSomething is a digital platform that mobilizes young people around the world to take social action in their communities through volunteering, promoting social change, or organizing civic action campaigns. The primary mode of communication with young people is by texting, and in hundreds of campaigns in any given year they average a 97% open rate. The management of DoSomething noticed that in every civic action campaign they received a dozen or so text messages that had nothing to do with the campaign but were about being bullied or having an addiction problem. In her TED Talk Lublin relates that "the worst message we ever got said exactly this: 'He won't stop raping me. It's my dad. He told me not to tell anyone. Are you there?'"

(TED Talk, www.ted.com/talks/nancy_lublin_the_heartbreaking_text_that_inspired_a_crisis_help_line/transcript?language=en#t-114119).

In response, DoSomething did something. They launched Crisis Text Line in Chicago and El Paso, and within a few months there were locally managed crisis text lines in every area code in the U.S., with no marketing. The private element of texting means that kids can text during lunch or from home and generally if they text, they want help. Crisis Text Lines average 2.41 active rescues every day, and 30% of the texts are about depression or suicide. As Lublin says in her TED Talk:

> The beautiful thing about Crisis Text Line is that these are strangers counseling other strangers on the most intimate issues, and getting them from hot moments to cold moments. It's exciting, and I will tell you that we have done a total of more than 6.5 million text messages in less than two years . . .

According to www.crisistrends.org, the repository of Crisis Text Line data made available to the public, more than 14,869,776 messages (on average) are exchanged every year. As a free, 24/7 service, the line is answered by trained volunteers who can work from anywhere with a computer and a secure connection. They receive training so they can learn how to manage the crisis text platform, be an active listener, help others solve problems, and create a safety plan, and the Crisis Text Line requests that every volunteer serve four hours each week to a minimum of 200 total hours. In her TED Talk, Lublin makes the point that because their work is text based, they can use data from calls to create algorithms, and the algorithms help the trained volunteers with appropriate and helpful responses to texters:

> We know that if you text the words "numbs" and "sleeve," there's a 99 percent match for cutting. We know that if you text in the words "mg" and "rubber band," there's a 99 percent match for substance abuse. And we know that if you text in "sex," "oral" and "Mormon," you're questioning if you're gay. Now that's interesting information that a counselor could figure out but that algorithm in our hands means that an automatic pop-up says, "99 percent match for cutting – try asking one of these questions" to prompt the counselor. Or "99 percent match for substance abuse, here are three drug clinics near the texter." It makes us more accurate.

Volunteers learn how to use the text line software and how to use the algorithms to help the person who is texting. More importantly, unlike a telephone hotline that must answer calls in the order in which they are received, the algorithms mean that individuals in suicidal crisis or in danger of self-harm are flagged and are triaged so they jump to number one in the queue.

Much like the National Suicide Prevention Lifeline, the Crisis Text Line is made up of a network of state-based locally operated crisis text lines, and although it started in the United States, it is operating also in Canada and the UK. Their tag line expresses the philosophy: "Strangers Helping Strangers via Text."

One example of this is HOPELINE, a text-based, free, 24/7 service in the state of Wisconsin that allows users to text from anywhere to receive emotional support. It offers a good example of what community volunteers working with textlines all over the United States are offering their communities. HOPELINE is not meant to be used as counseling, is not a suicide hotline, and is not meant to be used for medical purposes. In addition, HOPELINE is text-only and does not give the possibility of talking on the phone. Individuals text the word HOPELINE to 741741 and immediately receive a text back from a trained volunteer responding on a secure network using a computer or laptop.

Training of volunteers for crisis text lines is constantly evaluated and improved, and further development of the text line is through data evaluation. Because the text line is based on technology, Crisis Text Line has developed a large data set which is used to improve services. For example, responders who identify texter strengths (such as "you showed courage by texting us") receive higher satisfaction rates from texters. Data collected by Crisis Text Lines demonstrates that the "three most effective terms to use are brave, smart, and proud." www.crisistextline.org/philosophy

By partnering with the National Crisis Text Line, HOPELINE was able to become 24/7, have a standard training for all responders, collect data, and gain momentum in advertising and effectiveness. They have utilized social media in reaching individuals who may need the service, and have teamed up with the Tavern League to put HOPELINE pint glasses in bars while training their staff on the resource. Another awareness campaign has included the creation of the HOPELINE Challenge Coin used by law enforcement, VA's, and American Legions. https://centerforsuicideawareness.org/#HOPELINE

Areas of Growth

Despite the efforts of trained professionals and paraprofessionals there are still a vast majority of underserved individuals who never receive traditional mental health services (Walfish & Gesten 2008). Efforts to reach these individuals include the use of call centers, posting advertisements in emergency waiting rooms, peer referrals, and making contact through local places of worship. Limitations often include a lack of funding, or inability to properly allocate existing resources. Crisis centers and hotlines need leaders and administrators who know: 1) what training is needed, and 2) how to effectively run the program. Additionally, programs may have difficulty reaching or bringing in possible volunteers due to restrictions based on time, distance, language barriers, etc. These hindrances to recruiting, and keeping, trained staff mirror the difficulties in overcoming social barriers to those in need of mental health care, and suicide prevention. Truly, it takes a village to prevent a suicide, and trained paraprofessionals – ordinary people – demonstrate that mental health professionals are not the only means through which people can receive help; ordinary people can be good helpers. The use of paraprofessionals provides a cost-effective solution that, assuming proper training, can lead to successful outcomes (Walfish & Gesten 2008). By increasing awareness of the utility and *successfulness* of paraprofessionals, at local, and state, and federal levels, we would hope that more individuals would consider the role of the paraprofessional as an additional strategy in the fight against suicide, and for equal access to mental health services, and ultimately, for social justice.

References

Aakre, JM, Lucksted, A, & Browning-McNee, LA 2016, 'Evaluation of Youth Mental Health First Aid USA: A program to assist young people in psychological distress', *Psychological Services*, vol. 13, no. 2, pp. 121–126. doi: 10.1037/ser0000063

Abbey, J, Madsen, CH, & Polland, R 1989, 'Short-term suicide awareness curriculum', *Suicide and Life-Threatening Behavior*, vol. 19, no. 2, pp. 216–227.

Adamek, ME & Kaplan, MS 1996, 'Managing elder suicide: A profile of American and Canadian crisis prevention centers', *Suicide and Life-Threatening Behavior*, vol. 26, no. 2, pp. 122–131.

Aiken, LS, Losciuto, LA, Annausetts, M, & Brown, BS 1984, 'Paraprofessional versus professional drug counselors: Diverse routes to the same role', *International Journal of the Addictions*, vol. 19, no. 2, pp. 153–173.

Alley, S & Blanton, J 1976, 'A study of paraprofessionals in mental health', *Community Mental Health Journal*, vol. 12, no. 2, pp. 151–160.

Amodio, D 2009, 'Intergroup anxiety effects on the control of racial stereotypes: A psychoneuroendocrine analysis', *Journal of Experimental Social Psychology*, vol. 45, pp. 60–67. doi:10.1016/j.jesp.2008.08.009

Amodio, D & Hamilton, H 2012, 'Intergroup anxiety effects on implicit racial evaluation and stereotyping', *Emotion*, vol. 12, no. 6, 1273–1280. doi: 10.1037/a0029016

Andrews, JO, Felton, G, Wewers, ME, & Heath, J 2004, 'Use of community health workers in research with ethnic minority women', *Journal of Nursing Scholarship*, vol. 36, no. 1, pp. 358–365.

Armstrong, J 2003, 'Training for paraprofessional counsellors: Evaluating the meaning and impact of a common factors approach', *Counselling and Psychotherapy Research*, vol.3, no. 4, pp. 270–277.

Armstrong, J 2010, 'How effective are minimally trained/experienced volunteer mental health counsellors? Evaluation of CORE outcome data' *Counselling and Psychotherapy Research*, vol. 10, no. 1, pp. 22–31. doi: 10.1080/14733140903163284

Bartels, BD & Tyler, JD 1975, 'Paraprofessionals in the community mental health center', *Professional Psychology*, vol. 6, no. 4, pp. 442–452.

Bergsieker, H, Shelton, JN, and Richeson, J 2010, 'To be liked versus respected: Divergent goals in interracial interactions', *Journal of Personality and Social Psychology*, vol. 99, no. 2 pp. 248–264. doi: 10.1037/a0018474

Berman, JS & Norton, NC 1985, 'Does professional training make a therapist more effective?', *Psychological Bulletin*, vol. 98, no. 2, pp. 401–407.

Birenbaum, A & Ahmed, MB 1978, 'Career perspectives of paraprofessionals', *Administration in Mental Health*, vol. 6, no. 1, pp. 42–56.

Bright, JI, Baker, KD, & Neimeyer, RA 1999, 'Professional and paraprofessional group treatments for depression: A comparison of cognitive-behavioral and mutual support interventions', *Journal of Consulting and Clinical Psychology*, vol. 67, no. 4, pp. 491–501.

Bronfenbrenner, U 2005, 'Ecological systems theory' 1992, In U. Bronfenbrenner (ed), *Making human beings human: Bioecological perspectives on human development*, Thousand Oaks, CA: Sage Publications. pp. 106–173.

Burnette, C, Ramchand, R, & Ayer, L 2015, 'Gatekeeper training for suicide prevention: A theoretical model and review of the empirical literature', *Rand Health Quarterly*, vol. 5, no. 1, p. 16

Catanzarite, JA, & Robinson, MD 2013, 'Peer education in campus suicide prevention', *New Directions for Student Services*, vol. 2013, no. 141, pp. 43–53.

Christensen, A, Miller, WR, & Monoz, RF 1978, 'Paraprofessionals, partners, peers, paraphernalia, and print: Expanding mental health service delivery', *Professional Psychology*, vol. 9, no. 2, pp. 249–270.

Condron, D, Garraza, L, Walrath, C, McKeon, R, Goldston, D, and Heilbron, N 2015, 'Identifying and referring oyuths at risk for suicide following participation in school-based gatekeeper training', *Suicide and Life-Threatening Behavior*, vol. 45, no. 4, pp. 461–475.

Condron, S, Godoy Garraza, L, Kuiper, N, Sukumar, B, Walrath, C, & McKeon, R 2018, 'Comparing the effectiveness of brief versus in-depth gatekeeper training on behavioral outcomes for trainees', *Crisis: The Journal of Crisis Intervention and Suicide Prevention*. Advance online publication. doi: 10.1027/0227-5910/a000539

Constantino, M, Morrison, NR, Coyne, AE, & Howard, T 2017, 'Exploring therapeutic alliance training in clinical and counseling psychology graduate programs', *Training and Education in Professional Psychology*, vol. 11, no. 4, pp. 219–226. doi: 10.1037/tep0000157

Cooke, G, Wehmer, G, & Gruber, J 1975, 'Training paraprofessionals in the treatment of alcoholism: Effects on knowledge, attitudes and therapeutic techniques', *Journal of Studies on Alcohol and Drugs*, vol. 36, no. 1 pp. 938–948.

Cowen, EL, Trost, MA, & Izzo, LD 1973, 'Nonprofessional human-service personnel in consulting roles', *Community Mental Health Journal*, vol. 9, no. 4, pp. 335–341.

Creaser, JW & Carsello, CJ 1979, 'Isolating factors related to paraprofessional effectiveness', *Journal of Counseling Psychology*, vol. 26, no. 3, pp. 259–262.

Crisis Text Line 2018, *Purpose*. Viewed 21 September 2018, www.crisistextline.org/purpose

Cwik, MF, Barlow, A, Goklish, N, Larzelere-Hinton, F, Tingey, L, Craig, M, Lupe, R, & Walkup, J 2014, 'Community-based surveillance and case management for suicide prevention: An American Indian tribally initiated system', *American Journal of Public Health*, vol. 104, no. 3, pp. 18–23.

Daigle, MS, & Mishara, BL 1995, 'Intervention styles with suicidal callers at two suicide prevention centers', *Suicide and Life-Threatening Behavior*, vol. 25 no. 2, pp. 261–275.

Danish, SJ, & D'Augelli, AR 1976, 'Rationale and implementation of a training program for paraprofessionals', *Professional Psychology*, vol. 7 no. 1, *pp.* 38–46.

D'Augelli, AR, & Levy, M 1978, 'The verbal helping skills of trained and untrained human service paraprofessionals', *American Journal of Community Psychology*, vol. 6, no. 1, pp. 23–34.

Delworth, U 1974, 'Paraprofessionals as guerrillas: Recommendations for system change', *Journal of Counseling and Development*, vol. 53, no. 4, pp. 335–338.

Dew, MA, Bromet, EJ, Brent, D, & Greenhouse, JB 1987, 'A quantitative literature review of the effectiveness of suicide prevention centers', *Journal of Consulting and Clinical Psychology*, vol. 55, no. 2, pp. 239–244.

Dublin, LI 1969, 'Suicide prevention', In E. Shneidman (Ed.), *On the nature of suicide*, San Francisco, CA: Jossey-Bass. pp. 45–46

Durlak, JA 1979a, 'Assessment of paraprofessionals' on-the-job performance in an outpatient child guidance clinic', *Journal of Community Psychology*, vol. 7, no. 4, pp. 348–353.

Durlak, JA 1979b, 'Comparative effectiveness of paraprofessional and professional helpers', *Psychological Bulletin*, vol. 86, no. 1, pp. 80–92.

El-Amin, T, Anderson, BL, Leider, JP, Satorius, J, & Knudson, A 2018, 'Enhancing mental health literacy in rural America: Growth of Mental Health First Aid program in rural communities in the United States from 2008–2016', *Journal of Rural Mental Health*, vol. 42, no. 1, pp. 20–31. doi: 10.1037/rmh0000088

Enright, MF & Parsons, BV 1976, 'Training crisis intervention specialists and peer group counselors as therapeutic agents in the gay community', *Community Mental Health Journal*, vol. 12, no. 4, pp. 383–391.

Farberow, NL 1992, 'The Los Angeles Survivors-After-Suicide Program: An evaluation', *Crisis: Journal of Crisis Intervention and Suicide Prevention*, vol. 13, no. 1, pp. 23–34.

Frankish, CJ 1994, 'Crisis centers and their role in treatment: Suicide prevention versus health promotion', *Death Studies*, vol. 18, no. 4, pp. 327–339.

Gartner, A & Riessman, F 1974, 'The paraprofessional movement in perspective', *Journal of Counseling and Development*, vol. 53, no. 4, pp. 352–356.

Gatz, M, Hileman, C, & Amaral, P 1984, 'Older adult paraprofessionals: Working with and in behalf of older adults', *Journal of Community Psychology*, vol. 12, no. 4, pp. 347–358.

Getz, WL, Fujita, BN, & Allen, D 'The use of paraprofessionals in crisis intervention' *American Journal of Community Psychology*, vol. 3, no. 2, pp. 135–145. doi: 10.1007/BF00877788

Giblin, PT 1989, 'Effective utilization and evaluation of indigenous health care workers', *Public Health Reports*, vol. 104, no. 4, pp. 361–368.

Gilat, I & Shahar, G 2009, 'Suicide prevention by online support groups: An action theory-based model of emotional first aid', *Archives of Suicide Research*, vol. 13, no. 1, pp. 52–63.

Gilat, I, Tobin, Y, & Sharhar, G 2012, 'Responses to suicidal messages in an online support group: comparisons between trained volunteers and lay individuals', *Social Psychiatry*, vol. 47, no. 12.

Godsil, R & Richardson, LS 2017, 'Racial anxiety', *Iowa Law Review*, vol. 102, pp. 2235–2263. Available at https://ilr.law.uiowa.edu/print/volume-102-issue-5/racial-anxiety/

Goldston, DB, Walrath, CM, McKeon, R, Puddy, RW, Lubell, KM, Potter, LB, & Rodi, MS 2010, 'The Garret Lee Smith Memorial suicide prevention program', *Suicide and Life-Threatening Behavior*, vol. 40, no. 3, pp. 245–256.

Gone, JP & Alacantra, C 2007, 'Identifying effective mental health interventions for American Indian and Alaska Natives: A review of the literature', *Cultural Diversity and Ethnic Minority Psychology*, vol. 13, no. 4, pp. 356–363.

Gordon, DA & Arbuthnot, J 1988, 'The use of paraprofessionals to deliver home-based family therapy to juvenile delinquents', *Criminal Justice and Behavior*, vol. 15, no. 3, pp. 364–378.

Gould, MS & Kramer, RA 2001, 'Youth suicide prevention', *Suicide and Life-Threatening Behavior*, vol. 31, pp. 6–31.

Gould, MS, Kalafat, J, & Munfakh, JLH 2007, 'An evaluation of crisis hotline outcomes part 2: Suicidal callers', *Suicide and Life-Threatening Behavior*, vol. 37, no. 3, pp. 338–352.

Greenland, K, Xenias, D, & Maio, G 2012, 'Intergroup anxiety from the self and other: Evidence from self-report, physiological effects, and real interactions', *European Journal of Social Psychology*, vol. 42, no. 2, pp. 150–163. doi: 10.1002/ejsp.867

Gregory, A 2015, 'R U There? A new counseling service harnesses the power of the text message', *The New Yorker*, 9 February. Available at: www.newyorker.com/magazine/2015/02/09/r-u

Guerrero-Berroa, E & Phillips, RSC 2001, 'Health care paraprofessionals' awareness of the symptoms of geriatric depression', *Journal of Psychosocial Nursing and Mental Health Services*, vol. 39, no. 11, pp. 14–20.

Hadlaczky G, Hokby S, Mkrtchian A, Carli V, Wasserman D. 2014, Mental Health First Aid is an effective public health intervention for improving knowledge, attitudes, and behaviour: A meta-analysis. *International Review of Psychiatry*, 2014; 4; 467–475.

Hall, BL & Epp, HL 2001, 'Can professionals and nonprofessionals work together following a suicide?', *Crisis: Journal of Crisis Intervention and Suicide Prevention*, vol. 22, no. 2, pp. 4–78.

Hangartner, R, Totura, C, Labouliere, C, Gryglewicz, K, & Karver, M 2018, 'Benchmarking the "Question, Persuade, Refer" Program Against Evaluations of Established Suicide Prevention Gatekeeper Trainings', *Suicide Life-Threatening Behavior*. doi:10.1111/sltb.12430

Heilig, SM, Farberow, NL, Litman, RE, & Shneidman, ES 1968, 'The role of nonprofessional volunteers in a suicide prevention center', *Community Mental Health Journal*, vol. 4, no. 4, pp. 287–295.

Hetherington, K 1995, 'Professionals and nonprofessionals beyond the difference: The emergence of mutual compromise', *International Journal of Mental Health*, vol. 24, pp. 59–69.

Hoffman, AM & Warner, RW 1976, 'Paraprofessional effectiveness', *Journal of Counseling and Development*, vol. 10, pp. 494–497.

Jones, KH, & Bender, WN 1993, 'Utilization of paraprofessionals in special education: A review of the literature', *Remedial and Special Education*, vol. 14, no. 1, pp. 7–14.

Jorm, AF 2000, 'Mental health literacy: Public knowledge and beliefs about mental disorders', *The British Journal of Psychiatry*, vol. 177, 396–401. doi: 10.1192/bjp.177.5.396 Available at www.cambridge.org/core/services/aop-cambridge-core/content/view/5563369643662EC541F33D1DD307AD35/S000712500022730Xa.pdf/mental_health_literacy.pdf

Kalafat, J & Boroto, DR 1977, 'The paraprofessional movement as a paradigm community psychology endeavor', *Journal of Community Psychology*, vol. 5, no. 1, pp. 3–12.

King, R, Nurcombe, B, Bickman, L, Hides, L, & Rief, W 2003, 'Telephone counseling for adolescent suicide prevention: Changes in suicidality and mental state from beginning to end of a counseling session', *Suicide and Life-Threatening Behavior*, vol. 33, no. 4, pp. 400–411.

Kitchener, BA, & Jorm, AF 2008, 'Mental Health First Aid: An international programme for early intervention', *Early Intervention in Psychiatry*, vol. 2, no. 1, 55–61. doI: 10.1111/j.1751-7893.2007.00056.x Available at https://onlinelibrary.wiley.com/doi/epdf/10.1111/j.1751-7893.2007.00056.x

Kitchener, BA, & Jorm, AF 2002, 'Mental health first aid training for the public: Evaluation of effects on knowledge, attitudes and helping behavior', *BMC Psychiatry*, vol. 2. doi: 10.10.1186/1471-244X-2-10. Available at www.ncbi.nlm.nih.gov/pmc/articles/PMC130043/pdf/1471-244X-2-10.pdf

Krysinska, K, Westerlund, M, Niederkrotenthaler, T, Andriessen, K, Carli, V, Hadlaczky, G, . . . Wasserman, D 2017, 'A mapping study on the internet and suicide', *Crisis: The Journal of Crisis Intervention and Suicide Prevention*, vol. 38, no. 4, pp. 217–226. doi: 10.1027/0227-5910/a000444

Leenaars, AA & Lester, D 1995, 'Impact of suicide prevention centers on suicide in Canada', *Crisis: The Journal of Crisis Intervention and Suicide Prevention*, vol. 16, no. 1, p. 39.

Leenaars, AA., & Lester, D 2004, 'The impact of suicide prevention centers on the suicide rate in the Canadian provinces', *Crisis: The Journal of Crisis Intervention and Suicide Prevention*, vol. 25, no. 2, pp. 65–68.

Lenihan, G & Kirk, W 1990, 'Using student paraprofessionals in the treatment of eating disorders', *Journal of Counseling and Development*, 68, no. 3, pp. 332–335.

Lester, D 1997, 'The effectiveness of suicide prevention centers: A review', *Suicide and Life-Threatening Behavior*, vol. 27, no. 3, pp. 304–310.

Lester, D, Saito, Y, & Abe, K 1996, 'Have suicide prevention centers prevented suicide in Japan?' *Archives of Suicide Research* vol. 2, no. 2, pp. 125–128.

Lester, D, Saito, Y, & Abe, K 1997, 'The effect of suicide prevention centers on suicide in Japan', *Crisis: The Journal of Crisis Intervention and Suicide Prevention*, vol. 18, no. 1, pp. 48.

Levitt, AJ, Lorenzo, J, Yu, VY, Wean, C, & Miller-Solarino, S 2011, 'Suicide awareness and prevention workshop for social workers and paraprofessionals' *Journal of Social Work Education*, vol. 47, no. 3, pp. 607–613.

Lindsey, JD 1983, 'Paraprofessionals in learning disabilities' *Journal of Learning Disabilities*, vol.16, no. 8, pp. 467–472.

Lipson, SK 2013, 'A comprehensive review of mental health gatekeeper-trainings for adolescents and young adults', *International Journal of Adolescent Medicine and Health*, vol. 26, no. 3, pp. 1–12.

Littlefield, SN, & Koff, SZ 1986, 'Hotlines that burnout: A study of factors which contribute to the failure of crisis intervention centers', *Journal of Health and Human Resources Administration*, vol. 8, no. 3, pp. 279–295.

Lounsbury, JW, Roisum, KG, Pokorny, L, Sills, A, & Meissen, GJ 1979, 'An analysis of topic areas and topic trends in the Community Mental Health Journal from 1965 through 1977', *Community Mental Health Journal*, vol. 15, no. 4, pp. 267–276.

Lubin, N 2015, 'How data from a crisis text line is saving lives,' online video, TED Talk, viewed 5 September 2019, www.ted.com/talks/nancy_lublin_the_heartbreaking_text_that_inspired_a_crisis_help_line/transcript?language=en#t-114119

Lucksted, A, Mendenhall, AN, Frauenholtz, SI, & Aakre, JM 2015, 'Experiences of graduates of the Mental Health First Aid-USA course', *International Journal of Mental Health Promotion*, vol. 17, no. 3, pp. 169–183. http://dx.doi.org/10.1080/14623730.2015.1013670

McGuire, TG, & Miranda, J 2008, 'New evidence regarding racial and ethnic disparities in mental health: policy implications', *Health Affairs (Project Hope)*, vol. 27, no. 2, pp. 393–403.

McIntosh, JL 2017, 'Characteristics and effectiveness of suicide survivor support groups', in K Andriessen, K Krysinska, & OT Grad (eds.), *Postvention in action: The International Handbook of Suicide Bereavement Support*. Boston, MA: Hogrefe Publishing. pp. 117–130.

McWilliams, SA 1972, 'A process analysis of nonprofessional intervention with children' *Journal of School Psychology*, vol. 10, no. 4, pp. 367–377.

Miller, HL, Coombs, DW, Leeper, JD, & Barton, SN 1984, 'An analysis of the effects of suicide prevention facilities on suicide rates in the United States', *American Journal of Public Health*, vol. 74, no. 4, pp. 340–343.

Minore, B & Boone, M 2002, 'Realizing potential: Improving interdisciplinary professional/paraprofessional health care teams in Canada's northern Aboriginal communities through education', *Journal of Interprofessional Care*, vol. 16, no. 2, pp. 139–147.

Mishara, BL & Daigle, MS 1997, 'Effects of different telephone intervention styles with suicidal callers at two suicide prevention centers: An empirical investigation', *American Journal of Community Psychology*, vol. 25, no. 6, pp. 861–885.

Mo, P, Ko, TT, & Xin, MQ 2018, 'School-based gatekeeper training programmes in enhancing gatekeepers' cognitions and behaviours for adolescent suicide prevention: a systematic review', *Child and Adolescent Psychiatry and Mental Health*, vol. 12, no. 29, pp. 1–24. doi: 10.1186/s13034-018-0233-4

Mokkenstorm, JK, Eikelenboom, M, Huisman, A, Wiebenga, J, Gilissen, R, Kerkhof, AJFM, & Smit, JH 2017, 'Evaluation of the 113Online suicide prevention crisis chat service: Outcomes, helper behaviors and comparison to telephone hotlines', *Suicide and Life-Threatening Behavior*, vol. 47, no. 3, pp. 282–296. doi: 10.1111/sltb.12286

Morawska, A, Fletcher, R, Pope, S, Heathwood, E, Anderson, E, & McAuliffe, C 2013, 'Evaluation of mental health first aid training in a diverse community setting', *International Journal of Mental Health Nursing*, vol. 22, no. 1, pp. 85–92. doi: 10.1111/j.

Morgan, JP & King, GD 1975, 'The selection and evaluation of the volunteer paraprofessional telephone counselor', *American Journal of Community Psychology*, vol. 3, no. 3, pp. 237–247.

Morris, L 2011, 'History of Suicide Prevention Center' [Powerpoint Presentation]. Available at: http://file.lacounty.govSDSInterdmm166651_HistoryoftheSuicidePreventionCenter.pdf (Accessed 30 August 2018).

Nolan, KJ. & Cooke, ET 1970, 'The training and utilization of the mental health paraprofessional within the military: The social work/psychology specialist', *American Journal of Psychiatry*, vol. 127, no. 1, pp. 74–79.

Pattison, EM & Elpers, JR 1972, 'A developmental view of mental health manpower trends', *Psychiatric Services*, vol. 23, no. 11, pp. 325–328.

Okun, L, Chang, DF, Kanhai, G, Dunn, J, & Easley, H 2017, 'Inverting the power dynamic: The process of first sessions of psychotherapy with therapists of color and non-Latino white patients', *Journal of Counseling Psychology*, vol. 64, no. 4, pp. 443–452. doi: 10.1037/cou0000223

Office of the Surgeon General, National Action Alliance for Suicide Prevention 2012, 'National Strategy for Suicide Prevention: goals and objectives for action: A report of the US Surgeon General and of the National Action Alliance for Suicide Prevention.

Open Science Collaboration 2015, 'Estimating the reproducibility of psychological science', *Science*, vol. 349, no. 6251, pp. aac4716.

Pashler, H, & Harris, CR 2012, 'Is the replicability crisis overblown? Three arguments examined', *Perspectives on Psychological Science*, vol. 7, pp. 531–536.

Pless, IB & Satterwhite, B 1972, 'Chronic illness in childhood: Selection, activities and evaluation of non-professional family counselors', *Clinical Pediatrics*, vol. 11, no. 7, pp. 403–410.

Pope, B, Nudler, S, Norden, JS, & McGee, JP 1976, 'Changes in nonprofessional (novice) interviewers over a 3-year training period', *Journal of Consulting and Clinical Psychology*, vol. 44, no. 5, pp. 819–825.

Potter, LB, Powell, KE, & Kachur, SP 1995, 'Suicide prevention from a public health perspective', *Suicide and Life-Threatening Behavior*, vol. 25, no. 1, pp. 82–91.

Powell, ER 1976, 'Worker and caller variety in three crisis centers', *Suicide and Life-Threatening Behavior*, vol. 6, no. 4, pp. 202–208.

Rek, I & Dinger, U 2016, 'Who sits behind the telephone? Interpersonal characteristics of volunteer counselors in telephone emergency services', *Journal of Counseling Psychology*, vol. 63, no. 4, pp. 429–442.

Ribner, DS 1980, 'Psychiatrists and community mental health: Current issues and trends', *Psychiatric Services*, vol. 31, pp. 338–341.

Rickel, AU 1982, 'Perceptions of adjustment problems in preschool children by teachers and paraprofessional aides', *Journal of Community Psychology*, vol. 10, no. 1, pp. 29–35.

Robert, A, Suelves, JM, Armayones, M, & Ashley, S 2015, 'Internet use and suicidal behaviors: Internet as a threat or opportunity?', *Telemedicine and e-Health*, vol. 21, no. 4, pp. 306–311 doi: 10.1089/tmj.2014.0129

Robinson, J, Cox, G, Malone, A, Williamson, M, Baldwin, G, Fletcher, K, & O'Brien, M 2013, 'A systematic review of school-based interventions aimed at preventing, treating, and responding to suicide-related behavior in young people', *Crisis: The Journal of Crisis Intervention and Suicide Prevention*, vol. 34, no. 3, pp. 164–182. http://dx.doi.org/10.1027/0227-5910/a000168

Rosenbaum, A & Calhoun, JF 1977, 'The use of the telephone hotline in crisis intervention: A review', *Journal of Community Psychology*, vol. 5, pp. 325–339.

Sakowitz, ML & Hirschman 1975, 'Self-ideal congruency and therapeutic skill development in nonpaid paraprofessionals', *Journal of Community Psychology*, vol. 3, pp. 275–280.
Sameroff, A & Mackenzie, M 2003, 'A quarter-century of the Transactional Model: How have things changed? *Zero to Three*, 24.
Schinke, SP, Smith, TE, Myers, RK, & Altman, DC 1979, 'Crisis-intervention training with paraprofessionals', *Journal of Community Psychology*, vol. 7, no. 4, pp. 343–347.
Shybut, J 1982, 'Use of paraprofessionals in enhancing mental health service delivery in rural settings', *Journal of Rural Community Psychology*, vol. 3, no. 1, pp. 59–64.
Siegel, Jerome M 1973, 'Mental health volunteers as change agents', *American Journal of Community Psychology*, vol. 1, no. 2, pp. 138–158. doi: 10.1007/BF00880132
Signell, KA 1975, 'Training nonprofessionals as community instructors: A mental health education model of primary prevention', *Journal of Community Psychology*, vol. 3, no. 4, pp. 365–373.
Silverman, MM, & Felner, RD 1995, 'Suicide prevention programs: Issues of design, implementation, feasibility, and developmental appropriateness', *Suicide and Life-Threatening Behavior*, vol. 25, no. 1, pp. 92–104.
Simonson, NR & Bahr, S 1974, 'Self-disclosure by the professional and paraprofessional therapist', *Journal of Consulting and Clinical Psychology*, vol. 42, pp. 359–363.
Smith, RT 1973, 'Health and rehabilitation manpower strategy: New careers and the role of the indigenous paraprofessional', *Social Science and Medicine*, vol. 7, no. 4, pp. 281–290.
Snyder JA 1971, 'The use of gatekeepers in crisis management', *Bulletin of Suicidology*, vol. 8, pp. 39–44.
Sorensen, JL, & Galano, J 1976, 'Collaborative consultation in program evaluation with nonprofessionals', *Professional Psychology*, vol. 7, no. 4, pp. 541–546.
Stein, DM & Lambert, MJ 1984, 'Telephone counseling and crisis intervention: A review', *American Journal of Community Psychology*, vol. 12, no. 1, pp. 101–126.
Steisel, IM 1972, 'Paraprofessionals: Questions from a traditionalist', *Professional Psychology*, vol. 3, no. 4, pp. 331–334.
Stephan, WG 2014, 'Intergroup anxiety: Theory, research, and practice', *Personality and Social Psychology Review*, vol. 18, no. 3, pp. 239–255. doi: 10.1177/1088868314530518
Stephan, WG, & Stephan, CW 1985, 'Intergroup anxiety', *Journal of Social Issues*, vol. 41, no. 3, pp. 157–175. doi: 10.1111/j.1540-4560.1985.tb01134.xpp.
Stockdill, JW 2005, National Mental Health Policy and the Community Mental Health Centers, 1963–1981. In W. E. Pickren, Jr. & S. F. Schneider (eds.), *Psychology and the National Institute of Mental Health: A Historical Analysis of Science, Practice, and Policy* (pp. 261–293). Washington, DC: American Psychological Association. http://dx.doi.org/10.1037/10931-009
Strupp, HH & Hadley, SW 1979, 'Specific vs. nonspecific factors in psychotherapy: A controlled study of outcome', *Archives of General Psychiatry*, vol. 36, no. 10, pp. 1125–1136.
Summers, DA, Faucher, T, & Chapman, SB 1973, 'A note on nonprofessional judgements of mental health', *Community Mental Health Journal*, vol. 9, no. 2, pp. 169–177.

Taub, DJ, Servaty-Selb, HL, Miles, N, Watcher Morris, CA, Prieto-Welch, SL, & Werden, D 2013, 'The impact of gatekeeper training for suicide prevention on university resident assistants', *Journal of College Counseling*, vol. 16, no. 1, pp. 64–78.

Terrell, DL, McWilliams, SA, & Cowen, E 1972, 'Description and evaluation of group-work training for nonprofessional aides in a school mental health program', *Psychology in the Schools*, vol. 9, no. 1, pp. 70–75.

The Compassionate Friends 2018, 'Our Mission' Retrieved from: www.compassionatefriends.org/about/

Tierney, R, Ramsay, R, Tanney, B, & Lang, W 1990, 'Comprehensive school suicide prevention programs', *Death Studies*, vol. 14, no. 4, pp. 347–370.

Trawalter, S, Richeson, JA, & Shelton, JN 2009, 'Predicting behavior during interracial interactions: A stress and coping approach', *Personality and Social Psychology Review*, vol. 13, no. 4, pp. 243–268. doi: 10.1177/1088868309345850

Umbarger, C 1972, 'The paraprofessional and family therapy', *Family Process*, vol. 11, no. 2, pp. 147–162.

United Nations Department for Policy Coordination and Sustainable Development 1996, 'Prevention of suicide: guidelines for the formulation and implementation of national strategies'. New York: United Nations.

Vander Kolk, CJ 1973, 'Paraprofessionals as psychotherapeutic agents with moderately disturbed children', *Psychology in the Schools*, vol. 10, no. 2, pp. 238–242.

van Spijker, BA, Majo, MC, Smit, F, van Straten, A, & Kerkhof, AJ 2012, 'Reducing suicidal ideation: Cost effectiveness analysis of a randomized controlled trial of unguided web-based self-help', *Journal of Medical Internet Research*, vol. 14, no. 5, pp. 141.

Vorauer, JD 2006, 'An information search model of evaluative concerns in intergroup interaction', *Psychological Review*, vol. 113, no. 4, pp. 862–886. doi: 10.1037/0033-295X.113.4.862

Varah, C (ed.) 1985, *The Samaritans: Befriending the suicidal*. London: Constable & Robinson.

Walfish, S, & Gesten, E 2008, Supervision of paraprofessional human service workers. In A. K. Hess, K. D. Hess, & T. H. Hess (eds.), *Psychotherapy Supervision: Theory, Research, and Practice* (pp. 246–262). Hoboken, NJ: John Wiley & Sons.

Wallace, H 1970, 'The paraprofessional mental health worker: What are we all about?', Paper presented at the annual conference of the American Orthopsychiatric Association, New York, March 1970.

Wampold, BE, Baldwin, SA, Holtforth, MG, & Imel, ZE 2017, 'What characterizes effective therapists?', in LG Castonguay & CE Hill (eds.), *How and Why are Some Therapists Better than Others? Understanding Therapist Effects*. Washington, DC: American Psychological Association. pp. 37–53.

West, T, Pearson, A, and Stern, C 2014, 'Anxiety perseverance in intergroup interaction: When incidental explanations backfire', *Journal of Personality and Social Psychology*, vol. 107, no. 5, pp. 825–843. doi: 10.1037/a0037941

Zimmerman, J, and Bambling, M 2012, 'Influence of therapist variables on working alliance and therapy outcome', *Psychotherapy in Australia*, vol. 18, no. 2, pp. 76–82.

10 Availability and Quality of Mental Healthcare Services for Veterans at Risk for Suicide

Craig J. Bryan, AnnaBelle O. Bryan, David C. Rozek, Feea R. Leifker and Alexis M. May

In 2016, the Department of Veterans Affairs released the results of the most comprehensive analysis conducted to date focused on suicide among U.S. military veterans. Building on previous findings, these analyses highlighted the continued problem of increased suicide risk among military personnel and veterans, and yielded the frequently-cited statistic of "20 veterans per day." Since 2001, the suicide rate among all veterans has increased faster than the suicide rate among the U.S. general population (adjusting for age and gender to account for differences between veterans and civilians on these two variables), such that veterans are now approximately 22% more likely than civilians to die by suicide (Department of Veterans Affairs, 2016). Although the specific reasons for this disparity are not fully understood, one very likely factor is the significantly elevated rate of disability (defined as serious difficulties in hearing, vision, cognitive, ambulatory, self-care, and/or independent living) among veterans relative to civilians (U.S. Census Bureau, 2014) as well as high rates of poor community integration (Sayer et al., 2010). Disabled veterans are more likely to have lower socioeconomic levels, higher rates of homelessness, and higher levels of social isolation as compared to non-disabled veterans (Jordan et al., 1992; Murdoch et al., 2011). Perhaps not surprisingly, the majority of the disabilities reported among veterans are connected to their military service. Among these veterans, approximately 25% report extreme difficulty finding or keeping a job and up to half describe extreme difficulty taking part in "civilian" society, taking part in community activities, and maintaining friendships with non-veterans (Sayer et al., 2010). Taken together, these findings suggest that veterans are a vulnerable class, with greater vulnerability occurring among those with service-connected disabilities.

The rise in suicides among veterans varies across a number of important variables including age, gender, transition stage, and use of Veterans Health Association (VHA)[1] services. Among younger age groups (i.e., 18–39 years), for instance, the rate of suicide increased dramatically from 2001 to 2014 among veterans but changed very little among civilians. Among older age groups (40–69 years), the suicide rate increased for both veterans and civilians, but the male veteran rate increased more rapidly than the male civilian rate whereas the female veteran and female civilian rates increased to a comparable degree. Finally, among the oldest age groups (70 years and older), the male veteran rate is actually *lower* than the male civilian rate, although there was a pronounced decline among civilians but not veterans from 2001 to 2014. In contrast, female veterans and female civilians in this age group have comparable suicide rates. When comparing overall trends among female and male veterans over time, a stark difference becomes apparent: suicides have increased since 2001 three times faster among female veterans (35% increase) than male veterans (11% increase). This rapid increase in suicides among female veterans has contributed to a significant gender gap between veterans and civilians: whereas the male veteran rate is approximately 20% higher than the male civilian rate, the female veteran rate is approximately 250% higher than the female civilian rate. One contributor to this discrepancy is the elevated use of firearms as a suicide method among female veterans (Department of Veterans Affairs, 2016), which results in higher rates of fatal outcomes. Another possible contributor involves increased barriers to using VHA services among female veterans, which include lower income, knowledge gaps in eligibility criteria, and limited knowledge of medical services specific to women (Hoff & Rosenheck, 1998; Washington, Yano, Simon, & Sun, 2006).

Leaving the military and transitioning to civilian life marks an especially high risk period for this community. Upon separating from military service, a veteran's risk for suicide nearly doubles, especially for veterans with fewer years of military service and veterans who separated with a discharge status that was other than honorable (Reger et al., 2015). Another notable finding specific to veteran suicides surrounds healthcare utilization. Among veterans who receive medical and healthcare services from the VHA ("VHA users"), suicide rates have historically been higher than civilians and higher than veterans who do not receive medical or healthcare services from the VHA (i.e., "non-VHA users"). This difference seems to be explained in large part by the elevated rates of physical injury, mental illness, and disability among VHA users relative to the general population and non-VHA users. In other words, veterans who receive care from the VHA are much more likely than civilians and non-VHA users to have a medical and mental health condition that may contribute to their suicide risk. In addition, VHA users tend to have more severe health conditions than civilians and non-VHA users. However, from 2001 to 2014, suicides among non-VHA users increased approximately four times faster than VHA users, such that the historic gap in suicide rates between VHA users and non-VHA users has reduced by half.

These statistics lead to several key conclusions with respect to suicide. First, veterans comprise a vulnerable subgroup of the U.S. population owing to their elevated rates of physical and psychological injury and disability. Second, female veterans and young veterans have especially increased vulnerability to suicide. Third, separation from military service is an especially high risk period of time for veterans, especially for those whose discharge status is other than honorable. Fourth, suicide rates have risen among VHA users since 2001, but this increase (9%) is noticeably lower than the increase seen among adult civilians during that same timeframe (23%). This latter finding applies to both male and female veterans and suggests that, at a population level, VHA services provide a protective effect for veterans. Unfortunately, this protective effect is experienced only by only a minority of veterans: those who are eligible for VHA services and choose to use them. If we want to "bend the curve" of veteran suicide, we must pursue strategies for ensuring that all veterans, regardless of service history or disability status, have access to effective medical and mental healthcare. Rather than reaching out to help these veterans, however, many of our governmental and social institutions have instead excluded and marginalized them. In the end, good help is hard to find for most veterans; for some veterans, good help is nearly impossible to access.

Availability and Quality of Empirically-Supported Treatments for At-Risk Veterans

In response to the rising suicide rate among military personnel and veterans, the VA and the Department of Defense (DOD) have directed an unprecedented amount of resources towards suicide prevention. These efforts have included increased funding for suicide research, implementation of suicide prevention programs, and identification of effective suicide prevention strategies. Of the many things we have learned about military and veteran suicide over the past decade as a result of these efforts, the most important findings are arguably the identification of effective treatments and prevention strategies. Since 2015, for example, several treatment studies reporting suicide-related outcomes among military personnel and veterans have been published (Bryan et al., 2017; Jobes et al., 2017; Resick et al., 2017; Rudd et al., 2015; Trockel et al., 2015). Three of these studies tested treatments explicitly designed to reduce suicidal thoughts and behaviors among military personnel and veterans, regardless of diagnosis, gender, age, or background (Bryan et al., 2017; Jobes et al., 2017; Rudd et al., 2015), of which two showed significant effects on subsequent suicide attempt rates: brief cognitive behavioral therapy, a 12-session therapy that reduced suicide attempts by 60% (Rudd et al., 2015), and crisis response planning, a single-session, 30-minute intervention that reduced suicide attempts by 76% (Bryan et al., 2017). Two additional studies of PTSD-focused treatments (Bryan et al., 2016; Resick et al., 2017) and one study of an insomnia-focused treatment (Trockel et al., 2015) found significant reductions in suicidal thoughts among service members and veterans, suggesting that treatments targeting key risk factors among military personnel and veterans may also reduce suicide risk.

In addition to this, other treatments tested in non-veteran populations have shown promise for reducing suicidal thoughts and behaviors. For example, clozapine has been associated with significant reductions in suicidal behaviors among patients diagnosed with schizophrenia and lithium is associated with significant reductions in suicidal behaviors among patients diagnosed with bipolar disorder (Riesselman, Johnson, & Palmer, 2015). However, some have noted that many of the studies supporting the association of medication with reductions in suicidal behaviors have a number of confounds that could lead to overestimating their suicide prevention effects (Oquendo et al., 2011). It is possible that empirically-supported treatments developed for other psychological and behavioral disorders (e.g., substance use disorders, depression) also possess suicide prevention effects that are not yet known, as suicide-related outcomes have not been examined.

The availability of these empirically-supported treatments and practices across VHA facilities is a likely contributor to the protective effect of VHA services on the suicide rate among VHA users. A recent study by RAND Corporation (Watkins et al., 2011) found that eight out of nine empirically-supported treatments for common medical and psychiatric conditions became more available to VHA users across the U.S. over the past decade. For example, the number of VHA facilities with a dedicated suicide prevention coordinator, a mental health professional trained to provide empirically-supported suicide prevention interventions to high risk veterans and to help veterans access other indicated treatments and services, increased from 5% in 2007 to 99% in 2009 (Watkins et al., 2011). During that same two-year timeframe, the number of veterans with access to specialized therapies for PTSD like cognitive processing therapy (CPT; Resick, Monson, & Chard, 2017), which has been shown to reduce suicidal thinking among military personnel and veterans (Bryan et al., 2016; Resick et al., 2017), increased from 89% to 99%.

These positives are tempered by the worrying fact that, despite the wide availability of empirically-supported treatments across VHA facilities, a very small percentage of veterans actually receive them. The low rate of receiving empirically-supported treatments, despite their availability, seems to be associated with two primary factors. First, only a minority of U.S. veterans are VHA users: fewer than half of all U.S. veterans meet federal eligibility requirements and have enrolled in the system,[2] and only two-thirds of enrollees actually use VHA services (Bagalman, 2014). This means that, overall, less than one in three U.S. veterans actually receive treatment from the VHA. Second, although a particular VHA facility has at least one clinician who is trained to provide an empirically-supported treatment, a given VHA clinician may not offer these treatments and/or may not refer the veteran to a VHA clinician who does. This possibility is supported by a RAND report showing that only 20% of VHA users diagnosed with PTSD received an evidence-based treatment despite the availability of these treatments at 99% of the VHA facilities that served these veterans (Watkins et al., 2011). Thus, veterans with physical and psychiatric conditions that increase their risk for suicide are unlikely to receive the treatments that are most likely to ameliorate these conditions.

Considerable variability in the availability and quality of services across VHA facilities and regions of the U.S. has also been reported (Watkins et al., 2011), which suggests that further improvements in the quality of VHA care could be realized. Specific to suicide prevention, two recent studies highlight this issue. In both of these studies, researchers conducted reviews of VHA records to assess the quality of a suicide prevention strategy known as safety planning, an intervention that is intended to prevent suicidal behavior among high risk VHA users. The safety plan has a great deal in common with the empirically-supported crisis response plan mentioned above, and has been recommended as a suicide risk management procedure by suicide prevention experts and a number of accreditation agencies and bodies (e.g., Joint Commission, 2016; National Action Alliance for Suicide Prevention, 2018). Consistent with these recommendations, the safety plan was implemented by the VHA several years ago as a required part of a veteran's comprehensive suicide prevention plan. As part of this implementation, training manuals and resources were created and disseminated to VHA clinicians and staff members. These resources described the design and intent of the intervention, which emphasizes the importance of collaboratively developing the plan in several steps: first, identifying the veteran's warning signs for an emerging crisis; second, identifying self-management strategies the veteran can use when becoming emotionally overwhelmed; third, identifying specific sources of social support (e.g., family members, friends) who can be contacted; and fourth, identifying sources of professional assistance who can be contacted such as mental healthcare providers and crisis hotlines. Once a customized plan is created for the veteran, clinicians are supposed to review the plan regularly to assess its utility, efficacy, and acceptability to the veteran.

Results of two VHA studies (Gamarra et al., 2015; Green et al., 2016) have since found that, despite the availability of these resources to clinicians, there is considerable variability in the quality of safety plans created by VHA clinicians. Both studies also found that, overall, the quality of safety plans developed by VHA clinicians was poor, with the most frequently occurring deficit being insufficient specificity to maximize the procedure's utility. For example, 23% of veterans with elevated suicide risk had "generic, copied and pasted statements" instead of personalized and/or customized elements and 71% of veterans had no evidence of ongoing review of the plan by a VHA clinician. Perhaps not surprisingly, these researchers additionally found that the mere presence of safety plans did not correlate with the incidence of later suicide attempts. However, safety plans that were more complete and/or higher quality were correlated with reduced incidence of subsequent suicidal behaviors and psychiatric hospitalizations. In other words, this particular suicide prevention intervention was more likely to reduce suicide risk when VHA clinicians delivered them with high quality.

Despite these problems, the quality and performance of VHA care is actually as good as or even *better* than the quality and performance of providers in the private sector (Watkins et al., 2011). Specific to suicide prevention, the reduced quality of mental healthcare services from private providers seems to be attributable, at least in part, to deficient training practices among mental healthcare professional training programs. A recent report from the American Association of Suicidology (AAS; Schmitz et al., 2011) provides an overview of this issue. Across mental health disciplines, suicide-focused curriculum and training in mental healthcare professional programs are rare and, when offered, are very limited in scope: only half of psychology training programs, less than 25% of social work programs, 6% of marriage and family therapy programs, and 2% of counselor education programs provide any amount of education or training focused on suicide as a part of their curriculum. The profession of psychiatry seems to perform better, with over 90% of psychiatry program training directors reporting they provide suicide-specific education to psychiatry residents, although it is important to note that only 28% of psychiatry programs provide *skills-based* suicide-focused training opportunities. When suicide-focused education is available, it is therefore typically very limited and does not always include applied skills training. In many cases, this education is confined to only a few hours of coursework over the course of multiple years. The AAS report further notes that state licensing boards for most mental health professions—the bodies charged with protecting the public's health and safety from unqualified professionals—also do not require any exams or demonstration of competency in suicide risk assessment or intervention. This highlights an urgent and shocking reality: the vast majority of U.S. mental healthcare professionals receive little to no training in contemporary evidenced-based methods for managing suicide risk, which limits their preparedness and ability to effectively intervene with suicidal patients, and existing methods for regulating the mental healthcare professions employ strategies that do not sufficiently assess competency in this area.

These deficiencies in training and regulatory oversight adversely impact veterans (and nonveterans) because most of the VHA's mental healthcare professionals were trained in U.S. graduate programs and medical schools. By default, the majority of mental healthcare professionals hired by the VHA have little to no training or practical experience in the most effective methods for reducing suicide risk. This lack of training in empirically-supported treatments almost certainly contributes to the lower than expected provision of these treatments to veterans and the low to moderate quality of suicide prevention interventions provided by VHA clinicians noted above.

Deficient training across the mental health professions has an even greater impact on veterans accessing care from the private sector. As noted previously, over 70% of veterans who die by suicide are not VHA users, meaning they receive healthcare services from private providers typically located in their local communities, where empirically-supported treatments are even less available. Research focused on the implementation of trauma-focused treatments for individuals with PTSD highlights this issue. One study found that nearly half of mental healthcare professionals were unable to identify a preferred treatment to use for PTSD and fewer than one-third were able to name an empirically-supported treatment for PTSD (Sprang, Craig, & Clark, 2008). Another study found that less than 25% of licensed psychologists had received training or supervision in any empirically-supported treatment for PTSD (Becker, Zayfert, & Anderson, 2004), despite these treatments existing for over 15 years.

Even when clinicians have access to training in empirically-supported treatments, the receipt of training does not appear to be sufficient to ensure they provide these treatments to their patients: approximately half of clinicians who have been trained in empirically-supported treatments for PTSD nonetheless report they do not use them with patients due to low confidence and/or misconceptions about how the treatments work (Becker, Zayfert, & Anderson, 2004). This incredible statistic suggests that even when a veteran with PTSD finds a mental healthcare professional who knows how to effectively treat this condition, the veteran has only around a 50% chance of receiving the treatment from that provider. These trends are not limited to PTSD; similar gaps and issues have been identified for a wide range of psychological and behavioral conditions including panic disorder, substance use disorders, depression, marital problems, and suicide risk (Baker, McFall, & Shoham, 2008; Barlow, Levitt, & Bufka, 1999).

The reluctance of mental healthcare professionals to use empirically-supported treatments is perhaps best illustrated by the recent backlash against the American Psychological Association's (APA, 2018) *Clinical Practice Guideline for the Treatment of Posttraumatic Stress Disorder*. In 2013, a 12-member panel of researchers and clinicians overseen by the APA's Advisory Steering Committee was selected by the APA to develop the clinical practice guideline. After several years of work, which included opportunities for psychologists and members of the public to provide input and feedback on preliminary drafts of the report, the clinical practice guideline was published. Based on a review of all the available scientific and clinical evidence of efficacy, the clinical practice guideline strongly recommended several therapies for PTSD and conditionally recommended several other therapies. The guideline did not mandate these therapies or suggest that these recommended therapies should be provided to patients in all circumstances; rather, it simply identified those treatments that had consistently yielded the best outcomes. The hope was that practicing clinicians would be motivated to pursue training in these methods in order to improve the quality of care for patients, and that consumers of mental healthcare services would have better information about the treatment being provided from their clinicians. Contrary to this aspiration, however, the guideline's publication was met with considerable hostility and resistance by a large number of mental healthcare professionals, many of whom characterized the guideline as harmful because its conclusions were based largely on the results of randomized clinical trials (RCTs). RCTs provide the highest level of evidence to support (or fail to support) a treatment approach because it provides the greatest degree of confidence with respect to ruling out other potential explanations and causes for the findings. Perhaps not surprisingly, the most vocal opponents of the guideline were mental healthcare professionals who used treatment methods that were not recommended by the guideline as first-line treatments owing to their limited empirical support and/or empirically demonstrated inferiority as compared to the recommended treatments. The backlash eventually grew strong enough that an organized petition to repeal the guideline emerged online and was introduced at the APA's Council of Representatives, the organization's legislative body, who ultimately voted to maintain and uphold the practice guideline. Although a victory in its own right, the large number of mental healthcare professionals who publically resisted (and actively criticized) the use of empirically-supported treatments is unsettling.

The story of the APA's practice guideline reflects a pervasive obstacle for improving the quality of care for veterans: a shockingly large proportion of mental healthcare professionals are unwilling to change how they practice even when presented with clear data suggesting that this change could benefit the recipients of their services. This story may also provide some context for the aforementioned gap in receipt of empirically-supported treatments by VHA-users despite their wide availability across the VHA (e.g., only 20% of veterans receive an empirically-supported treatment from a VHA provider despite their availability to 99% of these veterans). Specifically, a large number of VHA clinicians were not trained to use these treatments prior to being hired and may have been trained to resist or even oppose their use (Lilienfeld, Ritschel, Lynn, Cautin, & Latzman, 2013). Knowing this, the VHA has produced multiple clinical practice guidelines and maintains an incredibly robust training system to support the use and implementation of best practices. It is important to note that public scrutiny likely provides additional incentives for preserving and maintaining the VHA's commitment to improving the quality of care for veterans. This combination of institutional commitment with public oversight has helped to increase in the availability and use of empirically-supported treatments within the VHA, but more work clearly needs to be done.

Outside the VHA, public scrutiny and institutional practices that support the use of empirically-supported treatments are much less common. The aggressive and intensive training programs that exist within the VHA do not exist in the private sector. These institutional discrepancies almost certainly contribute to the lower quality and performance of private sector providers as compared to the VHA. As a result, non-VHA users are even less likely than VHA-users to receive the most effective treatments for conditions associated with increased risk for suicide. Because 70% of U.S. veterans are non-VHA users (Bagalman, 2014), it becomes clear that empirically-supported treatments are largely unavailable to most veterans.

Without a doubt, deficient training among U.S. mental healthcare professional programs and unwillingness of mental healthcare professionals to use empirically-supported treatments has a negative impact on the veteran community, a group with elevated rates of physical and psychological injuries and disabilities that were often acquired as a consequence of their service to the nation's political interests. These issues disproportionately impact veterans who separated from military service with other than honorable discharges because VA benefits (including healthcare services) are withheld from this vulnerable subgroup. As noted above, veterans with other than honorable discharges are nearly twice as likely to die by suicide as veterans with an honorable discharge. Despite their clear need for services and resources, this subgroup paradoxically has the *fewest* services and resources available because many nonprofits and agencies in the private sector that serve veterans use the same eligibility criteria as the VA for determining access and provision of services. Veterans who are ineligible to receive assistance from federal agencies are also ineligible to receive assistance from many community agencies. As a result, the veterans with the greatest need for healthcare and support services are the veterans who are least likely to receive them.

Next Steps in Veteran Suicide Prevention

Reversing the trend of veteran suicide will require bold and innovative thinking at a national level that results in changes to existing policies and procedures, the development and creation of new initiatives, and places a priority on providing adequate training earlier in providers' careers. The data presented in this chapter suggest that an important component of any such national effort should address the availability and quality of healthcare services for veterans. Although the solution to veteran suicide certainly extends beyond the healthcare system, the existence of government and institutional systems that oversee and regulate the healthcare profession makes this particular piece of the puzzle more immediately amenable to change at a national level. Critically, availability, *and* quality of mental healthcare must be addressed simultaneously, as the targeting of only one of these two domains would only result in either improved access to poor quality care or limited access to high quality care, neither of which is likely to drive down veteran suicides. Improving both the availability and quality of care will require a number of significant shifts at a national level that will only be possible through the coordinated efforts of government and social institutions, and must extend beyond federal departments and agencies. Several possible strategies include the expansion of VHA healthcare services to all veterans, minimizing logistical barriers to care, improving the quality of mental healthcare professional training, and incentivizing the use of empirically-supported treatments.

Expanding VHA Healthcare Services to All Veterans

Data indicate that the receipt of healthcare services from the VHA is associated with a relative reduction in suicide risk. Although the suicide rate among VHA users has risen by 9% since 2001, this increase has been much less than the 38% increase seen among veterans who are non-VHA users and the 23% increase seen among civilians. VHA services therefore seem to confer an overall anti-suicide effect on its recipients. Unfortunately, less than 30% of U.S. veterans use VHA services. This low rate of utilization is due in part to low enrollment rates and eligibility restrictions. Specifically, fewer than half of all U.S. veterans have enrolled in the VA benefits system after meeting eligibility requirements, which are typically based on the length of previous military service and/or presence of service-connected disabilities (other less common factors can also influence a veteran's eligibility). Because enrollment serves as the first step in the benefits process, policy initiatives that remove barriers to enrollment and expand eligibility criteria could improve access to VHA services. For example, expanding eligibility criteria to include all veterans, regardless of discharge status, would improve the availability of healthcare services, especially for more vulnerable subgroups who are currently excluded from receiving VA benefits and other community-based resources. Although VHA services were recently expanded for veterans who served after November 11, 1998, and were discharged under other than honorable conditions, this expansion only applies to veterans who served in a combat theater. Further expansion of eligibility for VHA services, and specifically mental health services, to all veterans regardless of discharge status and disability status could also encourage a paradigm shift away from a benefits and service delivery model based on the demonstration of disability towards a model based on recovery.

Minimizing Logistical Barriers to Care

Separation from military service is associated with increased suicide risk for veterans. Currently, military personnel and veterans interested in receiving VA benefits must initiate the enrollment process via an application process that is perceived by many veterans as cumbersome and confusing. As a result, many veterans choose not to enroll in the VA system and do not learn about the benefits and services for which they may be eligible. Policy changes that institute automatic enrollment at the time of separation from military service could eliminate this barrier and improve access to healthcare for many veterans. Likewise, policy changes that remove practical barriers to care could significant improve access to care. Although discussions surrounding improved access to care for veterans often focus on mental health stigma, stigma-related barriers to care are actually relatively weak correlates of service utilization (Acosta et al., 2014). In contrast, logistical and practical barriers to care like cost of services, convenience of scheduling, and geographic proximity are much stronger correlates of service utilization. Consistent with these findings, the VHA has rapidly expanded telehealth technology, thereby extending healthcare services to veterans living in geographically remote areas and/or in regions with limited access to specialized services. Importantly, these telehealth services are shown to have comparable outcomes to in-person services (Morland et al., 2014). In addition to these advances, policy and institutional changes regarding the day-to-day operations of VA facilities could further improve utilization of VHA services among veterans. For example, many VA facilities have limited evening or weekend services or are not open at all during evenings or on weekends, which can limit access for veterans with scheduling barriers including employment, enrollment in classes, and/or childcare obligations. Policy changes that expand the operational hours of VHA facilities could reduce these barriers to care for many veterans.

Improving the Quality of Mental Healthcare Professional Training Programs

As previously discussed, U.S. mental healthcare professional training programs provide little to no training in state-of-the-art methods for assessing and intervening with patients at elevated risk for suicide. In addition, too few mental healthcare professionals receive education, training, and/or supervised experience in the delivery of empirically-supported treatments for psychological and behavioral disorders that are associated with increased risk for suicide. As a result, veterans pursuing mental health treatment are unlikely to find a clinician with sufficient knowledge or training to provide high quality services. The mental healthcare professional training system must therefore be redesigned to explicitly integrate such training. Change could be encouraged through each discipline's accrediting bodies, which could mandate educational curriculum focused on empirically-supported treatments and the effective management of suicide risk. State licensing boards could also require mental healthcare professionals to complete coursework and/or continuing education focused on empirically-supported methods for managing and reducing suicidal behaviors and other risk factors for suicide. This latter approach has already been pursued legislatively in several U.S. states: California, Indiana, Kentucky, Nevada, New Hampshire, Pennsylvania, Tennessee, Utah, Washington, and West Virginia. In these ten states, mental and behavioral healthcare professionals are required to complete training in suicide risk assessment and treatment. In three of these states (Nevada, Washington, and West Virginia), other healthcare professionals such as nurses and physicians are also required to complete such training.

Incentivizing the Use of Empirically-Supported Treatments

Mandating certain types of educational curriculum is unlikely to increase the use of empirically-supported treatments by itself. Unfortunately, the mental healthcare profession is replete with popular and widely-used practices and methods that would likely meet legislative and accreditation requirements because they are considered "evidence-based" despite their limited empirical foundation and, in some cases, inferior outcomes as compared to other, more effective methods. For example, animal-assisted therapies for veterans with PTSD have grown rapidly in popularity despite the near absence of scientific support for these methods (Anestis, Anestis, Zawilinski, Hopkins, & Lilienfeld, 2014). The response of mental healthcare professionals to the APA's clinical practice guideline for PTSD further highlights the considerable challenge involved in improving the quality of care for veterans (and nonveterans). Unfortunately, the frustrating reality is that mental healthcare professionals are unlikely to adopt and use methods that are unfamiliar to them even when those methods yield better outcomes for their patients.

Incentivizing the use of empirically-supported treatments and practices could increase clinicians' likelihood of using these treatments. For example, mental healthcare professionals who receive training and supervision in empirically-supported practices could receive discounts on professional liability insurance policies, similar to providing insurance discounts for "good practices" in other areas: discounts on car insurance for young drivers who attend and complete an approved driver's education class or for drivers whose cars contain certain safety features (e.g., air bags, antilock brakes), discounts on homeowner's insurance for homes with security alarm systems, and discounts on health insurance for being a nonsmoker. These incentives are provided because risk of adverse outcomes are reduced when these practices are employed. In mental healthcare, risk of adverse outcomes (i.e., suicide attempts, death by suicide) are similarly reduced when certain practices (i.e., empirically-supported treatments) are used by mental healthcare professionals. Insurance-based incentives would not require a mental healthcare professional to use a particular treatment or method (similarly, car insurance does not require a one to purchase a particular car and homeowners insurance does not require one to purchase a particular house), but would provide a financial benefit for using practices that yield better outcomes and, by default, decreased risk for malpractice claims and/or other litigation.

Another possible incentive system would include the development of "preferred provider" lists that include only those mental healthcare professionals who have successfully completed training in empirically-supported treatments and can demonstrate their routine use of these methods in day-to-day practice. An example of this approach is the publically-available roster of licensed mental healthcare providers who have completed training criteria for cognitive processing therapy (CPT) for PTSD (Resick et al., 2017), which is available online at www.cptforptsd.com. The CPT training program involves two levels of expertise: CPT Provider (the basic level), which designates clinicians who have demonstrated minimal competency in the treatment via participation in training and consultation with an approved trainer, and CPT Quality Provider (the advanced level), which designates clinicians who have additionally submitted audio or video recordings of their practice along with objectively-measured clinical outcomes (e.g., scores on validated symptom measures) to be reviewed and rated by an expert in the method. Because these rosters distinguish those clinicians with particular levels of experience and expertise, they could potentially provide economic and financial benefits through increased referrals. Such rosters could also be used by insurance providers as a method for verifying the training and experience of mental healthcare professionals to support discounts in insurance premiums.

Yet another possible incentive would be increasing the billable rate for psychological treatment when the treatment provided is empirically-supported. This approach could be useful because it may be seen as less coercive by mental healthcare professionals who may be less interested or willing to adopt or use empirically-supported treatments, and may incentivize early-career mental healthcare professionals to seek out training and supervision in empirically-supported treatments while in graduate school or soon thereafter. This approach may also align better with existing clinical practice guidelines, which differentiate first-line treatments from other treatment approaches that are provide an overall benefit to patients, albeit to a smaller degree relative to the first-line treatments.

Conclusions

U.S. military veterans are a vulnerable subgroup owing to their high rates of physical and psychological injury and disability. These vulnerabilities increase their risk for suicide. Unfortunately, many veterans receive low quality healthcare due in large part to deficient training practices in the U.S. mental healthcare professional training programs. These deficiencies should be corrected via several institutional and systems-based changes in accreditation requirements, regulatory processes, and institutional policies. A multipronged, systems-based approach to addressing these deficiencies could significantly improve the quality of mental healthcare services for veterans and, by extension, reduce suicide rates in this high risk community. Easy access to healthcare services is only one part of the solution; veterans must also have easy access to high-quality, empirically-supported care.

Notes

1 The Department of Veterans Affairs is functionally structured around three Administrations: Veterans Health Administration (VHA), Veterans Benefits Administration (VBA), and National Cemetery Administration (NCA). Healthcare and medical services are provided to eligible veterans through the VHA. Consistent with this structure, in the current chapter the abbreviation "VA" is used to refer to the federal department as a whole whereas the abbreviation "VHA" is used to refer to the medical and healthcare functions of the VA.

2 The federal eligibility requirements to receive VHA services are quite complicated, and involve factors including (but not limited to) period and length of military service, recency of military service, deployment history, service-connected disability, military awards, and discharge type. The complexity of VHA eligibility requirements, which are established by Congress, contributes to considerable confusion among service members and veterans (and the general public), and likely serves as a barrier to enrollment for many service members and veterans who may actually be eligible. The VA has attempted to mitigate this issue by creating a range of user-friendly eligibility determination tools, including automated systems available online (http://hbexplorer.vacloud.us).

References

Acosta, J.D., Becker, A., Cerully, J., Fisher, M.P., Martin, L.T., Vardavas, R., Slaughter, M.E., & Schell, T.L. (2014). *Mental Health Stigma in the Military*. Santa Monica, CA: RAND Corporation.

American Psychological Association (2018). *Clinical Practice Guideline for the Treatment of PTSD*. Washington, DC: American Psychological Association.

Anestis, M.D., Anestis, J.C., Zawilinski, L.L., Hopkins, T.A., & Lilienfeld, S.O. (2014). Equine-related treatments for mental disorders lack empirical support: A systematic review of empirical investigations. *Journal of Clinical Psychology*, *70*, 1115–1132.

Bagalman, E. (2014). *The Number of Veterans That Use VA Health Care Services: A Fact Sheet*. Washington, DC: Congressional Research Service.

Baker, T.B., McFall, R.M., & Shoham, V. (2008). Current status and future prospects of clinical psychology: Toward a scientifically principled approach to mental and behavioral health care. *Psychological Science in the Public Interest*, *9*, 67–103.

Barlow, D.H., Levitt, J.T., & Bufka, L.F. (1999). The dissemination of empirically supported treatments: A view to the future. *Behaviour Research and Therapy, 37 (Suppl 1)*, S147–S162.

Becker, C.B., Zayfert, C., & Anderson, E. (2004). A survey of psychologists' attitudes towards and utilization of exposure therapy for PTSD. *Behaviour Research and Therapy*, *42*, 277–292.

Bryan, C.J., Clemans, T.A., Hernandez, A.M., Mintz, J., Peterson, A.L., Yarvis, J.S., & Resick, P.A. (2016). Evaluating potential iatrogenic suicide risk in trauma-focused group cognitive behavioral therapy for the treatment of PTSD in active duty military personnel. *Depression and Anxiety*, *33*, 549–557.

Bryan, C.J., Mintz, J., Clemans, T.A., Leeson, B., Burch, T.S., Williams, S.R., Maney, E., & Rudd, M.D. (2017). Effect of crisis response planning vs. contracts for safety on suicide risk in U.S. Army Soldiers: a randomized clinical trial. *Journal of Affective Disorders*, *212*, 64–72.

Department of Veterans Affairs (2016). *Suicide Among Veterans and Other Americans, 2001–2014*. Washington, DC: Department of Veterans Affairs Office of Mental Health and Suicide Prevention.

Gamarra, J.M., Luciano, M.T., Gradus, J.L., & Stirman, S.W. (2015). Assessing variability and implementation fidelity of suicide prevention safety planning in a regional VA Healthcare System. *Crisis*, *36*, 433–439.

Green, J.D. , Kearns, J., Marx, B., Nock, M., Rosen, R., & Keane, T. (2016). Evaluating safety plan effectiveness: do safety plans tailored to individual veteran characteristics decrease risk? In D.J. Lee (Chair), *Preventing Suicide Among Military and Veteran Population*. Paper presented at the annual meeting of the Association for Behavioral and Cognitive Therapies, New York.

Hoff, R.A., & Rosenheck, R.A. (1998). Female veterans' use of Department of Veterans Affairs health care services. *Medical Care*, *36*, 1114–1119.

Jobes, D.A., Comtois, K.A., Gutierrez, P.M., Brenner, L.A., Huh, D., Chalker, S.A., . . ., & Crow, B. (2017). A randomized controlled trial of the Collaborative Assessment and Management of Suicidality versus enhanced care as usual with suicidal soldiers. *Psychiatry: Interpersonal and Biological Processes*, *80*, 339–356.

Jordan, B.K., Marmar, C.R., Fairbank, J.A., Schlenger, W.E., Kulka, R.A., Hough, R.L., & Weiss, D.S. (1992). Problems in families of male Vietnam veterans with posttraumatic stress disorder. *Journal of Consulting and Clinical Psychology*, *60*, 916–926.

Kliem, S., Kröger, C. & Kosfelder, J. (2010). Dialectical behavior therapy for borderline personality disorder: a meta-analysis using mixed-effects modeling. *Journal of Consulting and Clinical Psychology*, *78*, 936–951.

Lilienfeld, S. O., Ritschel, L. A., Lynn, S. J., Cautin, R. L., & Latzman, R. D. (2013). Why many clinical psychologists are resistant to evidence-based practice: Root causes and constructive remedies. *Clinical Psychology Review*, *33*, 883–900.

Morland, L. A., Mackintosh, M. A., Greene, C. J., Rosen, C. S., Chard, K. M., Resick, P., & Frueh, B. C. (2014). Cognitive processing therapy for posttraumatic stress disorder delivered to rural veterans via telemental health: a randomized noninferiority clinical trial. *The Journal of Clinical Psychiatry*, *75*, 470–476.

Murdoch, M., Sayer, N.A., Spoont, M.R., Rosenheck, R., Noorbaloochi, S., Griffin, J.M., Arbisi, P.A., & Hagel, E.M. (2011). Long-term outcomes of disability benefits in US veterans with posttraumatic stress disorder. *JAMA Psychiatry*, *68*, 1072–1080.

National Action Alliance for Suicide Prevention (2018). *Recommended Standard Care for People with Suicide Risk: Making Health Care Suicide Safe*. Washington, DC: Education Development Center, Inc.

Oquendo, M.A., Galfalvy, H.C., Currier, D., Grunebaum, M.F., Sher, L., Sullivan, G.M., . . ., & Mann, J.J. (2011). Treatment of suicide attempters with bipolar disorder: a randomized clinical trial comparing lithium and valproate in the prevention of suicidal behavior. *American Journal of Psychiatry*, *168*, 1050–1056.

Reger, M.A., Smolenski, D.J., Skopp, N.A., Metzger-Abamukang, M.J., Kang, H.K., Bullman, T.A., Perdue, S., & Gahm, G.A. (2015). Risk of suicide among U.S. military service members following Operation Enduring Freedom or Operation Iraqi Freedom deployment and separation from the U.S. military. *JAMA Psychiatry*, *72*, 561–569.

Resick, P.A., Monson, C.M., & Chard, K.M. (2017). *Cognitive Processing Therapy for PTSD: A Comprehensive Manual*. New York: Guilford Press.

Resick, P.A., Wachen, J.S., Dondanville, K.A., Pruiksma, K.E., Yarvis, J.S., Peterson, A.L., & Mintz, J. (2017). Effect of group vs individual cognitive processing therapy in active-duty military seeking treatment for posttraumatic stress disorder: a randomized clinical trial. *JAMA Psychiatry*, *74*, 28–36.

Riesselman, A., Johnson, E., & Palmer, E. (2015). Lithium and clozapine in suicidality: shedding some light to get out of the dark. *Mental Health Clinician*, *5*, 237–243.

Rudd, M. D., Bryan, C. J., Wertenberger, E. G., Peterson, A. L., Young-McCaughan, S., Mintz, J., . . ., & Wilkinson, E. (2015). Brief cognitive-behavioral therapy effects on post-treatment suicide attempts in a military sample: results of a randomized clinical trial with 2-year follow-up. *American Journal of Psychiatry*, *172*, 441–449.

Sayer, N. A., Noorbaloochi, S., Frazier, P., Carlson, K., Gravely, A., & Murdoch, M. (2010). Reintegration problems and treatment interests among Iraq and Afghanistan combat veterans receiving VA medical care. *Psychiatric Services*, *61*, 589–597.

Schmitz, W.M., Allen, M.H., Feldman, B.N., Gutin, N.J., Jahn, D.R., Kleespies, P.M., Quinnett, P., & Simpson, S. (2012). Preventing suicide through improved training in suicide risk assessment and care: an American Association of Suicidology task force report addressing serious gaps in U.S. mental health training. *Suicide and Life-Threatening Behavior*, *42*, 292–304.

Sprang, G., Craig, C., & Clark, J. (2008). Factors impacting trauma treatment practice patterns: The convergence/divergence of science and practice. *Journal of Anxiety Disorders*, *22*, 162–174.

The Joint Commission (2016). *Sentinel Event Alert 56: Detecting and Treating Suicide Ideation in All Settings*. Available online at https://www.jointcommission.org/assets/1/18/SEA_56_Suicide.pdf

Trockel, M., Karlin, B.E., Taylor, C.B., Brown, G.K., & Manber, R. (2015). Effects of cognitive behavioral therapy for insomnia on suicidal ideation in veterans. *Sleep*, *38*, 259–265.

United States Census Bureau (2014). *American Community Survey*. Available from https://www.census.gov/acs/www/data/data-tables-and-tools/data-profiles/2014/.

Washington, D.L., Yano, E.M., Simon, B., & Sun, S. (2006). To use or not to use—what influence why women veterans choose VA healthcare? *Journal of General Internal Medicine, 21 (Suppl 3)*, S11–S18.

Watkins, K.E., Pincus, H.A., Smith, B., Paddock, S.M., Mannle, T.E., Woodroffe, A., . . ., & Call, C. (2011). *The Cost and Quality of VA Mental Health Services*. Santa Monica, CA: The RAND Corporation.

11 Hello Cruel World!

Embracing a Collective Ethics for Suicide Prevention

Jennifer White

The world we live in can be unspeakably cruel. More so for some than others. While heartache, sickness, grief, loneliness and pain are universal human experiences, the suffering caused by structural violence and inequalities, social and environmental injustices, or racist colonial policies, is by no means equally borne by people across the globe. These institutionalized and structural forms of oppression complicate and intensify the experience of human despair in profound ways. Yet, the response to the experiences of human suffering from the mainstream suicide prevention field has generally been to ignore the political, historical, and social arrangements that contribute to despair (e.g. white supremacy, heteropatriarchy, colonial violence, transphobia, corporate greed, hegemonic masculinity) in favour of a narrow focus on treating and managing individuals who have been conceptualized as mentally ill and in need of expert intervention. This approach is undoubtedly helpful to some, and even life-saving for others. And yet, if we fail to challenge narrow biomedical formulations of suffering, or never ask how our suicide prevention practices (as cultural products) actively shape ideas about what it means to be human, or overlook how we may be implicated in the problem, our efforts to shore up our collective capabilities, support others to endure, and stay accountable to our joint future, will remain partial and inadequate.

In this chapter, I argue for richer and more nuanced vocabularies to reflect more politically informed, historically situated, and relational conceptualizations of living, dying, suffering and suicide. Such a move requires a reconsideration of the project of suicide prevention itself. Inspired by Alexis Shotwell (2016) who argues for a collective form of ethics that eschews purity, I attempt to map out what a re-vitalized ethical and political vision for suicide prevention might look like. This includes reckoning with the fact that we are always living and working in the midst of interlocking systems, structures, and discourses that both (re-)produce harm and also shape understandings of what it means to be human or live a worthwhile life. If, as Shotwell suggests, we are always implicated in others' suffering, then it seems like we need an ethical vision for suicide prevention that can capture our deep interdependency, complicity, and potential for collective action.

I begin with a review of some of mainstream suicidology's prevailing ideas, the practices it makes possible, and the view of human and collective life it seems to articulate. Drawing on Shotwell's (2016) discourses of purity, I suggest that mainstream suicidology aspires to a world that can be ultimately tamed and "made pure" through the techniques of science and an abiding faith in expert knowledge. And yet, despite all of the efforts of the past several decades, including widespread public education efforts, means restriction campaigns, media reporting guidelines, specialized training for professionals, dissemination of research knowledge, promotion of evidence-based treatments, and support for local community-based coalitions, the suicide rates in Canada and the United States have either remained stable or increased over the past 15 years (Curtin, Warner and Hedegaard, 2016; Statistics Canada, 2013). Rates of suicide among Indigenous peoples have also remained disproportionately high, relative to the general population, although there is a high degree of variation across Indigenous communities, and some First Nations communities have zero rates of suicide (Chandler and Lalonde, 1998). In the second part of the paper, I turn back to Shotwell (2016), who offers an ethical vision for living in compromised times, that I think holds promise for suicidology and suicide prevention work. Two of Shotwell's core ideas are particularly germane to my argument. First, "we are not, ever, pure" (p. 7) and second, "being co-constituted with the world, ontologically inseparable, just seems to be our condition" (p. 7). I would also add that this latter point is something Indigenous peoples have known and practiced for thousands of years, and it would be an egregious error to suggest that concepts like holism, interdependence, interconnectedness, collectivism, ecologies of practice, or relational ontologies are new (Euro-Western) ideas (Todd, 2016). By embracing the mess of our interdependent, co-constituted, and ethically compromised realities, and giving up any pretense of our own innocence, I argue that we may be able to respond more fully and creatively to the suffering and potentialities of others. In the final section of the paper, I attempt to map out what a collective ethics for suicide prevention might look like. It resonates with the dynamic sophistication of an "all my relations" Indigenous worldview (Battiste, 2014; Todd, 2016), with an emphasis on "living in compromised times" (Shotwell, 2016) and "staying with the trouble" (Haraway, 2016), which I argue, are required elements for responding to the complexities and challenges of the 21st century. Specifically, I propose an ethical vision that is predicated on our deep *relationality and interdependence* with the whole living world. It is one that is grounded in a recognition that we are always acting under *compromised conditions*. It is a vision inspired by *collective action and accountability* for our shared future, and does not shy away from acknowledging and addressing our potential *complicity with harm*.

Mainstream Suicidology and the Search for Purity

Shotwell (2016) begins her book by arguing that we are currently living in a time when the pursuit and desire for purity (in our ethics, politics, ideologies, and material existence) has never been greater. It is her contention that many of us (especially privileged, white, Euro-western settlers who benefit the most from global inequality) aspire to live in a world that is natural, innocent and pure, free of contamination; a world where we are not implicated in others' suffering or the destruction of the planet; where we can 'forget' about things like slavery, genocide, colonial violence and begin anew. We want to believe that there are answers to complex problems. We want to believe that our choices, whether it is practicing yoga, volunteering in the community, eating vegan, de-toxifying, participating in protest marches, or "buying local," can somehow wipe the slate clean and enable us to escape our implication in "complex webs of suffering" (p. 5). No matter how well-intentioned the efforts, they are all variants on purism or purity politics according to Shotwell.

I suggest that some contemporary suicide prevention practices might also be usefully thought of as a type of purism, whereby we seek to "meet and control a complex situation that is fundamentally outside our control" (Shotwell, 2016, p. 8). The stubborn persistence of suicide rates, despite decades of research, intervention, and public awareness campaigns, attests to our lack of control over this complex phenomenon. Erasing the contradictions, cultural contingencies, and uncertainties surrounding suicide (Petrov, 2013) in favour of more singular and authoritative accounts that draw on scientific and psychological conceptualizations (Marsh, 2010) is an example of suicidology's aspirations towards purism. Moreover, by developing suicide prevention programs that reflect the state's interest in promoting, maximizing, and legislating life itself (i.e. Foucault's bio-power) (Marsh, 2010; Petrov, 2013), mainstream suicidology, with all its scientific pretensions, becomes a tool in the pursuit of purity. As Petrov (2013) notes, "it is no coincidence that it was in the age of such bio-power with its optimistic view of development and growth prospects that suicide – a bio-political thorn in the side – appeared as a scientific problem" (p. 354).

As Shotwell (2016) makes clear, being "against purity" is not the same as saying we are *for* continued suffering, inequality, violence, or other forms of human despair. Nor does it mean that just because the problem of suicide may be beyond our ability to control it, we should give up trying to respond in compassionate ways to those who are contemplating ending their lives. On the contrary, we need to respond to the challenge by thinking about the issue of suicide, and our implication in it, differently. Admittedly, this is a very difficult shift to make. Shotwell writes,

> It is hard for us to examine our connection with *unbearable pasts* with which we might reckon better, our implication in *impossibly*

> *complex presents* through which we might craft different modes of response, and our aspirations for *different futures* toward which we might shape different worlds-yet-to-come.
>
> (p. 8, emphasis in original)

Mainstream suicidology and suicide prevention efforts, like other human service fields, have emerged out of a Euro-western, liberal humanist tradition and are strongly influenced by the ideals of the Enlightenment era (Saraceno, 2012; White, 2017). Among other things, this includes the acceptance of the bounded, autonomous and individual Western self as natural and desirable, combined with an unquestioned faith in the value of professional interventions and expertise (Wexler and Gone, 2012; White, 2011). Recognizing the diversity of the broad field of suicidology, and making no claims to represent the field in its entirety, listed below are some examples of prevailing ideas that could be considered "purity moves" in Shotwell's parlance. Several of these points have been well articulated through previous critiques (Hjelmeland, 2016; Marsh, 2016; Marsh and White, 2015; Petrov, 2013; Wexler and Gone, 2012; White, 2017).

- Reducing complexity by framing suicide as an exclusively individual (mental health) problem
- Likening suicide prevention to first-aid or medical treatment
- Reading stigma through a singular lens of mental illness or suicidality (erasing the effects of race, gender, age, ability, sexual orientation)
- Controlling the narrative/policing the language of suicide prevention as a response to "contagion"
- Privileging positivism as the most valued mode of inquiry
- Over estimating the value of professional help-seeking and expert knowledge
- Making individuals the primary unit of analysis and placing the onus for change on individuals
- Supporting specific modes of being (e.g. self-regulating, cognitively congruent) over others through "evidence-based" therapeutic practices
- "Forgetting" histories of genocide, slavery, and colonial violence in accounts of suicide risk
- Drawing on rhetorical strategies that suggest *all* suicides are preventable (e.g. "Zero Suicide"), without consideration for potentially unintended consequences such as increased coercion or involuntary hospitalizations

Suicidology and Suicide Prevention Are Conflated

Another way to think about purism within suicidology is to consider some of its unspoken assumptions. For example, it is taken as a given that the field of suicidology is organized around a common goal of reducing the number of people who take their own lives (Fitzpatrick, Hooker and Kerridge, 2015). Even though very few would quibble with the idea that preventing people from killing themselves is a laudable goal, how we conceptualize what suicide *is* (illness, crime, sin, weapon, protest), the justifications we provide for our interventions, and the unexamined consequences of our professional practices should not be beyond interrogation. This was a point well-articulated by Szasz (1999) almost two decades ago.

Fitzpatrick (2016) draws attention to some of the potential hazards of unreflexively linking the study of suicide with the goals of suicide prevention. Specifically, 'solving' the problem of suicide may appear to be a self-evident goal of suicidology, and yet having such a narrow instrumental aim can potentially interfere with asking certain kinds of questions about suicide itself and/or diminish the value of problem-*raising*. A narrow problem-solving approach can lead us to neglect the broader social and historical contexts of human suffering and rarely invites critical scrutiny into the construction of the problem or its purported solutions (White, 2012).

This type of critique has also been raised by those working in the allied field of critical criminology. For example, McAra (2016) suggests that in order to resist being tamed by the existing policy and practice discourses that preserve the status quo, criminologists might be better conceptualized as reflexive "cultural workers" [whose role is] "to be disruptive rather than ameliorative, confrontational rather than collaborative" (p. 2). In her account, "crime science" is distinguished from 'public criminology,' with the latter focused on understanding criminology as a political strategy, an institutional performance, and an embodied practice (for those who become objects of regulation). This analysis offers some useful parallels and lessons for a more reflexive, critical, and public suicidology.

Suicidology Shapes Ways of Being a Self

It is also worth considering some of the unarticulated ontological conceptions of human beings that prevail within mainstream suicidology. The influence of the psy-discourses in shaping particular subjectivities is something that Nikolas Rose (1989) explored in his seminal book, *Governing the Soul: The Shaping of the Private Self*. He writes,

> rather than trying to analyze how human individuals have been formed by particular social processes, I ask how persons have been understood within particular practices, how these understandings might have come about, what kinds of techniques for acting on human beings were linked to these understandings, what kind of consequences followed.
>
> (Rose, 1989, p. xvii)

In other words, mainstream suicidology not only reflects a set of preferred practices for addressing the problem of suicide, it also actively shapes ideas about living and desired ways of being human. For example, Wexler and Gone (2012) critique western understandings of selfhood that permeate most contemporary suicide prevention practices. They argue that the idea of the bounded, unencumbered, self, is not universal or required. In many ways, the liberal humanist view of the self is out of step with Indigenous cosmologies and understandings, which are deeply relational; inextricably linked to the land, animals and the natural world; and actively engaged with the spirit world (Battiste, 2014).

Unspoken psychological understandings about suicidality also produce normative ideas about what counts as "good mental health," which in turn have implications for how we come to think about persons. As Ian Hacking (2008) has pointed out, with the increasing medicalization of suicide in the 19th century, "the idea of a special kind of person, 'the suicidal person,' was launched" (p. 6). For example, we have largely come to accept that, 'suicidal persons' are those who, given their risky status, should be subject to regular questioning, assessment, monitoring, and in some cases containment. They are understood to carry the risks for suicide "inside of them," often turning persons into categories who can then be read through distinct identity markers such as "high risk" or "medium risk" or "low risk." This orientation is made evident in the way that we organize our clinical interviews to systematically and thoroughly assess such things as suicidal histories, thoughts, plans, and intentions. Contemporary approaches to suicide risk assessment are often predicated on the assumption that 'suicidal thoughts' are individual, private and solitary cognitions that can be accurately accessed through skillful interviewing techniques and questions (Shea, 1999). Prominent voices within the field of suicidology have recently suggested that suicide is a form of "pathological derangement" that has no adaptive function and that 100% of suicidal persons suffer from a mental disorder (Joiner et al., 2016). This clearly has implications for how we come to think about persons.

Purism Has its Limits

Rogers and Soyka (2004) made the observation that many contemporary approaches to suicide prevention, which are based on a crisis intervention model (i.e. risk management, standardized procedures), may actually be part of the reason we are failing to see a decline in suicide rates. They suggest that these procedural approaches may create unnecessary distance between clinicians and those who seek their help, and can be experienced as de-humanizing. Others have argued that by forbidding, denying or condemning suicide (which are all purity moves) "one risks not only being blind to what is *fundamentally common to all human beings*, but we are also, paradoxically, more vulnerable to anxiety, shame, boredom, fear of death and—suicide" (Petrov, 2013, p. 349, emphasis added). Thinking about suicide's fundamentally common human quality sits in stark contrast to those efforts that conceptualize suicide as "pathological derangement" (Joiner et al., 2016) and instead finds resonance with those who read suicide as an *understandable response* or protest against violence, injustice, hate, and cruelty (Button, 2016; Reynolds, 2016).

In the next section, I explore the potentials of understanding human suffering, including suicidal despair, as part of a greater interconnected web of social relations. This expanded view is based on an understanding that "all forms of suffering involve layers of personal history, embedded in a nexus of meaningful relationships that are, in turn, embedded in cultural and political systems" (Bracken et al., 2012, p. 433). I suggest that by strengthening our collective capacity to imagine and enact a more just and compassionate world, we may discover that suicide prevention work can become something bigger and bolder – an ethical vision for living well together.

Embracing the Mess of Our Embodied Co-Existence

Recognizing the relevance and value of Indigenous worldviews and knowledge systems for theorizing and responding to our current times (Battiste, 2013; Todd, 2016), and drawing on the contributions of critical, post-structural, and feminist scholars (Gergen, 2011; Jaworski, 2014; St. Pierre, 2014), I begin from the premise that it is only through ongoing social practices and relational entanglements that we emerge as selves (including suicidal selves). We never truly think, exist, or act alone. This has important implications for how we think about suicide. Instead of assuming suicide to be the ultimate final act of an unencumbered and de-contextualized individual who suffers from a mental disorder, we can draw on richer, more irreducible conceptualizations of suicide that are less singular, more culturally situated, and historically contingent (Marsh, 2010). Suicide is always collective, performative, and situated (Jaworski, 2014; White, 2017). It is always a relational response. It always has a history. Once we accept that distress, suffering and suicide can never be understood outside of an embodied, co-constituted, relational ontology then the only type of response that makes sense is one that is based on a "collective web of responsibility" (Shotwell, 2016, p. 54).

Simply by being alive, we are already entangled with other human and non-human lives, both near and distant. The implication of our embodied co-existence is that "to live, we rely on others intimately – we use them, and our actions shape the conditions for their lives and deaths" (Shotwell, 2016, p. 108). Where we live, what we eat, how we consume the earth's finite resources to support our ongoing existence, and how we think about concepts like land, property, natural resources, and nationhood immediately brings us all into complex ethical relations with one another. The kinds of ethical dilemmas that these embodied entanglements pose, which reflect our deep interdependence, cannot always be worked out by a self-contained moral agent who carefully and rationally weighs out the best course of moral action, contrary to what many western approaches to ethics suggest. Shotwell (2016) acknowledges that many ethical problems may be appropriately addressed at the level of the individual, including for example, decisions about whether to steal, lie, cheat, harm or murder. Other problems, including many that are relevant to suicide require a more robust, politicized, and collective form of ethics that reflects the densely layered complexity of our current condition under late stage capitalism, where many are "worn out by the activity of reproducing life" (Berlant, 2007, p. 759). In other words, many people are experiencing what Berlant describes as a "slow death." And as Jabir Puar (2017) asks, what kinds of slow deaths have been ongoing that a suicide might represent an escape from" (p. 11)? This is an important question to think with.

To say that we are all implicated in others' suffering, does not mean that we are all *equally* implicated. This is because harms are not equally distributed. In the context of Canada, where both Shotwell (2016) and I are writing from, this means acknowledging that we are working and living on stolen Indigenous lands and an "aspect of our role [as non-Indigenous white settlers] is actively participating in a politics of responsibility . . . actively challenging our own and others' ignorance and occluded thinking, and taking up practices of decolonization" (p. 25). The implication for suicide prevention work is that our privilege (whether it is related to our skin color, gender, status as educated professionals, or place of residence) typically comes at some cost to others. By politicizing suicide prevention work, we are acknowledging the ways that complex relations of power contribute to, and complicate, experiences of dislocation, dispossession, and despair. In short, the lived experiences of suffering cannot always be remediated by individually focused psychological interventions.

Others Are Always Involved

In contrast to the mainstream suicidology discourse, where pinning down the private thoughts and specific intentions of an individual are a central concern, a more relational view of suicidal despair begins from the premise that "[even] when you think, someone else is always involved" (Parker, 2007, p. 5). As such, suicide ideation is no longer lodged in the head of the individual person, but rather ideas about suicide are always co-constituted through language, relationships, bodies, culture, materials, relations of power, and histories (Jaworski, 2014; White and Kral, 2014). This is why asking questions that re-locate experiences of despair and suffering within a broader relational and sociopolitical context can produce very different effects from those that individualize and medicalize distress (Aldarondo, 2007). Such questions might include those inspired by narrative therapists (Madigan, 2011; Reynolds, 2016; Sather and Newman, 2016), including: "With these suicidal thoughts, what are you taking a stand against?" or "Do you think it's fair that we live in a world that places more value on some lives more than others?" or "Were there ever times that you questioned someone's view of you as less than worthy or legitimate?" or "Do you ever think that what you're up against may not entirely of your own making?" or "Who would be the least surprised to learn that you are taking this stand against this [hate, injustice, cruelty, patriarchy, colonial violence, toxic masculinity]?" Beyond having value within the therapeutic context, these questions and ways of thinking can also influence the broader field of suicide prevention as a whole by decentering the individual, and contextualizing problems and their histories.

Finding Cracks and Opportunities for Resistance

Wherever you find an applied professional field dedicated to the provision of social care, health, or education, you will almost certainly find a network of critical scholars, service users and practitioners who are pushing against the status quo, pursuing critically oriented research agendas, and mobilizing for radical social change. This is because no field of practice or academic community can sustain a monolithic hold on the truth, and "where there is power there is resistance, and . . . in every dominant practice there are contradictions and spaces for us to work to challenge and change the existing state of affairs" (Parker, 2007, p. 2).

Whether it is critical criminology, critical public health, critical psychology or critical social work, these movements very often turn the critical gaze on their own professional practices to illuminate how structural forces, social determinants, and ruling relations work together to perpetuate injustice and harm. United in their recognition that the world we live in is profoundly unjust, conferring structural advantages on some groups over others, these intellectual and social movements draw on a diverse range of Indigenous, critical, post-structural, feminist, queer, social constructionist, and postcolonial theoretical frameworks to challenge and subvert the status quo. Thus, critical suicidology's (White, Marsh, Kral and Morris, 2016) greatest influence may be judged by how well it challenges mainstream assumptions about the causes of suicidal despair, how often it makes room for the contributions and perspectives of those with lived experience and local knowledge, and how successfully it resists being tamed or co-opted by existing policy discourses (McAra, 2016; Parker, 2007; White, 2012; 2016).

In the next section I suggest that what seems to be missing from the mainstream approach to suicide prevention is an adequate analysis of human distress and suffering that moves beyond the familiar individual psychological frame towards a more complicated view of our co-existence. It is an invitation to re-think how we might go on together in a world that is admittedly cruel, but not only that; it is also a world that holds the possibility for us to imagine alternative (impure) futures. In other words, "[p]erhaps we could be-do-live something different" (St. Pierre, 2014, p. 5).

Collective Ethics for a Shared Future

Shotwell offers some useful resources for living into an impure future, inspired by Donna Haraway's commitment to an ethics of flourishing in the 'real world.' For Haraway (2016), the ethical task is not to "make an imaginary future safe," rather it is about "learning to be truly present" and "staying with the trouble" (p. 1). Specifically,

> The task is to make kin in lines of inventive connection as a practice of learning to live and die well with each other in a thick present. Our task is to make trouble, to stir up potent response to devastating events, as well as to settle troubled waters and rebuild quiet places.
>
> (Haraway, 2016, p. 1)

Would it be possible, for example, when attempting to make sense of suicidality, to begin with a recognition of our ontological, material, and relational co-existence and deep interdependence (Shotwell, 2016)? And if we were to start there, with an understanding of our relational accountability to one another, what would that enable in terms of how we might respond to expressions of suffering, protest, or despair in our fellow kin (both human and non-human; near and distant) (Haraway, 2016)? What new conversational spaces and alliances might get opened up if we helped individuals to recognize that we are relationally entangled with history and with each other? What would it mean to learn that the struggles we face and the challenges we are up against, are not always of our own making (Aldarondo, 2007; Prilleltensky, Rossiter and Walsh-Bowers, 1996)? Could we also ensure that the social, institutional and political arrangements that produce oppression, do not fall from view when trying to understand the emergence of suicide as a response to inequality, injustice, oppression, generational trauma and colonial violence (Button, 2016; Reynolds, 2016)? These questions are obviously grounded in a radically different starting place from most mainstream suicide prevention conversations that frame suicidality as "pathological derangement" or the product of mental disorders (Joiner et al., 2016).

Learning from and with Indigenous Knowledge Systems

What I am calling for is a more capacious, relational, situated, and precarious view of suicide and suicide prevention. It is a bold vision that gestures towards the future and asks: what can we become together when we centre our interdependence, complicity and co-constitution? I seek to honor and give proper credit to Indigenous epistemologies that exemplify living knowledge systems and ethical relations that are intimately tied to land, place, human and non-human entities. As Todd (2016) writes, it is unconscionable when non-Indigenous scholars fail "to credit Indigenous thinkers for their millennia of engagement with sentient environments, with cosmologies that enmesh people into complex relationships between themselves and *all* relations, and with climates and atmospheres as important points of organization" (p. 6, emphasis in original).

For non-Indigenous, white settlers living in Canada, we need to learn from, and hold with respect, the knowledge and contributions of Indigenous thinkers, whose intellectual, legal and ethical traditions are grounded in specific places, where the idea of the interconnectedness of all living things is deeply understood and embodied (Battiste, 2013; Todd, 2016; Wilson, 2008). From there, we need to figure out how we might re-situate suicide prevention work so that it can become a collective effort or social movement that capably undermines the cruelties, forms of dispossession, and injustices of the present, while at the same time never "forgetting" the historical harms that have contributed to the experience of suffering and suicidal despair.

Paying Attention Differently

With these moves, we might just get a glimpse of what suicide prevention can become. To make the shift that I am envisioning will require paying attention differently so that our layered social histories and unequal sites of privilege are brought into view. This mode of attention would increase the visibility of those interlocking structures and systems that contribute to, and exacerbate, human suffering. Such an analysis of human suffering would attend to the following: the economic and social structures that benefit the rich; the racist policies that reproduce white supremacy; the ableist and normative discourses that govern what is to count as a worthwhile life; the profit-seeking values that drive pharmaceutical companies to push pharmacological interventions over structural changes; the colonial practices that deny Indigenous peoples their rights to reclaim their stolen lands and sacred territories; the patriarchal structures and beliefs that perpetuate violence against women while promoting hegemonic versions of masculinity for men; the hetero- and cis-normative discourses that fuel hatred and disqualify queer, gender non-conforming, or gender fluid identities; the ageist assumptions that de-value old people and convey disdain for dependency; the corporate greed and extractive mentalities that threaten human and non-human life on this planet; and the conceit that humans are the pinnacle or endpoint of evolution.

Recognizing and engaging with the complexity of this interconnected web of suffering will hopefully help us to understand and respond to suicide in more creative and useful ways, and at the same time might also help us address other threats to our individual, collective, and planetary well-being (Haraway, 2016; Shotwell, 2016; Zylinska, 2014). As just one example, the recent documentary film from the United States, entitled "Beyond Standing Rock" (Inside Energy, 2017) tells the story of how Indigenous young people from the Standing Rock Sioux Nation and their allies came together to protest the Dakota Access pipeline, and in the process of fighting for land rights, justice, and tribal sovereignty, they experienced a profound sense of solidarity and collective healing. Not surprisingly, pursuing a joint goal, taking pride in their cultural traditions, and collectively organizing against injustice and corporate greed reportedly led to lowered incidences of substance use, depression and suicide among community members (Reveal, 2017).

Reckoning with the cruel world, imagining other possible futures for ourselves and others, and grounding our work in a shared understanding of our interdependence and relational accountability, is the task before us. This work is deeply ethical and political. Suicide prevention, in all its complexity and impurity, can become a site for re-imagining the world.

References

Aldarondo, E. (ed.) (2007) *Advancing social justice through clinical practice.* Mahwah, NJ: Lawrence Erlbaum Associates.

Battiste, M. (2013) *Decolonizing education: nourishing the learning spirit.* Saskatoon, SK: Purich Publishing.

Berlant, L. (2007) 'Slow death (Sovereignty, obesity, lateral agency)', *Critical Inquiry*, 33, p754–780.

Bracken, P., Thomas, P., Timimi, S., & Asen, E. (2012) 'Psychiatry beyond the current paradigm', *British Journal of Psychiatry*, 201, p430–434.

Button, M. (2016) 'Suicide and social justice: toward a political approach to suicide', *Political Research Quarterly*, 69(2), p270–280.

Chandler, M., & Lalonde, C. (1998) Cultural continuity as a hedge against suicide in Canada's First Nations. *Transcultural Psychiatry*, 35(2), p191–219.

Curtin, S. Warner, M. and Hedegaard, H. (2016) 'Increase in suicide in the United States, 1999–2014. National Center for Health Statistics', *NCHS Data Brief*, p241.

Fitzpatrick, S. (2016) 'Stories of suicide and social justice' *Project Muse: Philosophy, Psychiatry, and Psychology*, 23(3/4), p285–287.

Fitzpatrick, S., Hooker, C., and Kerridge, I. (2015) 'Suicidology as a social practice', *Social Epistemology*, 29(3), p303–322.

Gergen, K. (2011) 'The self as social construction', *Psychological Studies*, 56(1), p108–116.

Hacking, I. (2008) 'The suicide weapon' *Critical Inquiry*, 35(1), p1–32.

Haraway, D. (2016) *Staying with the trouble: Making kin in the Chthulucene.* Durham, NC: Duke University Press.

Hjelmeland, H. (2016) 'A critical look at current suicide research' in J. White, I. Marsh, M. Kral, and J. Morris (eds.) *Critical suicidology: Transforming suicide research and prevention for the 21st century*. Vancouver: University of British Columbia Press, pp. 31–55.

Inside Energy (2017). *Beyond Standing Rock: Energy, environment and tribal control*. Available at: www.beyondstandingrock.org/ (Accessed: 21 June 2017).

Jaworski, K. (2014) *The gender of suicide: Knowledge production, theory and suicidology*. Burlington, VT: Ashgate Publishing.

Joiner, T., Hom, M., Hagan, C., and Silva, C. (2016) 'Suicide as a derangement of the self-sacrificial aspect of eusociality', *Psychological Review*, 123(3), p235–254.

Madigan, S. (2011) *Narrative therapy*. Washington, DC: American Psychological Association.

Marsh, I (2010) *Suicide: Foucault, history and truth*. Cambridge: Cambridge University Press.

Marsh, I. (2016) 'Critiquing contemporary suicidology' in J. White, I. Marsh, M. Kral, and J. Morris (eds.) *Critical suicidology: Transforming suicide research and prevention for the 21st century*. Vancouver: University of British Columbia Press, pp. 15–30.

Marsh, I. and White, J. (2015) 'Boundaries, thresholds and the liminal in youth suicide prevention work' in H. Skott-Myhre, V. Pacini-Ketchabaw and K. Skott-Myhre (eds.) *Youth work, early education, and psychology: Liminal encounters*. New York: Palgrave MacMillan, pp. 69–89.

McAra, L. (2016) 'Can criminologists change the world? Critical reflections on the politics, performance and effects of criminal justice' *British Journal of Criminology*, 57(4), p767–788.

Parker, I. (2007) 'Critical psychology: what it is and what it is not', *Social and Personality Psychology Compass*, 1(1), p1–15.

Petrov, K. (2013) 'The art of dying as an art of living: historical contemplations on the paradoxes of suicide and the possibilities of reflexive suicide prevention', *Journal of Medical Humanities*, 34(3), p347–368.

Prilleltensky, I., Rossiter, A., and Walsh-Bowers, R. (1996) 'Preventing harm and promoting ethical discourse in the helping professions: conceptual, research, analytical, and action frameworks', *Ethics and Behavior*, 6(4), p287–306.

Puar, J. K. (2017) *The right to maim: Debility, capacity, disability*. Durham, NC: Duke University Press.

Reveal (2017). *Standing rock and beyond*. Reveal: The Center for Investigative Reporting. Available at: www.revealnews.org/episodes/standing-rock-and-beyond/ (Accessed 21 June 2017).

Reynolds, V. (2016) 'Hate kills: a social justice response to suicide', in J. White, I. Marsh, M. Kral and J. Morris (eds.) *Critical suicidology: transforming suicide research and prevention for the 21st century* Vancouver: UBC Press, pp. 169–187.

Rogers, J. and Soyka, K. (2004). '"One size fits all": an existential constructivist perspective on the crisis intervention approach with suicidal individuals', *Journal of Contemporary Psychotherapy*, 34(1), p7–21.

Rose, N. (1989) *Governing the soul: the shaping of the private self*. London: Free Association Books.

Saraceno, J. (2012) 'Mapping whiteness and coloniality in the human service field: possibilities for a praxis of social justice in child and youth care', *International Journal of Child, Youth and Family Studies*, 3(2/3), p248–271.

Sather, M. and Newman, D. (2016). "Being more than just your final act:" elevating the multiple storylines of suicide with narrative practice,' in J. White, I. Marsh, M. Kral and J. Morris (eds.) *Critical suicidology: Transforming suicide research and prevention for the 21st century*. Vancouver: UBC Press, pp. 115–132.

Shea, S. (1999) *The practical art of suicide assessment: A guide for mental health professionals and substance abuse counselors*. Hoboken, NJ: John Wiley and Sons.

Shotwell, A. (2016) *Against purity: Living ethically in compromised times*. Minneapolis: University of Minnesota Press.

Statistics Canada (2013). Suicides and suicide rate, by sex and by age group. Available at: www.statcan.gc.ca/tables-tableaux/sum-som/l01/cst01/hlth66a-eng.htm (Accessed 23 June 2017).

St. Pierre, E. (2014) 'A brief and personal history of post qualitative research: Toward "post inquiry"', *Journal of Curriculum Theorizing*, 30(2), p2–19.

Szasz, T. (1999) *Fatal freedom: The ethics and politics of suicide*. Westport, CT: Praeger Publishers.

Todd, Z. (2016) 'An Indigenous feminist's take on the ontological turn: "Ontology" is just another word for colonialism' *Journal of Historical Sociology*, 29(1), p4–22.

Wexler, L. and Gone, J. (2012) 'Culturally responsive suicide prevention in Indigenous communities: unexamined assumptions and new possibilities' *American Journal of Public Health*, 102(5), p800–806.

White, J. (2012) 'Youth suicide as a 'wild problem:'implications for prevention practice', *Suicidology Online*, 3, p42–50.

White, J. and Kral, M. (2014) 'Re-thinking youth suicide: language, culture and power', *Journal of Social Action for Counseling and Psychology*, 6, p122–142.

White, J., Marsh, I., Kral, M. & Morris, J. (2016) (eds.) *Critical suicidology: Transforming suicide research and prevention for the 21st century*. Vancouver: UBC Press.

White, J. (2017) 'What can critical suicidology *do*?', *Death Studies*, 41(8), p472–480.

Wilson, S. (2008) *Research is ceremony: Indigenous research methods*. Halifax: Fernwood Books.

Zylinska, J. (2014) *Minimal ethics for the anthropocene*. Ann Arbor, MI: Open Humanities Press.

Index

Page numbers in *italics* refer to information in tables. Those followed by 'n' refer to notes followed by the note number.